Process in Relationship

Marriage and Family

SECOND EDITION

Edward A. Powers

Iowa State University

Mary W. Lees

Iowa State University

WEST PUBLISHING CO.

St. Paul · New York · Boston

Los Angeles · San Francisco

COPYRIGHT © 1974 By WEST PUBLISHING CO.
COPYRIGHT © 1976 By WEST PUBLISHING CO.

Printed in the United States of America
Library of Congress Cataloging in Publication Data

Main entry under title:
Process in relationship.
    Includes bibliographical references and indexes.
    1. Sex role—Addresses, essays, lectures.
2. Marriage—Addresses, essays, lectures. 3. Interpersonal relations— Addresses, essays, lectures.
I. Powers, Edward A., 1941–   II. Lees, Mary W., 1926–
HQ728.P75   1976   301.41   75–40423
ISBN   0–8299–0082–9

To Paige
    Courtney
    Mary Kay & Tom
    Marty
    Debbie & Jim
    Judy
    Susan
    Rebecca
    David

May your encounter with these concerns be a gentle one

*

PROLOGUE

In any college class dealing with the family, particularly in a class in Courtship and Marriage, some students enroll with the expectation of finding a "snap" course. Others will be merely fulfilling departmental requirements with an interesting course. Most enroll, however, with a very different motivation: The need and desire to confront the basic issues of interpersonal living. Who am I? Who are you? How do we find out who we are? How do we learn to live in the same world with at least a semblance of inner integrity and peace?

In our classroom experience and through contact with persons searching for such direction and answers, we have found serious gaps and inadequacies in available resource material. Student questions usually come in one of the five areas explored here—femaleness/maleness, love, sex, conflict and termination. Although other issues are raised, they usually are reducible to these five areas of interpersonal relations. But text and journal treatment generally does not present the significance of such issues nor challenge the readers to find the meaning from their experiences. Resource materials on femaleness/maleness and love are not lacking. However, they are most often oriented to one of three perspectives: 1) theoretical statements; 2) research or statistical reports; or 3) demythologizing beliefs. While there is a need for theoretical statements and research reports, many of these are difficult enough for the scholar to comprehend, let alone the introductory student. Although myths need to be questioned, the writers who do so seem to make little effort to provide new insights to replace the older notions they have demolished.

Resource material on sex most likely is either a statistical presentation of how many do or don't and when, or else it is technique and performance oriented. While this may be useful in a certain context, such material does not challenge students to put sex within the framework of a life perspective.

For the areas of conflict and termination, there are fewer available references. What is available, more often than not, is designed to help avoid or minimize the reality of conflict and termination in human relationships. For instance, much has been written on how to be adjusted and have a happy marriage (i. e., don't fight!), but there is little on the meaning of conflict or how to handle it constructively. Similarly, "termination" usually implies death or divorce, and is discussed in terms of its effect on children and individual adjustment. We propose to deal with the reality of conflict and termination as an ongoing process of relationships at all stages throughout life.

Within each of the five chapters, readings are presented that demonstrate how the pertinent issues continually arise in living. Identity and role in female-male relationships are not established once and for all in pre-teen interaction, but are important in all subsequent relationships as well. The female-male relationship is basic to the reality of love, conflict and termination, and is basic at all ages. Love is not an issue decided upon finding the "right one". In growing and changing we must learn to give and receive love in new ways. The importance of sexual behavior and the personal and interpersonal satisfaction it provides is constantly changing throughout life. Conflict in a relationship is not necessarily an indication of weakness or impending failure. Conflict is a reality of every relationship from infancy through death. It affects female-male interaction, love, and the endings-beginnings of all interpersonal contacts. Finally, termination does not mean simply death or divorce. In every relationship some phase is dying as other elements in the interaction are developing or growing.

This is the second edition of *Process in Relationship*. The first edition was well received but suggestions from readers convinced us we could better address the concerns of students by greatly revising the previous volume. Many of the ideas in this reader reflect the thinking of Frank Fear and J. P. Golinvaux who were involved in an earlier version of the reader.

These readings have been selected partly because we feel they are interesting and not statistically oriented. More basically, however, two decisions have guided our choices. First, we have selected authors whose works demonstrate the actualities of theoretical issues. Such issues are encountered throughout life and must be faced and handled constructively. Second, we have presented materials that will challenge the individual to begin the process of finding meaning in these areas. We cannot answer questions but we can hope that the readings will give rise to relevant questions.

Finally, we have avoided the perspective that presents the "problems" of sex-roles, or the "problems" of love and sex or of conflict, or termination. We present these areas as realities of living. The question is not how to avoid, minimize, or adjust to these "problems", but rather:

What shall we do about these realities?

How do we learn to handle them?

How do we find meaning on which to build for the future?

EDWARD A. POWERS
MARY W. LEES

Iowa State University
Ames, Iowa

January, 1976

CONTENTS

CONTENTS

PROCESS
IN
RELATIONSHIP:
Marriage and Family

FEMALE-MALE RELATIONSHIP

Pictures by Susan Brown Nicholson.

INTRODUCTION

Gender somehow is intricately woven into virtually every human relationship. Accordingly, one of life's most perplexing tasks, that of resolving how to be acceptable to both ourselves and others, is influenced by our interpretation of what is expected of us as men and women. Perhaps an understanding of why females and males are so often pitted against one another begins with the realization that we often do not share the same reality. That is, our gender not only influences what we deem is meaningful in life but also affects how we view our environment. Even the same words may have different meanings for males and females. For example, "ambition" would likely have a positive connotation for males but a negative connotation for females.

Our gender is implicit in any relationship and influences much of what follows the initial encounter. When the relationship is going well, the perceived significance of gender is not as great. Conversely, when things are not going well we may frequently conclude that our dissatisfaction stems from someone's failure to do what is "naturally" expected of a female or male. However hard we may try, the socialization process is so strong we seldom escape the trap of basing our social expectations on what is the "normal" behavior for men and women.

What assumptions are implicit in our personal interpretations of what is "natural" for persons of the same or opposite sex? How do we come to have these ideas? What affects our understanding of what it is to be a woman or a man? These are a few of the issues examined by the authors whose works comprise this section.

Shulman portrays a young girl's dilemma of physical attractiveness versus intelligence as the criteria for womanhood. Lester felt his physique inadequate for his maleness but knew no other standards by which he could gauge his growth. Both were caught in the cultural trap of assessing maturity and gender by physical standards alone. The early age and the process by which these norms become internalized is discussed by Howe.

Balswick and Peek see these norms for adult men resulting in a syndrome of male inexpressiveness. Whether they result in the playboy or John Wayne type, maleness in our society does not include the honest expression of emotions and feelings in relationship to women. Steinmetz goes further in proposing liberation for men in areas other than just emotional expression. The point is well taken that both men and women need freeing from the stereotypic sex roles prevalent in our culture.

The last three readings in this section deal with the roles, expectations and realities of relationship in marriage. Rollin challenges the "Motherhood Myth", the idea that "having babies is something all normal women want and need and will enjoy doing". Congdon explores the progression of his emotions during his wife's pregnancy. In "Flood Tide", Lohmann questions her own identity and possible changes in her husband's emotional response to her, now that she is no longer pregnant and the children are gone.

Whatever the difference in perspective of these authors there is a commonality: although problems and barriers encountered differ according to gender, both must be confronted and managed to achieve our full potential as men and women.

MEMOIRS OF AN EX-PROM
QUEEN (EXCERPT) *

Alix Kates Shulman

There were weekly opinion polls called Slam Books which told in black and white what people thought of each other; yet even they told me almost nothing. Filled between classes in composition books from the five-and-ten, one charm per page, when completed the Slam Books yielded one perfect Composite Girl. As early as the eighth grade my name began to turn up in their pages, and by the ninth grade it appeared regularly. But it was usually on the NOSE page, or under BEST COMPLEXION. True, my skin concealed me well enough, and I was pert in profile, but what about inside and straight on? My avowed distinctions were purely negative; they did not even photograph well. The excellence of my nose was its insignificance; the virtue of my skin was its odd refusal to erupt. When everyone else's pimples cleared up, what then? Could my looks outlive the disappearance of their blackheads? Could I base my future on anything so trivial as skin? Unlike BUST, CHARM, SEX APPEAL, PERSONALITY, POISE, SENSE OF HUMOR, and HAIR, which as they grew in mass grew in value, my acknowledged assets were self-limiting. While the girls with positive charms, even immaterial ones, could look for daily gains, the best I could hope for was relief that no flaws had yet surfaced. There was nothing I could do to help. Baffled, I clung to my rock, filtering data from the passing stream, and withdrew further into myself. If I couldn't control my body, at least I could control my mind. Self-control, my father said, is the key to the world.

My father was proof of it. He had lifted himself from a ghetto high school to a position of eminence in Cleveland's legal establishment by sheer will, or so the family story went. Now I realize that my father was merely filling his destined slot in the professional scheme of things for hard-working sons of frugal and ambitious Jewish immigrants: his older brother had become a doctor, his younger brother a dentist, and all his sisters teachers until they turned into wives. My father, the middle son, had of course

* From MEMOIRS OF AN EX–PROM   Alix Kates Shulman. Reprinted by
    QUEEN, by Alix Kates Shulman,   permission of Alfred A. Knopf, Inc.
    Copyright © 1969, 1971, 1972 by

to be a lawyer. But close up it is hard to distinguish ambition from destiny, and I heard only my family's version. In high school my father had used his cunning to study shorthand and typing instead of shop, and landed a job as private secretary to one of Cleveland's industrial tycoons. He played chess with the boss, attended law school at night, and in between, with that single-mindedness he passed to me, he learned at least ten new multisyllable words a day, practiced oratory before the mirror, and studied the classics of literature in the tiny nickel volumes of the Little Leather Library series. When the time came for him to take the bar exam, he passed with the highest score in Ohio. It was predicted he would have a brilliant career.

My mother, as clever and ambitious as he, heeded the predictions and married him. Already loved by my father at a distance, my mother, the youngest and fairest of a family of lovely sisters on my father's ghetto block, had no trouble at all—so went the story. In America beautiful clever girls do not long remain schoolteachers.

They passed their hopes to their children. My mother, wanting happiness for me, gave me braces and dancing lessons; my father, valuing learning and success, gave me his library of Little Leather books. My brother Ben mastered the Baybury hills no-handed on his bike and managed a paper route; and I entered the Little Leather Library. I read and reread each volume, fleeing from my baffling outer life. Their contents came in such small, sweet packages that I could digest them piecemeal and savor them at length. I never suspected that a book measuring three inches by four inches might be considered suitable only for adults or that in larger bindings those very treasures might have struck me as impossibily difficult. Starting with the fairy tales and the *Arabian Nights,* I moved easily through *Candide, Gulliver,* and *Rasselas* without noticing any difference in genre, and then on to the plays, stories, and essays my father had studied. While my brother played football and read baseball books, and my classmates read beauty books and movie magazines, I went through plays by Ibsen, Strindberg, Oscar Wilde, and Moliére; stories of Tolstoy, Kipling, Balzac, William Morris, de Maupassant; meditations of Marcus Aurelius; words of Jesus; addresses of Lincoln; essays of Mill, Thoreau, Shaw, Voltaire, and Emerson; dialogues of Plato; and even selected reflections of Madame de Sévigné. They were so fanciful and cerebral that they made me forget I was a piece of meat, albeit a prime piece according to the specifications of my mounting pile of *Seventeen* magazines. My father, glowing with pride to see me following behind him, discussed the classics with me as an equal, using long, latinate words (a language I dubbed "lawish"); and my mother, imagining me in a better college, saw me marrying a better man. To me, however, the little books imparted Truth, all dipped out of a single vat of life's wisdom. My one-time belief in miracles mellowed to a belief in the printed word, and wide-eyed still, I read every romance as a parable for the future, every essay as personal advice. Coupled with looks, knowledge was surely power.

A cunning freak, I learned to keep my knowledge and ambitions to myself. In school, I tried to pass as smart instead of studious. I refused to learn typing and shorthand out of the same wisdom that had led my father to study them. I wanted to be admired, not a secretary. I realized that for a girl "business skills" were sure to lock the very doors they had opened for my father. Instead, I cultivated other, more useful skills. Without neglecting to brush my hair assiduously according to the instructions in *Seventeen,* I used my electives on math and commercial law, and mastered forging my father's signature for report cards and excuses. I started a notebook, with sections for words to learn, quotations to contemplate, reforms to accomplish. Ten resolutions each New Year's Eve. In everything I set myself records to beat, as I did at night with my joy button. What I couldn't master, like spelling, I disdained, claiming I could always use a dictionary. I wouldn't compete unless I could win. Borrowing from Marcus Aurelius a philosophy of sour grapes, I hedged all my bets: I wanted to be the smartest since I couldn't be sure I was the prettiest; I wanted to be the prettiest since I couldn't be sure I was the smartest. With a vanity refined to perversion, I cut school to hide that I cared to be smart, telling no one about my books, and I affected sloppiness to hide how much I wanted to be beautiful, locking away my beauty charts in my desk drawer. I began to look for trouble so it wouldn't take me by surprise. If I asked for it, I thought, maybe I could control it.

Unlike other truants who cut school to shoplift, go to the movies or a burlesque show, miss a test, or play pool, I had another purpose. I went downtown where no one knew me and, standing at a bus stop on some busy corner, I tried to stare down strange men on buses that passed by, testing my audacity. I would stare at someone till I caught his eye, then force myself to continue no matter what he did, until I stared him down and made him look away. I wanted to beat the boys at their own vile game. I would rather hate them than fear them; best of all I would make them fear me. I wanted to pick my mark, hold his eye, control his mind, bend his will to mine. I didn't dare try it in Baybury. Instead, I cut school and went downtown to play my Bus Stop Game. It was a dangerous game, for I could never tell when a man would call my bluff by leering back and force my eyes into humiliating retreat. But I had to do it: it was part of my nameless joy-life. If I succeeded at the Bus Stop Game by outstaring my mark, I rewarded myself with my button's joy; but if I failed by looking away first, I forbade myself to touch it. My father's daughter, I was very strict.

Eventually I got so good at the game that I was able to board the buses and try it on passengers from whom I couldn't escape. I selected the most frightening men to root out my fear. I wanted to make my eyes into such powerful beams that I could bend strangers and enemies to my will. I studied audacity, determined that if I couldn't be sure I had the power that comes with beauty, I would have another kind of power.

But it all turned out to be unnecessary. One balmy Friday night in early October—a Round Table night—I suddenly got the proof I had lacked that I was indeed beautiful.

The seventeen girls of Sigma Lambda Tau (the best sorority? the second-best?) all sat cross-legged in a circle on the plush cranberry carpet of Maggie West's living room. The previous Friday and the following were for business; but this one was for Round Table only: pure confrontation. Around the circle clockwise the word would pass, exploding in scandal, wrath, or outrage. One at a time the month's transgressions and oversights would be named, complaints registered, warnings given, accusers faced.

In our pleated skirts and cashmere sweaters over white dickies, we sat fiddling with our charm bracelets and straightening our sox, waiting for the President to start. Some of us gave last-minute orders to the pledges, writing merits and demerits in their conduct books. Others of us checked our new breasts in their Carousel bras like tips of sausages in their casings, looking from one to the other: were the straps adjusted evenly?

Beverly Katz, President, whispered something surreptitiously in someone's ear, then, smoothing down the pleats of her baby-blue skirt, called the meeting to order. How was it, I wondered, that her pimples did not affect her eminence? Neither her big bosom (BEST BUST) nor her sly black eyes that so perfectly expressed disdain explained her mysterious authority. She ruled by mean glances, not good looks. I studied her, wondering why everyone laughed when she cracked those jokes I never got; why even I laughed.

"Okay, let's get going. You wanna start, Sally?" said Beverly Katz, turning to the girl at her side. And off went Sally, around the circle, loosing her rhetoric on us, passing compliments and hurling insults. When she finally came to me, she frowned and hesitated a moment; then, changing her mind as I held my breath, passed on to the next sister. I was still cringing when she began on my neighbor in a voice that, like everyone's, emulated Beverly's. "I'm not saying who told me," she said, "but I happen to know . . ."

I tuned out, relieved. Why had she even hesitated over me? How could I have offended her? From my bayside perch I tried only to please, giving offense to no one. I went to their meetings, observed their taboos, admired their figures, studied their styles, always keeping my mouth carefully shut. My joy-life was secret. I wanted only to belong.

Some of the girls—perhaps the guilty ones—hung on Sally's words. Others scanned their notes, rehearsing for their own turns to talk, soon to come up. Between turns Beverly Katz popped bubbles or cracked jokes, though, as everyone knew, she had little reason to be jovial. It was already three weeks since she had received her S.L.T. pin back from Iggy Friedman, tackle, with whom she was certainly still in love and had probably already gone too far. And without Iggy, as everyone knew, she would never be re-elected President.

If Beverly Katz was at twelve o'clock, then I was at nine o'clock. Around the circle passed the word, coming closer to me. Each girl in turn had a chance to speak her mind to all or none, as she was moved. From Sally to Sue to Maggie to May. Six o'clock, seven o'clock, eight o'clock.

"Sasha?" said Beverly, popping a bubble.

I shook my head. My thoughts, questions all, were too tentative to expose to them, the slightest of whom seemed so certain, so powerful. As always, I passed.

On we moved toward the ultimate moment after Round Table when the Cokes and potato chips would be passed around, a record would be started on the phonograph, we would separate, the doors would be thrown open, and the boys, who had been waiting noisily on the lawn outside, would at last be invited in. We were all needles for that moment. Rumor had it that the football team was gradually defecting to Alpha Phi Beta. Not many of them had shown up at our meeting the week before, and without the right boys we'd never get the right pledges, and then before we knew it S.L.T. would be going down; perhaps it was already slipping. As the last few sisters spoke, we shifted on our pastel skirts and plucked at our sweaters, combing our hair and checking our bras again, till finally, circle completed, we were back to the President.

"Before we adjourn," began Beverly, holding everyone back with her black eyes, "I have a few things to say myself." She turned directly to me. Smoothing the pleats of her skirt she rose on her knees and measured the distance between our eyeballs before going into her venomous trance.

I was ready. Our eyeballs met. *Now.*

"You don't seem to care who you step on to get a guy. You think you're pretty hot shit. But watch out. We're all on to you now. We know how you operate!"

I take off, slowly at first, then at increasing speeds, swimming through space.

I hear my mother shouting in comforting farewell from some vast distance, "Just you wait, someday they'll be sorry!" while "Liar! Schemer!" resounds in my ears.

Sitting on pastel clouds receding rapidly, the sisters glance at each other with assenting smiles. They are passing a long bubble pipe from cloud to cloud, all in cahoots. In their center a black-eyed medium sings out the prophecy, Katz's Curse. (Of course she is only a medium with acne and not responsible for what she says.) "You can't get away with this shit forever!" she shouts.

I am shocked. Can she know about the Bus Stop Game? My joy button? If not, what can she be talking about? Jimmy Brennan's thing? Iggy's phone calls?

"Glub, glub, glub," she mouths, diving under a circle of white-caps and up through baby-blue waves.

At last I come to rest on my rock. Up she swims to my face inside a huge, expanding bubble. "You think that just because you're beautiful you can do anything you please and get away with it. But you can't! Someday it'll all catch up with you and then you'll pay! You'll pay for everything!"

The bubble bursts, drenching us all.

Everything? I wonder, as in the bubble's circular wake the prophecy echoes like a curse.

Though I decide it is a sane prophecy, the conclusions reasonable—no one should expect to get away with anything indefinitely—I nevertheless begin to tremble.

When the wave recedes, Beverly sits down again, being careful that the pleats in her skirt are smooth. She surveys the circle with triumphant eyes and everyone smiles back at her. I smile too, trying not to offend.

I remember something, but I don't know what. It is something strong and delicious, stuck between my teeth. Strong enough, I wonder, to sweeten the rue? I suck it out and roll it over my tongue, and then I realize: *Beverly Katz has called me beautiful, and not one word about nose or skin.*

She gets up to open the door. Out come the Cokes.

Surely I must be beautiful if she hates me for it! Well, let her hate me then, what do I care? Obviously this hatchery is not the world.

In come the boys. "Hi." "Hi." "Hi." "Hi, Sasha. Who got it tonight?" says, of all people, Iggy Friedman.

"I did," I say, surpassing protocol, and trying to master my pain by naming it. "From Beverly."

"Gee. That's too bad." Iggy looks down, slightly embarrassed. I shrug. Nat King Cole proposes that it's only a paper moon hanging over a cardboard sea.

"C'mon," says Iggy, touching my elbow. "I'll take you home tonight. We can go to Lenny's for a Lennyburger and you can tell me about it if you want to."

I taste sin. "Swell," I say. "Just let me get my sweater." For the first of what will be many times, I toss my head with a hint of defiance, like Veronica Lake. Beverly Katz may not see me, but she will hear.

I return in a moment with my sweater. "Ready," I say flashing my prettiest smile. And linking my arm in Iggy's I walk with him out the door.

What but destiny or extraordinary luck could have kept me apart from them, clinging to my rock? To have swum along with them once would have meant forever. I would make my way differently. With an eye at the end of each of my rays, I was better off a starfish. After having studied all the fairy tales and *Candide* and *Rasselas,* I knew there were some who crossed over the mountains and seas. At fourteen I believed that somewhere there must be a vast green ocean, deep and mysterious, with other currents more swift and powerful than those of this bay. There were some who escaped. Let my sisters curse me then, since their love was out of the question. Beautiful, I could try for the ocean.

BEING A BOY *

JULIUS LESTER

As boys go, I wasn't much. I mean, I tried to be a boy and spent many childhood hours pummeling my hardly formed ego with failure at cowboys and Indians, baseball, football, lying, and sneaking out of the house. When our neighborhood gang raided a neighbor's pear tree, I was the only one who got sick from the purloined fruit. I also failed at setting fire to our garage, an art at which any five-year-old boy should be adept. I was, however, the neighborhood champion at getting beat up. "That Julius can take it, man," the boys used to say, almost in admiration, after I emerged from another battle, tears brimming in my eyes but refusing to fall.

My efforts at being a boy earned me a pair of scarred knees that are a record of a childhood spent falling from bicycles, trees, the tops of fences, and porch steps; of tripping as I ran (generally from a fight), walked, or simply tried to remain upright on windy days.

I tried to believe my parents when they told me I was a boy, but I could find no objective proof for such an assertion. Each morning during the summer, as I cuddled up in the quiet of a corner with a book, my mother would push me out the back door and into the yard. And throughout the day as my blood was let as if I were a patient of 17th-century medicine, I thought of the girls sitting in the shade of porches, playing with their dolls, toy refrigerators and stoves.

There was the life, I thought! No constant pressure to prove oneself. No necessity always to be competing. While I humiliated myself on football and baseball fields, the girls stood on the sidelines laughing at me, because they didn't have to do anything except be girls. The rising of each sun brought me to the starting line of yet another day's Olympic decathlon, with no hope of ever winning even a bronze medal.

Through no fault of my own I reached adolescence. While the pressure to prove myself on the athletic field lessened, the overall situation got worse—because now I had to prove myself with girls.

* Reprinted with permission from Ms.
Magazine.

Just how I was supposed to go about doing this was beyond me, especially because, at the age of 14, I was four foot nine and weighed 78 pounds.   (I think there may have been one 10-year-old girl in the neighborhood smaller than I.)   Nonetheless, duty called, and with my ninth-grade gym-class jockstrap flapping between my legs, off I went.

To get a girlfriend, though, a boy had to have some asset beyond the fact that he was alive.   I wasn't handsome like Bill McCord, who had girls after him like a cop-killer has policemen.   I wasn't ugly like Romeo Jones, but at least the girls noticed him: "That ol' ugly boy better stay 'way from me!"   I was just there like a vase your grandmother gives you at Christmas that you don't like or dislike, can't get rid of, and don't know what to do with.   More than ever I wished I were a girl.   Boys were the ones who had to take the initiative and all the responsibility.   (I hate responsibility so much that if my heart didn't beat of itself, I would now be a dim memory.)

It was the boy who had to ask the girl for a date, a frightening enough prospect until it occurred to me that she might say no! That meant risking my ego, which was about as substantial as a toilet-paper raincoat in the African rainy season.   But I had to thrust that ego forward to be judged, accepted, or rejected by some girl.   It wasn't fair!   Who was she to sit back like a queen with the power to create joy by her consent or destruction by her denial?   It wasn't fair—but that's the way it was.

But if (God forbid!) she should say Yes, then my problem would begin in earnest, because I was the one who said where we would go (and waited in terror for her approval of my choice).   I was the one who picked her up at her house where I was inspected by her parents as if I were a possible carrier of syphilis (which I didn't think one could get from masturbating, but then again, Jesus was born of a virgin, so what did I know?).   Once we were on our way, it was I who had to pay the bus fare, the price of the movie tickets, and whatever she decided to stuff her stomach with afterward. (And the smallest girls are all stomach.)   Finally, the girl was taken home where once again I was inspected (the father looking covertly at my fly and the mother examining the girl's hair).   The evening was over and the girl had done nothing except honor me with her presence.   All the work had been mine.

Imagining this procedure over and over was more than enough: I was a sophomore in college before I had my first date.

I wasn't a total failure in high school, though, for occasionally I would go to a party, determined to salvage my self-esteem. The parties usually took place in somebody's darkened basement. There was generally a surreptitious wine bottle or two being passed furtively among the boys, and a record player with an insatiable appetite for Johnny Mathis records. Boys gathered on one side of the room and girls on the other. There were always a few boys and girls who'd come to the party for the sole purpose of grinding away their sexual frustrations to Johnny Mathis's falsetto, and they would begin dancing to their own music before the record player was plugged in. It took a little longer for others to get started, but no one matched my talent for standing by the punch bowl. For hours, I would try to make my legs do what they had been doing without effort since I was nine months old, but for some reason they would show all the symptoms of paralysis on those evenings.

After several hours of wondering whether I was going to die ("Julius Lester, a sixteen-year-old, died at a party last night, a half-eaten Ritz cracker in one hand and a potato chip dipped in pimiento-cheese spread in the other. Cause of death: failure to be a boy"), I would push my way to the other side of the room where the girls sat like a hanging jury, I would pass by the girl I wanted to dance with. If I was going to be refused, let it be by someone I didn't particularly like. Unfortunately, there weren't many in that category. I had more crushes than I had pimples.

Finally, through what surely could only have been the direct intervention of the Almighty, I would find myself on the dance floor with a girl. And none of my prior agony could compare to the thought of actually dancing. But there I was and I had to dance with her. Social custom decreed that I was supposed to lead, because I was the boy. Why? I'd wonder. Let her lead. Girls were better dancers anyway. It didn't matter. She stood there waiting for me to take charge. She wouldn't have been worse off if she'd waited for me to turn white.

But, reciting "Invictus" to myself, I placed my arms around her, being careful to keep my armpits closed because, somehow, I had managed to overwhelm a half jar of deodorant and a good-size bottle of cologne. With sweaty armpits, "Invictus," and legs afflicted again with polio, I took her in my arms, careful not to hold her so far away that she would think I didn't like her, but equally careful not to hold her so close that she could feel the catastrophe which had befallen me the instant I touched her hand. My penis, totally disobeying the lecture I'd given it before we left home, was as rigid as Governor Wallace's jaw would be if I asked for his daughter's hand in marriage.

God, how I envied girls at that moment. Wherever *it* was on them, it didn't dangle between their legs like an elephant's trunk. No wonder boys talked about nothing but sex. That thing was always there. Every time we went to the john, there it was, twitching around like a fat little worm on a fishing hook. When we took baths, it floated in the water like a lazy fish and God forbid we should touch it! It sprang to life like lightning leaping from a cloud. I wished I could cut it off, or at least keep it tucked between my legs, as if it were a tail that had been mistakenly attached to the wrong end. But I was helpless. It was there, with a life and mind of its own, having no other function than to embarrass me.

Fortunately, the girls I danced with were discreet and pretended that they felt nothing unusual rubbing against them as we danced. But I was always convinced that the next day they were all calling up all their friends to exclaim: "Guess what, girl? Julius Lester got one! I ain't lyin'!"

Now, of course, I know that it was as difficult being a girl as it was a boy, if not more so. While I stood paralyzed at one end of a dance floor trying to find the courage to ask a girl for a dance, most of the girls waited in terror at the other, afraid that no one, not even I, would ask them. And while I resented having to ask a girl for a date, wasn't it also horrible to be the one who waited for the phone to ring? And how many of those girls who laughed at me making a fool of myself on the baseball diamond would have gladly given up their places on the sidelines for mine on the field?

No, it wasn't easy for any of us, girls and boys, as we forced our beautiful free-flowing child-selves into those narrow, constricting cubicles labeled female and male. I tried, but I wasn't good at being a boy. Now, I'm glad, knowing that a man is nothing but the figment of a penis's imagination, and any man should want to be something more than that.

SEXUAL STEREOTYPES START EARLY *

FLORENCE HOWE

"I remember quite clearly a day in six grade," a college fresh-man told me a year ago, "when the class was discussing an article from a weekly supplementary reader. The story was about a chef, and someone in the class ventured the opinion that cooking was women's work, that a man was a 'sissy' to work in the kitchen. The teacher's response surprised us all. She informed us calmly that men make the best cooks, just as they make the best dress designers, singers, and laundry workers. 'Yes,' she said, 'anything a woman can do a man can do better.' There were no male students present, my teacher was a woman."

Children learn about sex roles very early in their lives, proba-bly before they are eighteen months old, certainly long before they enter school. They learn these roles through relatively simple patterns that most of us take for granted. We throw boy-babies up in the air and roughhouse with them. We coo over girl-babies and handle them delicately. We choose sex-related colors and toys for our children from their earliest days. We encourage the energy and physical activity of our sons, just as we expect girls to be quieter and more docile. We love both our sons and daughters with equal fervor, we protest, and yet we are disappointed when there is no male child to carry on the family name.

A hundred fifty years ago, Elizabeth Cady Stanton learned to master a horse and the Greek language in an attempt to com-fort her father who had lost his only son and heir. No matter what evidence of brilliance Cady Stanton displayed, her father could only shake his head and murmur, "If only you were a boy, Elizabeth," much to the bafflement of the girl who had discern-ed that riding horses and studying Greek were the activities that had distinguished her dead brother from her living sisters. Only thirty years ago, at family gatherings, I remember hearing whispers directed at my brother and me: "Isn't it a pity that he has all the looks while she has all the brains." Others could contribute similar anecdotes today.

* Reprinted from *Saturday Review*,
October, 1971, 76–94, by permission
of *Saturday Review*.

The truth of it is that while we in the West have professed to believe in "liberty, equality, and fraternity," we have also taken quite literally the term "fraternity." We have continued to maintain, relatively undisturbed, all the ancient edicts about the superiority of males, the inferiority of females. Assumptions current today about woman's alleged "nature" are disguised psychological versions of physiological premises in the Old Testament, in the doctrines of the early church fathers, and in the thinking of male philosophers, writers, educators—including some who founded women's colleges or opened men's colleges to women. In short, what we today call the "women's liberation movement" is only the most recent aspect of the struggle that began with Mary Wollstonecraft's *Vindication of the Rights of Women* in 1795—a piece of theory that drew for courage and example on the fathers of the French and American revolutions. It is, of course, only one hundred years since higher education was really opened up to women in this country, and many people know how dismal is the record of progress for professional women, especially during the past fifty years.

How much blame should be placed on public education? A substantial portion, although it is true that schools reflect the society they serve. Indeed, schools function to reinforce the sexual stereotypes that children have been taught by their parents, friends, and the mass culture we live in. It is also perfectly understandable that sexual stereotypes demeaning to women are also perpetuated by women—mothers in the first place, and teachers in the second—as well as by men—fathers, the few male teachers in elementary schools, high school teachers, and many male administrators and educators at the top of the school's hierarchy.

Sexual stereotypes are not to be identified with sexual or innate differences, for we know nothing about these matters. John Stuart Mill was the first man (since Plato) to affirm that we could know nothing about innate sexual differences, since we have never known of a society in which either men or women lived wholly separately. Therefore, he reasoned, we can't "know" what the pure "nature" of either sex might be: What we see as female behavior, he maintained, is the result of what he called the education of "willing slaves." There is still no "hard" scientific evidence of innate sexual differences, though there are new experiments in progress on male hormones of mice and monkeys. Other hormonal experiments, especially those using adrenaline, have indicated that, for human beings at least, social factors and pressures are more important than physiological ones.

Sexual stereotypes are assumed differences, social conventions or norms, learned behavior, attitudes, and expectations. Most stereotypes are well-known to all of us, for they are simple—not to say simple-minded. Men are smart, women are dumb but beautiful, etc. A recent annotated catalogue of children's books (distributed by the National Council of Teachers of English to thousands of teachers and used for ordering books with federal funds) lists titles under the headings "Especially for Girls" and "Especially for Boys." Verbs and adjectives are remarkably predictable through the listings. Boys "decipher and discover," "earn and train," or "foil" someone; girls "struggle," "overcome difficulties," "feel lost," "help solve," or "help [someone] out." One boy's story has "strange power," another moves "from truancy to triumph." A girl, on the other hand, "learns to face the real world" or makes a "difficult adjustment." Late or early, in catalogues or on shelves, the boys of children's books are active and capable, the girls passive and in trouble. All studies of children's literature—and there have been many besides my own—support this conclusion.

Ask yourself whether you would be surprised to find the following social contexts in a fifth-grade arithmetic textbook:

1) girls playing marbles; boys sewing;
2) girls earning money, building things, and going places; boys buying ribbons for a sewing project;
3) girls working at physical activities; boys babysitting and, you guessed it, sewing.

Of course you would be surprised—so would I. What I have done here is to reverse the sexes as found in a fifth-grade arithmetic text. I was not surprised, since several years ago an intrepid freshman offered to report on third-grade arithmetic texts for me and found similar types of sexual roles prescribed: Boys were generally making things or earning money; girls were cooking or spending money on such things as sewing equipment.

The verification of sexual stereotypes is a special area of interest to psychologists and sociologists. An important series of studies was done in 1968 by Inge K. Broverman and others at Worcester State Hospital in Massachusetts. These scientists established a "sex-stereotype questionnaire" consisting of "122 bipolar items"—characteristics socially known or socially tested as male or female. Studies by these scientists and others established what common sense will verify: that those traits "stereotypically masculine   .   .   .   are more often perceived as socially desirable" than those known to be feminine. Here are some "male-valued items" as listed on the questionnaire:

very aggressive
very independent
not at all emotional
very logical
very direct
very adventurous
very self-confident
very ambitious

These and other characteristics describe the stereotypic male. To describe the female, you need only reverse those traits and add "female-valued" ones, some of which follow:

very talkative
very tactful
very gentle
very aware of feelings of others
very religious
very quiet
very strong need for security

and the one I am particularly fond of citing to men who control my field—"enjoys art and literature very much."

The Worcester scientists used their 122 items to test the assumptions of clinical psychologists about mental health. Three matched groups of male and female clinical psychologists were given three identical lists of the 122 items unlabeled and printed in random order. Each group was given a different set of instructions: One was told to choose those traits that characterize the healthy adult male; another to choose those of the healthy adult female; the third, to choose those of the healthy adult —a person. The result: The clinically healthy male and the clinically healthy adult were identical—and totally divergent from the clinically healthy female. The authors of the study concluded that "a double standard of health exists for men and women." That is, the general standard of health applies only to men. Women are perceived as "less healthy" by those standards called "adult." At the same time, however, if a woman deviates from the sexual stereotypes prescribed for her—if she grows more "active" or "aggressive," for example—she doesn't grow healthier; she may, in fact, if her psychiatrist is a Freudian, be perceived as "sicker." Either way, therefore, women lose or fail, and so it is not surprising to find psychologist Phyllis Chesler reporting that proportionately many more women than men are declared "sick" by psychologists and psychiatrists.

The idea of a "double standard" for men and women is a familiar one and helps to clarify how severely sexual stereotypes constrict the personal and social development of women. Studies by child psychologists reveal that while boys of all ages clearly identify with male figures and activities, girls are less likely to make the same sort of identification with female stereotypes. With whom do girls and women identify? My guess is that there is a good deal of confusion in their heads and hearts in this respect, and that what develops is a pattern that might be compared to schizophrenia: The schoolgirl knows that, for her, life is one thing, learning another. This is like the Worcester study's "double standard"—the schoolgirl cannot find herself in history texts or as she would like to see herself in literature; yet she knows she is not a male. Many women may ultimately discount the question of female identity as unimportant, claiming other descriptions preferable—as a parent, for example, or a black person, or a college professor.

Children learn sexual stereotypes at an early age, and, by the time they get to fifth grade, it may be terribly difficult, perhaps hardly possible by traditional means, to change their attitudes about sex roles—whether they are male or female. For more than a decade, Paul Torrance, a psychologist particularly interested in creativity, has been conducting interesting and useful experiments with young children. Using a Products Improvement Test, for example, Torrance asked first-grade boys and girls to "make toys more fun to play with." Many six-year-old boys refused to try the nurse's kit, "protesting," Torrance reports, "I'm a boy! I don't play with things like that." Several creative boys turned the nurse's kit into a doctor's kit and were then "quite free to think of improvements." By the third grade, however, "boys excelled girls even on the nurse's kit, probably because," Torrance explains, "girls have been conditioned by this time to accept toys as they are and not to manipulate or change them."

Later experiments with third, fourth, and fifth-graders using science toys further verify what Torrance calls "the inhibiting effects of sex-role conditioning." "Girls were quite reluctant," he reports, "to work with these science toys and frequently protested: 'I'm a girl; I'm not supposed to know anything about things like that!' " Boys, even in these early grades, were about twice as good as girls at explaining ideas about toys. In 1959, Torrance reported his findings to parents and teachers in one school and asked for their cooperation in attempting to change the attitudes of the girls. In 1960, when he retested them, using similar science toys, the girls participated willingly and even with apparent enjoyment. And they performed as well as the boys. But in one significant respect nothing had changed: The boys' contributions were more highly valued—both by other boys and by girls—than the girls' contributions, regardless of the fact that, in terms of sex, boys and girls had scored equally. "Apparently," Torrance writes, "the school climate has helped to make it more acceptable for girls to play around with science things, but boys' ideas about science things are still supposed to be better than those of girls."

Torrance's experiments tell us both how useful and how limited education may be for women in a culture in which assumptions about their inferiority run deep in their own consciousness as well as in the consciousness of men. While it is encouraging to note that a year's effort had changed behavior patterns significantly, it is also clear that attitudes of nine-, ten-, and eleven-year-olds are not so easily modifiable, at least not through the means Torrance used.

Torrance's experiments also make clear that, whatever most of us have hitherto assumed, boys and girls are not treated alike in elementary school. If we consider those non-curricular aspects of the school environment that the late anthropologist Jules Henry labeled the "noise" of schools, chief among them is the general attitude of teachers, whatever their sex, that girls are likely to "love" reading and to "hate" mathematics and science. As we know from the Rosenthal study of teacher expectations, *Pygmalion in the Classroom,* such expectations significantly determine student behavior and attitudes. Girls are not expected to think logically or to understand scientific principles; they accept that estimate internally and give up on mathematics and science relatively early. And what encouragement awaits the interested few in high school? For example, in six high school science texts published since 1966 and used in the Baltimore city public schools—all of the books rich in illustrations—I found photographs of one female lab assistant, one woman doctor, one woman scientist, and Rachel Carson. It is no wonder that the percentage of women doctors and engineers in the United States has remained constant at 6 per cent and 1 per cent respectively for the past fifty years.

Though there is no evidence that their early physical needs are different from or less than boys', girls are offered fewer activities even in kindergarten. They may sit and watch while boys, at the request of the female teacher, change the seating arrangement in the room. Of course, it's not simply a matter of physical exercise or ability: Boys are learning how to behave as males, and girls are learning to be "ladies" who enjoy being "waited on." If there are student-organized activities to be arranged, boys are typically in charge, with girls assisting, perhaps in the stereotyped role of secretary. Boys are allowed and expected to be noisy and aggressive, even on occasion to express anger; girls must learn "to control themselves" and behave like "young ladies." On the other hand, boys are expected not to cry, though there are perfectly good reasons why children of both sexes ought to be allowed that avenue of expression. Surprisingly early, boys and girls are separated for physical education and hygiene, and all the reports now being published indicate preferential treatment for boys and nearly total neglect of girls.

In junior high schools, sexual stereotyping becomes, if anything, more overt. Curricular sex-typing continues and is extended to such "shop" subjects as cooking and sewing, on the one hand, and metal- and woodworking, printing, ceramics, on the other. In vocational high schools, the stereotyping becomes outright channeling, and here the legal battles have begun for equality of opportunity. Recently, the testimony of junior high and high school girls in New York has become available in a pamphlet prepared by the New York City chapter of NOW (*Report on Sex Bias in the Public Schools,* available from Anne Grant West, 453 Seventh St., Brooklyn, N. Y. 11215). Here are a few items:

- Well, within my physics class last year, our teacher asked if there was anybody interested in being a lab assistant, in the physics lab, and when I raised my hand, he told all the girls to put their hands down because he was only interested in working with boys.

- There is an Honor Guard . . . students who, instead of participating in gym for the term, are monitors in the hall, and I asked my gym teacher if I could be on the Honor Guard Squad. She said it was only open to boys. I then went to the head of the Honor Guard . . . who said that he thought girls were much too nasty to be Honor Guards. He thought they would be too mean in working on the job, and I left it at that.

- We asked for basketball. They said there wasn't enough equipment. The boys prefer to have it first. Then we will have what is left over. We haven't really gotten anywhere.

Finally, I quote more extensively from one case:

MOTHER: I asked Miss Jonas if my daughter could take metal-working or mechanics, and she said there is no freedom of choice. That is what she said.

THE COURT: That is it?

ANSWER: I also asked her whose decision this was, that there was no freedom of choice. And she told me it was the decision of the board of education. I didn't ask her anything else because she clearly showed me that it was against the school policy for girls to be in the class. She said it was a board of education decision.

QUESTION: Did she use that phrase, "no freedom of choice"?

ANSWER: Exactly that phrase—no freedom of choice. That is what made me so angry that I wanted to start this whole thing.

· · ·

THE COURT: Now, after this lawsuit was filed, they then permitted you to take the course; is that correct?

DAUGHTER: No, we had to fight about it for quite a while.

QUESTION: But eventually they did let you in the second semester?

ANSWER: They only let me in there.

Q: You are the only girl?

A: Yes.

Q: How did you do in the course?

A: I got the medal for it from all the boys there.

Q: Will you show the court?

A: Yes (indicating).

Q: And what does the medal say?

A: Metal 1970 Van Wyck.

Q: And why did they give you that medal?

A: Because I was the best one out of all the boys.

THE COURT: I do not want any giggling or noises in the court-room.   Just do the best you can to control yourself or else I will have to ask you to leave the courtroom.   This is no picnic, you know.   These are serious lawsuits.

Such "serious lawsuits" will, no doubt, continue, but they are not the only routes to change.   There are others to be initiated by school systems themselves.

One route lies through the analysis of texts and attitudes.   So long as those responsible for the education of children believe in the stereotypes as given, rather than as hypothetical con-structs that a patriarchal society has established as desired norms—so long as the belief continues, so will the condition. These beliefs are transmitted in the forms we call literature and history, either on the printed page or in other media.

Elementary school readers are meant for both sexes.   Primers used in the first three grades offer children a view of a "typical" American family: a mother who does not work, a father who does, two children—a brother who is always older than a sister— and two pets—a dog and sometimes a cat—whose sexes and ages mirror those of the brother and sister.   In these books, boys build or paint things; they also pull girls in wagons and push merry-go-rounds.   Girls carry purses when they go shop-ping;   they help mother cook or pretend that they are cooking; and they play with their dolls.   When they are not making mess-es, they are cleaning up their rooms or other people's messes. Plots in which girls are involved usually depend on their inabili-ty to do something—to manage their own roller skates or to ride a pony.   Or in another typical role, a girl named Sue ad-mires a parachute jumper: "What a jump!" said Sue.   "What a jump for a man to make!"   When her brother puts on a show for the rest of the neighborhood, Sue, whose name appears as the title of the chapter, is part of his admiring audience.

The absence of adventurous heroines may shock the innocent; the absence of even a few stories about women doctors, lawyers, or professors thwarts reality; but the consistent presence of one female stereotype is the most troublesome matter:

> Primrose was playing house. Just as she finished pouring tea for her dolls she began to think. She thought and thought and she thought some more: "Whom shall I marry? Whomever shall I marry?
>
> "I think I shall marry a mailman. Then I could go over to everybody's house and give them their mail.
>
> "Or I might marry a policeman. I could help him take the children across the street."

Primrose thinks her way through ten more categories of employment and concludes, "But now that I think it over, maybe I'll just marry somebody I love." Love is the opiate designated to help Primrose forget to think about what she would like to do or be. With love as reinforcer, she can imagine herself helping some man in his work. In another children's book, Johnny says, "I think I will be a dentist when I grow up," and later, to Betsy, he offers generously, "You can be a dentist's nurse." And, of course, Betsy accepts gratefully, since girls are not expected to have work identity other than as servants or helpers. In short, the books that schoolgirls read prepare them early for the goal of marriage, hardly ever for work, and never for independence.

If a child's reader can be pardoned for stereotyping because it is "only" fiction, a social studies text has no excuse for denying reality to its readers. After all, social studies texts ought to describe "what is," if not "what should be." And yet, such texts for the youngest grades are no different from readers. They focus on families and hence on sex roles and work. Sisters are still younger than brothers; brothers remain the doers, questioners, and knowers who explain things to their poor, timid sisters. In a study of five widely used texts, Jamie Kelem Frisof finds that energetic boys think about "working on a train or in a broom factory" or about being President. They grow up to be doctors or factory workers or (in five texts combined) to do some hundred different jobs, as opposed to thirty for women.

Consider for a moment the real work world of women. Most women (at least for some portion of their lives) work, and if we include "token" women—the occasional engineer, for instance—they probably do as many different kinds of work as men. Even without improving the status of working women, the reality is

distinctly different from the content of school texts and literature written for children. Schools usually at least reflect the
society they serve; but the treatment of working women is one
clear instance in which the reflection is distorted by a patriarchal
attitude about who *should* work and the maleness of work. For
example, there are women doctors—there have been women
doctors in this country, in fact, for a hundred years or so. And
yet, until the publication this month of two new children's books
by the Feminist Press (Box 334, Old Westbury, N. Y. 11568),
there were no children's books about women doctors.

In a novel experiment conducted recently by an undergraduate
at Towson State College in Maryland, fourth-grade students answered "yes" or "no" to a series of twenty questions, eight of
which asked, in various ways, whether "girls were smarter than
boys" or whether "daddies were smarter than mommies." The
results indicated that boys and girls were agreed that 1) boys
were not smarter than girls, nor girls smarter than boys; but 2)
that daddies were indeed smarter than mommies! One possible
explanation of this finding depends on the knowledge that daddies, in school text and on television (as well as in real life),
work, and that people who work know things. Mommies, on
the other hand, in books and on television, rarely stir out of the
house except to go to the store—and how can someone like that
know anything? Of course, *we* know that half of all mothers in
the United States work at some kind of job, but children whose
mommies do work can only assume—on the basis of evidence
offered in school books and on television—that their mommies
must be "different," perhaps even not quite "real" mommies.

If children's readers deny the reality of working women, high
school history texts deny women their full historical role. A
recent study by Janice Law Trecker of thirteen popular texts
concludes with what by now must seem a refrain: Women in
such texts are "passive, incapable of sustained organization or
work, satisfied with [their] role in society, and well supplied
with material blessings." Women, in the grip of economic and
political forces, rarely fighting for anything, occasionally receive
some "rights," especially suffrage in 1920, which, of course,
solves all *their* problems. There is no discussion of the struggle
by women to gain entrance into higher education, of their efforts
to organize or join labor unions, of other battles for working
rights, or of the many different aspects of the hundred-year-long
multi-issue effort that ended, temporarily, in the suffrage act of

1920. Here is Dr. Trecker's summary of the history and contributions of American women as garnered from the thirteen
texts combined:

> Women arrived in 1619 (a curious choice if meant to be their
> first acquaintance with the New World). They held the Seneca
> Falls Convention on Women's Rights in 1848. During the
> rest of the nineteenth century, they participated in reform
> movements, chiefly temperance, and were exploited in fac-
> tories. In 1920, they were given the vote. They joined the
> armed forces for the first time during the Second World War
> and thereafter have enjoyed the good life in America. Add
> the names of the women who are invariably mentioned: Har-
> riet Beecher Stowe, Jane Addams, Dorothea Dix, and Frances
> Perkins, with perhaps Susan B. Anthony, Elizabeth Cady
> Stanton . . . [and you have the story].

Where efforts have been made in recent years to incorporate
black history, again it is without attention to black women, either with respect to their role in abolitionist or civil rights movements, for example, or with respect to intellectual or cultural
achievements.

Just as high school history texts rely on male spokesmen and
rarely quote female leaders of the feminist movement—even
when they were also articulate writers such as Charlotte Perkins
Gilman, or speakers such as Sojourner Truth—so, too, literary
anthologies will include Henry James or Stephen Crane rather
than Edith Wharton or Kate Chopin. Students are offered James
Joyce's *Portrait of the Artist as a Young Man* or the *Autobi-
ography of Malcolm X,* rather than Doris Lessing's *Martha Quest*
or Anne Moody's *Coming of Age in Mississippi.* As a number
of studies have indicated, the literary curriculum, both in high
school and college, is a male-centered one. That is, either male
authors dominate the syllabus or the central characters of the
books are consistently male. There is also usually no compen-
sating effort to test the fictional portaits—of women and men—
against the reality of life experience. Allegedly "relevant" textbooks for senior high school or freshman college composition
courses continue to appear, such as Macmillan's *Representative
Men: Heroes of Our Time.* There are two women featured in
this book: Elizabeth Taylor, the actress, and Jacqueline Onassis,
the Existential Heroine. Thirty-five or forty men—representing
a range of racial, political, occupational, and intellectual inter-

ests—fill the bulk of a book meant, of course, for both men and women. And some teachers are still ordering such texts.

It's not a question of malice, I assume, but of thoughtlessness or ignorance. Six or seven years ago I too was teaching from a standard male-dominated curriculum—and at a women's college at that. But I speak from more than my own experience. Last fall at this time I knew of some fifty college courses in what has come to be known as women's studies. This fall, I know of more than 500, about half of which are in literature and history. I know also of many high school teachers who have already begun to invent comparable courses.

School systems can and should begin to encourage new curricular developments, especially in literature and social studies, and at the elementary as well as the high school level. Such changes, of course, must include the education and re-education of teachers, and I know of no better way to re-educate them than to ask for analyses of the texts they use, as well as of their assumptions and attitudes. The images we pick up, consciously or unconsciously, from literature and history significantly control our sense of identity, and our identity—our sense of ourselves as powerful or powerless, for example—controls our behavior. As teachers read new materials and organize and teach new courses, they will change their views. That is the story of most of the women I know who, like me, have become involved in women's studies. The images we have in our heads about ourselves come out of literature and history; before we can change those images, we must see them clearly enough to exorcise them and, in the process, to raise others from the past we are learning to see.

That is why black educators have grown insistent upon their students' learning black history—slave history, in fact. That is also why some religious groups, Jews for example, emphasize their history as a people, even though part of that history is also slave history. For slave history has two virtues: Not only does it offer a picture of servitude against which one can measure the present; it offers also a vision of struggle and courage. When I asked a group of young women at the University of Pittsburgh last year whether they were depressed by the early nineteenth-century women's history they were studying, their replies were instructive: "Certainly not," one woman said, "we're angry that we had to wait until now—after so many years of U. S. history in high school—to learn the truth about some things." And another added, "But it makes you feel good to read about those tremendous women way back then. They felt some of the same things we do now."

Will public education begin to change the images of women in texts and the lives of women students in schools? There will probably be some movement in this direction, at least in response to the pressures from students, parents, and individual teachers. I expect that parents, for example, will continue to win legal battles for their daughters' equal rights and opportunities. I expect that individual teachers will alter their courses and texts and grow more sensitive to stereotypic expectations and behavior in the classroom. But so far there are no signs of larger, more inclusive reforms: no remedial program for counselors, no major effort to destereotype vocational programs or kindergarten classrooms, no centers for curricular reform. Frankly, I don't expect this to happen without a struggle. I don't expect that public school systems will take the initiative here. There is too much at stake in a society as patriarchal as this one. And schools, after all, tend to follow society, not lead it.

THE INEXPRESSIVE MALE: A TRAGEDY OF AMERICAN SOCIETY *

Jack O. Balswick and Charles W. Peek

The problem of what it means to be "male" and "female" is a problem which is faced and dealt with in its own way in every society. Through cross-cultural research one now surmises that culture rather than "nature" is the major influence in determining the temperamental differences between the sexes. It may be no accident that a woman, Margaret Mead, did the classic study demonstrating that temperamental differences between the sexes are explained very little in terms of innateness, but rather in terms of culture. In her book, *Sex and Temperament*, Mead reported on the differences in sex roles for three New Guinea societies.[1] Using ethnocentric western standards in defining sex roles, she found that the ideal sex role for both the male and female was essentially "feminine" among the Arapesh, "masculine" among the Mundugumor, and "feminine" for the male and "masculine" for the female among the Tchambuli. The Tchambuli represents a society that defines sex roles in a complete reversal of the traditional distinctions made between masculine and feminine roles in the United States.

It is the purpose of this paper to consider a particular temperament trait that often characterizes the male in American society. As sex role distinctions have developed in America, the male sex role as compared to the female sex role, carries with it prescriptions which encourage inexpressiveness. In some of its extreme contemporary forms, the inexpressive male has even come to be glorified as the epitome of a real man. This will be discussed later in the paper when two types of inexpressive male are examined.

THE CREATION OF THE INEXPRESSIVE MALE

Children, from the time they are born both explicitly and implicitly are taught how to be a man or how to be a woman. While the girl is taught to act "feminine" and to desire "feminine" ob-

* Reprinted from *The Family Coordinator*, October, 1971, pp. 363–368, by permission of the authors and the National Council on Family Relations.

jects, the boy is taught how to be a man. In learning to be a man, the boy in American society comes to value expressions of masculinity and devalue expressions of femininity. Masculinity is expressed largely through physical courage, toughness, competitiveness, and aggressiveness, whereas femininity is, in contrast, expressed largely through gentleness, expressiveness, and responsiveness. When a young boy begins to express his emotions through crying, his parents are quick to assert, "You're a big boy and big boys don't cry." Parents often use the term, "he's all boy," in reference to their son, and by this term usually refer to behavior which is an expression of aggressiveness, getting into mischief, getting dirty, etc., but never use the term to denote behavior which is an expression of affection, tenderness, or emotion. What parents are really telling their son is that a real man does not show his emotions and if he is a real man he will not allow his emotions to be expressed. These outward expressions of emotion are viewed as a sign of femininity, and undesirable for a male.

Is it any wonder, then, that during the most emotional peak of a play or movie, when many in the audience have lumps in their throats and tears in their eyes, that the adolescent boy guffaws loudly or quickly suppresses any tears which may be threatening to emerge, thus demonstrating to the world that he is above such emotional feeling?

THE INEXPRESSIVE MALE AS A SINGLE MAN

At least two basic types of inexpressive male seem to result from this socialization process: the cowboy and the playboy. Manville has referred to the *cowboy type* in terms of a "John Wayne Neurosis" which stresses the strong, silent, and two-fisted male as the 100 percent American he-man.[2] For present purposes, it is especially in his relationship with women that the John Wayne neurosis is particularly significant in representing many American males. As portrayed by Wayne in any one of his many type-cast roles, the mark of a real man is that he does not show any tenderness or affection toward girls because his culturally-acquired male image dictates that such a show of emotions would be distinctly unmanly. If he does have anything to do with girls, it is on a "man to man" basis: the girl is treated roughly (but not sadistically), with little hint of gentleness or affection. As Manville puts it:

> The on-screen John Wayne doesn't feel comfortable around women. He does like them sometimes—God knows he's not *queer*. But at the right time, and in the right place—which he chooses. And always with his car/horse parked directly outside, in/on which he will ride away to his more important business back in Marlboro country.[3]

Alfred Auerback, a psychiatrist, has commented more directly on the cowboy type.[4] He describes the American male's inexpressiveness with women as part of the "cowboy syndrome." He quite rightly states that "the cowboy in moving pictures has conveyed the image of the rugged 'he-man,' strong, resilient, resourceful, capable of coping with over-whelming odds. His attitude toward women is courteous but reserved." As the cowboy equally loved his girlfriend and his horse, so the present day American male loves his car or motorcycle and his girlfriend. Basic to both these descriptions is the notion that the cowboy does have feelings toward women but does not express them, since ironically such expression would conflict with his image of what a male is.

The *playboy type* has recently been epitomized in *Playboy* magazine and by James Bond. As with the cowboy type, he is resourceful and shrewd, and interacts with his girlfriend with a certain detachment which is expressed as "playing it cool." While Bond's relationship with women is more in terms of a Don Juan, he still treats women with an air of emotional detachment and independence similar to that of the cowboy. The playboy departs from the cowboy, however, in that he is also "non-feeling." Bond and the playboy he caricatures are in a sense "dead" inside. They have no emotional feelings toward women, while Wayne, although unwilling and perhaps unable to express them does have such feelings. Bond rejects women as women, treating them as consumer commodities; Wayne puts women on a pedestal. The playboy's relationship with women represents the culmination of Fromm's description of a marketing-oriented personality in which a person comes to see both himself and others as persons to be manipulated and exploited. Sexuality is reduced to a packageable consumption item which the playboy can handle because it demands no responsibility. The woman in the process, becomes reduced to a playboy accessory. A successful "love affair" is one in which the bed was shared, but the playboy emerges having avoided personal involvement or a shared relationship with the woman.

The playboy, then, in part is the old cowboy in modern dress. Instead of the crude mannerisms of John Wayne, the playboy is a skilled manipulator of women, knowing when to turn the lights down, what music to play on the stereo, which drinks to serve, and what topics of conversation to pursue. The playboy, however, is not a perfect likeness; for unlike the cowboy, he does not seem to care for the women from whom he withholds his emotions. Thus, the inexpressive male as a single man comes in two types: the inexpressive feeling man (the cowboy) and the inexpressive non-feeling man (the playboy).

THE INEXPRESSIVE MALE AS A MARRIED MAN

When the inexpressive male marries, his inexpressiveness can become highly dysfunctional to his marital relationship *if* he continues to apply it across-the-board to all women, his wife included. The modern American family places a greater demand upon the marriage relationship than did the family of the past. In the typical marriage of 100 or even 50 years ago, the roles of both the husband and the wife were clearly defined as demanding, task-oriented functions. If the husband successfully performed the role of provider and protector of his wife and family and if the wife performed the role of homemaker and mother to her children, chances were the marriage was defined as successful, both from a personal and a societal point of view. The traditional task functions which in the past were performed by the husband and wife are today often taken care of by individuals and organizations outside the home. Concomitant with the decline of the task functions in marriage has been the increase in the importance of the companionship and affectionate function in marriage. As Blood and Wolfe concluded in their study of the modern American marriage, "companionship has emerged as the most valued aspect of marriage today." [5]

As American society has become increasingly mechanized and depersonalized, the family remains as one of the few social groups where what sociologists call the primary relationship has still managed to survive. As such, a greater and greater demand has been placed upon the modern family and especially the modern marriage to provide for affection and companionship. Indeed, it is highly plausible to explain the increased rate of divorce during the last 70 years, not in terms of a breakdown in marriage relationships, but instead, as resulting from the increased load which marriage has been asked to carry. When the husband and wife no longer find affection and companionship from their marriage relationship, they most likely question the wisdom of attempting to continue in their conjugal relationship. When affection is gone, the main reason for the marriage relationship disappears.

Thus, within the newly defined affectively-oriented marriage relationship male inexpressiveness toward *all* women, wife included, would be dysfunctional. But what may happen for many males is that through progressively more serious involvements with women (such as going steady, being pinned, engagement, and the honeymoon period of marriage), they begin to make some exceptions. That is, they may learn to be *situationally rather than totally inexpressive*, inexpressive toward women in most situations but not in all. As the child who learns a rule and then, through further experience, begins to understand the exceptions to it, many American males may pick up the principle of inexpressiveness toward women, discovering its exceptions as they become more and more experienced in the full range of man-woman relationships. Consequently, they may become more expressive toward their wives while remaining essentially inexpressive toward other women; they learn that the conjugal relationship is one situation that is an exception to the cultural requirement of male inexpressiveness. Thus, what was once a double *sexual* standard, where men had one standard of sexual conduct toward their fiancee or wife and another toward other women, may now be primarily a double *emotional* standard, where men learn to be expressive toward their fiancee or wife but remain inexpressive toward women in general.

To the extent that such situational inexpressiveness exists among males, it should be functional to the maintenance of the marriage relationship. Continued inexpressiveness by married males toward women other than their wives would seem to prohibit their forming meaningful relationships with these women. Such a situation would seem to be advantageous to preserving their marital relationships, since "promiscuous" expressiveness toward other women could easily threaten the stability of these companionship-oriented marital relationships.

In short, the authors' suggestion is that situational inexpressiveness, in which male expressiveness is essentially limited to the marital relationship, may be one of the basic timbers shoring up many American marriages, especially if indications of increasing extramarital sexual relations are correct. In a sense, then, the consequences of situational inexpressiveness for marital relationships do not seem very different from those of prostitution down through the centuries, where prostitution provided for extramarital sex under circumstances which discouraged personal affection toward the female partner strong enough to undermine the marital relationship. In the case of the situationally inexpressive husband, his inexpressiveness in relations with women other than his wife may serve as a line of defense against the possible negative consequences of such involvement toward marital stability. By acting as the cowboy or playboy, therefore, the married male may effectively rob extramarital relationships of their expressiveness and thus preserve his marital relationship.

The inexpressiveness which the American male early acquires may be bothersome in that he has to partially unlearn it in order to effectively relate to his wife. However, if he is successful in partially unlearning it (or learning a few exceptions to it), then it can be highly functional to maintaining the conjugal relationship.

But what if the husband does not partially unlearn his inexpressiveness? Within the newly defined expressive function of the marriage relationship, he is likely to be found inadequate. The possibility of an affectionate and companionship conjugal relationship carries with it the assumption that both the husband and wife are bringing into marriage the expressive capabilities to make such a relationship work. This being the case, American society is ironically short changing males in terms of their ability to fulfill this role expectation. Thus, society inconsistently teaches the male that to be masculine is to be inexpressive, while at the same time expectations in the marital role are defined in terms of sharing affection and companionship which involves the ability to communicate and express feelings. What exists apparently, is another example of a discontinuity in cultural conditioning of which Benedict (1938) spoke more than 30 years ago.

Conclusion and Summary

It has been suggested that many American males are incapable of expressing themselves emotionally to a woman, and that this inexpressiveness is a result of the way society socialized males into their sex-role. However, there is an alternative explanation which should be explored, namely, that the learning by the male of his sex-role may not actually result in his inability to be expressive, but rather only in his thinking that he is not supposed to be expressive. Granted, according to the first explanation, the male cannot express himself precisely because he was taught that he was not supposed to be expressive, but in this second explanation inexpressiveness is a result of present perceived expectations and not a psychological condition which resulted from past socialization. The male perceives cultural expectations as saying, "don't express yourself to women," and although the male may be capable of such expressiveness, he "fits" into cultural expectations. In the case of the married male, where familial norms do call for expressiveness to one's wife, it may be that the expectations for the expression of emotions to his wife are not communicated to him.

There has been a trickle of evidence which would lend support to the first explanation, which stresses the male's incapacity to be expressive. Several studies have suggested that especially among the lowly educated, it is the wife playing the feminine role who is often disappointed in the lack of emotional concern shown by her husband.[6, 7, 8, 9] The husband, on the other hand, cannot understand the relatively greater concern and emotional expressiveness which his wife desires, since he does not usually feel this need himself. As a result of her research, Komarovsky has suggested that "the ideal of masculinity into which . . . (men are) . . . socialized inhibits expressiveness both directly, with its emphasis on reserve, and indirectly, by identifying personal interchange with the feminine role."[10] Balswick found that males are less capable than females of expressing or receiving companionship support from their spouses.[11] His research also supports the view than inadequacy of expressiveness is greatest for the less educated males. Although inexpressiveness may be found among males at all socioeconomic levels, it is especially among the lower class male that expressiveness is seen as being inconsistent with his defined masculine role.

There may be some signs that conditions which have contributed toward the creation of the inexpressive male are in the process of decline. The de-emphasis in distinctiveness in dress and fashions between the sexes, as exemplified in the "hippy" movement can be seen as a reaction against the rigidly defined distinctions between the sexes which have characterized American society. The sexless look, as presently being advanced in high fashion, is the logical end reaction to a society which has superficially created strong distinctions between the sexes. Along with the blurring of sexual distinctions in fashion may very well be the shattering of the strong, silent male as a glorified type. There is already evidence of sharp criticisms of the inexpressive male and exposure of him as constituting a "hangup." Marriage counselors, sensitivity group leaders, "hippies," and certainly youth in general, are critical of inexpressiveness, and candid honesty in interpersonal relations. Should these views permeate American society, the inexpressive male may well come to be regarded as a pathetic tragedy instead of the epitome of masculinity and fade from the American scene. Not all may applaud his departure, however. While those interested in more satisfactory male-female relationships, marital and otherwise, will probably gladly see him off, those concerned with more stable marital relationships may greet his departure less enthusiastically. Although it should remove an important barrier to satisfaction in all male-female relationships via an increase in the male's capacity for emotional response toward females, by the same token it also may remove a barrier against emotional entanglement in relations with females outside marital relationships and thus threaten the stability of marriages. If one finds the inexpressive male no longer present one of these days, then, it will be interesting to observe whether any gains in the stability of marriage due to increased male expressiveness *within* this relationship will be enough to offset losses in stability emanating from increasing displays of male expressiveness *outside* it.

MALE LIBERATION—DESTROYING
THE STEREOTYPES *

SUZANNE K. STEINMETZ

Discrimination against minorities has, as a topic of current interest, captured a large audience. This focus has tended to be on discrimination against Blacks, Chicanos, Indians, as well as women. Little by little the picture is emerging—one cannot discriminate against another group without suffering losses. We all pay for discrimination. When we discriminate against others, we lose not only potential talent, but suffer increases in crime, lack of security, and costly and inefficient welfare programs. Males, however, are usually not considered to be discriminated against; therefore, research in this area is notably missing.

This paper is concerned with a variety of male stereotypes which are seen as limiting the personal freedom of both males and females. Although there has been a tendency for the women's movement to emphasize the injustices to women, it is increasingly evident that this is not a zero-sum game—men's losses are not necessarily women's gains. The following are examples of male stereotypes and how they operate to limit the personal freedom of both men and women.

HEAD OF THE FAMILY: A MALE PREROGATIVE

Male employment in our society is the means for participating in the family and is the major mechanism for conferring adult status. Research on unemployed men and their families during the depression suggests that loss of power and influence in the family is tied to the loss of employment. The importance of being employed, for the male, is further supported by the literature on family violence. It has been found that when unemployment increases, violence between husbands and wives likewise increases. The mental retardation literature still further supports this importance of successfully filling the earner-provider role. Given the same degree of retardation, women are less likely to be viewed

* Originally presented at the annual meeting of the National Council on Family Relations, Toronto, Canada, October, 1973.

By permission of the author, Suzanne K. Steinmetz, University of Delaware.

as unsuccessful in fulfilling expected roles than men, since for women, unlike men, successfully holding a full-time paid job is not a prerequisite of adequate adult functioning.

According to a statement of the Association for Women Psychologists of the American Psychological Association, sex role stereotyping, while it may enable men to hold higher prestige jobs with greater financial rewards, and a greater chance for promotion, also causes them " . . . crippling pressure to compete, achieve, produce, to stifle emotional sensitivity, and gentleness." [1]

The research suggests that even when the man is employed, having an employed wife appears to constitute a threat to his position as head.[2] Aldous suggests that " . . . the opportunity to practice an occupation, therefore, is a community tie that enables the male to perform the role of provider, a role that for most men appears a prerequisite for their performing other family roles." [3] Astrid Shømberg notes that: "It is always assumed that the husbands have a duty from which their wives are exempt of providing for their families." [4] Thus while man has the advantage in the labor market, the woman is compensated in that she is not taxed on the economic value of the work she performs or on the payment in the form of housing, food, or clothes for this work.

Thus even in these days of increasing sexual equality, it is still customary for males to be the *main* provider. Although we are willing to admit that a woman may enjoy working for the intrinsic value of work, there is a tendency to view the wife's working as a resource, in the Blood and Wolfe sense, which improves her position relative to her spouse.[5] We tend to see her gains as something her husband loses. This overlooks the fact that the husband often gains many advantages if his spouse is employed: additional income; less need to become "insurance poor"; security in knowing that one's wife is capable of carrying on, if necessary; greater independence—the clinging vine now has her own interests making her more interesting in her own right; and finally, pride in gains from having family members who are successfully employed since employment holds a high value in the work-ethic oriented America.

One objection leveled at the advantages of having one's wife employed concerns the increased expenses incurred as a result of her employment. This makes the economic value of her employment

questionable. The media, which is quite good at reinforcing traditional stereotypes has as its familiar family situation the wife
who, upon entering the labor force not only runs up expenses,
e. g., travel, clothes, eating out, but also turns the house into a
shambles and neglects her housekeeper/organizer/hostess role.
The message is that any gains she might have incurred from work
are insignificant compared to the family's cost of having her employed.

This view is discriminatory in that the club membership, expensive car, and well stocked bar are not, except for tax purposes,
deducted from the male's income. Instead they are considered a
form of conspicuous consumption which gives added prestige and
status to one's job. As Settles notes, "Usually when discussing
the economic benefit of a woman's job to her family, her 'expenses' due to working are pulled out and subtracted from her
take-home salary to yield the possible added income. This practice ignores the subtle increase in standard of living for the family
which the so-called expenses may bring. For example, the second
car may be as much a convenience to the adolescents and the husband as it is a commuting expense to the mother. Often the
clothes needed for work are said to be more expensive than those
for housewives, but isn't that the whole point? (Nicer clothes
reflect an increased family standard of living). One may want to
wear nice clothes not only for work, but to go out to dinner that
night with your husband—eating out more frequently is also supposedly an expense for the working wife." [6]

Yet, so entrenched is society in the traditional role of *male* head
of household, that even when the wife is head in terms of occupation and financial support of the family, the census edits these returns to have the husband shown as head. This emphasis on the
importance of the male as head of household, to the point of having the census bureau edit the "deviant" cases, places an unnecessary social stigma on males who have no desire or, for a variety
of reasons, are unable to fulfill this role according to expected
standards.

THE FUNCTION OF THE BUMBLING MALE: SEXISM IN THE MEDIA

Not only does the census reinforce traditional sex roles in the
collecting and analyzing of data, for example, the categorizing of
respondents as "head, wife of head, son or daughter of head", but

this trend is further strengthened in the media. A major portion of the literature on discrimination has focused on the inferior treatment regarded women. This literature informs us that women are awarded less prestigious jobs, make less money, have less authority, and that the woman's proper place is at the foot of her husband. These views of women are reinforced in the media. In all fairness, however, in the last few TV seasons there has been an attempt to show women in professionally employed capacities not only in their traditional occupational roles as teachers and nurses, but also as doctors, lawyers, detectives, and airplane pilots. In a sizeable portion of the media, however, it is the husband who is shown as an inferior being. This occurs in the typical family situation comedy where, for a variety of reasons, the male finds himself temporarily in charge of the house, and is depicted as too incompetent to make a cup of tea. A recent Dick Van Dyke episode showed the star attempting to make breakfast. The water in the tea kettle boiled away, the oatmeal had the consistency of thick putty, in attempting to flip a fried egg it missed the pan and splattered over the stove, the toast burned, and the kitchen was a total disaster.

Although the sequence was extremely funny, the message clearly told of the consequences when males invade female's territory. Thus men should avoid at all costs female tasks and instead concentrate on male tasks—the office. Not only is this a rather untrue statement of male's ability to cope with household chores, but it is uncomplimentary in assuming that the normal male would be unable to follow simple directions (the recipe) or use common sense.

This stereotye has its counterpart in the helpless housewife who attempts to take a job outside the home, and reinforces the view that the wife's place is in the home. It also places the husband/male in the awkward position of trying not to do as well as his wife in housekeeping chores since that would deprive her of her only source of self-image. (Remember when girls were told not to display their knowledge of football or mechanics or they would show up their date and thereby risk not being asked for a second date?)

Although there are studies which show that men do perform numerous "female" household chores, the sex-typed data gathering has resulted in limited knowledge about how men feel about these jobs or how well they perform them.[7] We are all aware of numerous male chefs, dress designers, and on a more local scale, the increasing number of male participants and winners in cooking and baking contests. We also have evidence which would suggest that most men are probably as competent in housekeeping/childrearing chores as are women if the necessity arises, and in some cases are more efficient in performing these chores.[8] Neither men nor women gain from this stereotyping of activities according to gender since it restricts the number and range of activities which men and women can engage in without being labeled "deviant". Except in emergencies, few men are willing to admit that they do the cooking or laundry. This sex-restrictive outlook denies men an outlet for creative, noncompetitive endeavors such as cooking, baking and sewing. This view of the male as a bumbling idiot is untrue, and an insult to man's intelligence. It can only serve to reinforce outmoded and useless sex role stereotypes as to the "proper" tasks for males.

THE NON-DEPENDENT MALE: SEX-BASED DENIAL OF BENEFITS

Although women are no longer considered the property of their husbands as they were in Biblical times, women still give up their independent status when they marry and are considered part of an equivalent unit of evaluation based on their husbands socioeconomic status.[9] As early as 1862, Blackstone noted that when a woman married, she lost her separate legal status:

> . . . By marriage the husband and wife are one person in the law: that is the very being or legal existence of the women is suspended during marriage, or at least is incorporated and consolidated into that of her husband.[10]

Given this long tradition, it seemed logical that the 1939 Social Security Act "in an attempt to avoid detailed investigations of family financial relationships . . . found it expedient . . . to base dependency determination on the generally accepted presumption that a man is responsible for the support of his wife and children." [11] The retirement age was 62 for women and 65 for men, until the 1972 Social Security Act amendment when it was changed to 62 for both.[12]

When Social Security was first organized children received benefits payable on the earning record of the working mother without a husband, but not a working wife when her husband was present, nor were benefits payable to the husband or widower or of the working wife. Amendments in 1950 and 1967 enabled children to receive benefits on the death, disability or retirement of mothers regardless of their marital status and a man ". . . is now eligible for benefits as a dependent husband or widower *if* his wife has been providing at least half of his support." [13]

Interestingly, for a woman to claim benefits on her husband's earnings, it is not necessary for him to have contributed to more than half her support. Given the still existing inequality in occupational positions and pay scales, it is not likely that many wives contribute at least half the support of their husband, especially since housekeeping (unpaid work) is not counted toward support. At the end of 1971 fewer than 9,000 men were entitled as dependent husbands and only 3,000 as dependent widowers.[14]

Therefore discrimination occurs—unequal protection for the same money—based on sex. Unlike the widowed mother, the widower father with children to care for is not entitled to a benefit for himself. A divorced husband or a surviving divorced husband, age 62 or over, does not have rights to benefits which a divorced wife or surviving divorced wife may receive.[15] As is pointed out, ". . . up to now, it has seemed reasonable to most people either to assume that men generally are not dependent on their wives or to require a test of dependency for wives or widows." [16] The time, however, has come. FICA is not collected on the basis of sex or dependency—the working woman, regardless of her marital state, pays the same amount as the working male. Therefore, benefits should be distributed on the basis of one's earning record. This is an increasing issue. In 1971 only about 12,000 men could claim benefits as dependent husbands or widowers. Today 3,200,000 husbands could qualify since their wives earn more than they and therefore contribute more than half to their support.[17] This issue is currently being tested in the U. S. District Court on behalf of a New Jersey resident whose wife died in childbirth.[18]

Stephen Wisenfeld, whose application for mother's insurance benefits was turned down has enlisted the aid of the Women's Rights Project of American Civil Liberties Union, and is trying to prove that he deserves as much help as any widow. Because he is a father and widower instead of a mother and widow, he is not receiving equal protection under the law.

MALE AND HIS HEREDITARY TITLE: THE FAMILY NAME

As Rossi notes, "men are the symbolic carriers of the temporal continuity of the family" and ". . . it is the son who is important for the social prestige and perpetuation of the family name." [19]   Again, we can turn to history for a long tradition.   The importance of the practice of primogeniture, the custom whereby the eldest son inherits the property of his father, is suggested by Goode to have been an important variable in Japan's move towards westernization.[20]   Since the management of family property became the responsibility of the eldest son, other sons were free to become "innovators", move to the city, learn a trade or marry an heiress.[21]

In China, often a noble class family would "adopt" a talented youth to carry on the family line if there were no suitable male heirs.[22]   Although our society is not as extreme, cases are common in which couples decide to "try for another" because they desire to have a son (or daughter if they have several sons).

There is also indication that in certain segments of our society, notably among working-class families, a male child is necessary to prove one's masculinity.   This is especially true in societies where Macho is of prime importance, e. g. Mexico.[23]   With the current trend of women opting to retain their maiden name, perhaps some of the pressure will be removed from "sonless" fathers.

MALE DEPRIVATION: THE NON-EXISTENT TERM

Language is not just a means for communication, but gives insights into culture, values, lifestyles and experiences.   Eskimos, for example, have numerous words for "snow" while the English language has but one word.   Snow of course is a more important part of the Eskimos' life than in ours.   Thus language gives an indication of the values held and the importance placed on certain phenomena.   This label becomes an important indicator of our feelings.

It is interesting ". . . that the term is maternal deprivation for women and father absence for men." [24]   Funk and Wagnalls states that "absence" means simply not there or non-existent, while "deprivation" connotes the loss or taking away of something. The literature on maternal deprivation would seem to indicate not only its importance, but the fact that the child's loss of the mother, even if only for a few hours a day, is considered a real deprivation. Research and the literature on father absence suggests that not only is the father's contribution to rearing children less important, but his absence tends to be viewed as an economic loss—reflected in the lowering of the mother and child's socioeconomic status.

In addition, while there is an awareness that length of absence and the quality of care provided by mother substitutes are important variables in the study of maternal deprivation, they are not considered in studies dealing with father absence.[25] Instead, all types of absences tend to be lumped together without regard to the differential effect of sanctioned absence (armed services, hospital illness) vis-à-vis unsanctioned absence (desertion, divorce), or the length and permanency of the father's absence.[26]

Until recently, pregnant women could not remain on the job after a certain stage in the pregnancy. Leaves of absence for childbirth were, in essence, job termination. This negative attitude towards women taking time off for childbirth and child care is intensified for men. One must remember that one common method for discriminating against women in the job market is to suggest that their stay would be short lived because of pregnancy and childrearing, and thus costly to train and replace. Although discrimination on the basis of sex, in this case questioning the woman's plans regarding pregnancy, is against the law, the practice still persists. (The Sociologists for Women in Society, at the 1973 annual meeting noted that women, while being interviewed during the ASA meeting, were being asked these questions, with clear disregard for the equal employment guidelines.)

If women are facing discrimination because they desire to take time off for childrearing, imagine the conflicts men face when they desire similar privileges. A recent study, *Motherless Families,* suggests that one of the biggest problems for these fathers was combining the role of worker and homemaker.[27] While the middle-class man had a more flexible schedule and was able to purchase homemaking help, the working-class father frequently faced job termination as the result of lateness or time off for child care responsibilities. Thus, in the working class where sex-role segregation was the strongest (and where workers were more easily replaceable), employers were unwilling to adjust to the need for flexible hours or extra time for child care. Men are faced with a conflict. While society finds it desirable for women to give up outside employment to remain at home and care for their children, society does not extend this to men. Thus the father must cope with the strain to remain at home to care for small children (who already are suffering the loss of their mother) and the need to fulfill the status-conferring role of paid employment. Yet in the Victor and Wilding study, 49 percent decided or were forced because of inadequate alternatives to remain at home with their children, feeling that their children needed them, usually considered a female reaction.[28]

So prevalent is the idea that mothers are the important parent in child rearing, almost to the exclusion of fathers, that a student research project investigating the teaching behavior of working-class fathers with pre-school children found fathers pleased and surprised to be asked about child rearing techniques as they thought that child development researchers cared only about mothers.[29]

There are new regulations which might open the way for men to take a more active role in child rearing. These regulations state that an employer who grants maternity leaves must likewise grant paternity leaves. This creates a legal sanction for child rearing to be left to the choice of the individual parents, giving fathers not only societal sanction for desiring to take an early active part in the rearing of their children, but provides financial compensation and the assurance of a job when the father is able to return to work. With this change will hopefully come a more neutral view towards the single parent family, regardless of who is missing, and consider maternal deprivation no more or less important than paternal absence.

THE "HAPPY" BACHELOR: THE BIGGEST MYTH

So far we have been concerned with the male in the context of his family. One of the biggest myths, however, is that of the happy bachelor. While women are considered successful when they finally trap their man, men are usually considered defeated—

trapped, freedom lost, fun and games ended.   The evidence, however, is quite to the contrary.

Durkheim, in his study of suicide, found that married individuals tended to have higher coefficients of preservation, and Gove
noted in an analysis of data from 1959–61 that single males are
97 percent more likely to commit suicide than are married
males.[30]   He concludes that "the data on suicide for the United
States are consistent with the data on mental illness and psychological well-being which indicate that marriage is more advantageous to males than to females." [31]

Lest one think that with age a bachelor adjusts to his "blissful"
state, Bellin and Hardt found with a sample of respondents age 65
or over, that more than 26 percent of the males showed evidence
of mental disorders.[32]   This supports Adler's hypothesis that
".   .   .   emotional security and social stability afforded by married life makes for low incidence of mental illness".[33]   Other studies indicate that the single male is least likely to be "very happy"
when compared to single females and married males and females.[34, 35, 36, 37]   Single males are also most likely to consider
themselves "not too happy" or, when classified by psychiatric
judges for symptom formation, to be considered "impaired".[38]
Bradburn and Caplovitz also found that marriage was more important for males than females in describing their happiness.[39]

In an in-depth study of single men, Stark notes that during the
interviews it was not uncommon for the men to break down and
weep, so overcome with their own unhappiness.[40]   One bachelor,
38, a psychology professor, stated his feelings on marriage:

> It's easy to put it down if you've had it. You know I some-
> times spend the whole night on the phone calling to get some-
> one to come over. People I don't really want to see. You get
> used to being put down. I get so I don't even want to be with
> couples. I get so nervous some nights I get diarrhea, so I
> watch TV. But you can't dig a horror film by yourself.

Another bachelor, 36, describes his feelings this way:

> I'm tired being man with a capital M. Even really hip chicks
> lay everything on you. You're supposed to start and finish it,
> making good and apologize if it's bad. This woman I'm seeing
> went home and cried after we made love. She had to be back
> to take the babysitter home. She called and she was really
> depressed. I realized all my life I've been doing that, going

in and going home. So when do I get to cry and be depressed? Most women will tell you it's okay to show your
feelings. But if you really do, where are they? Back home
with the kids or moving with some other guy who's cool like
ice. I'm laying off sex for awhile to see what happens. Hell,
it's better than putting on a show.

One may wonder, in view of the generally unhappy, unstable,
bachelors studied by researchers why this myth persists. One
possible explanation concerns the exploitive nature of the dat-
ing/mating game. The object for men is to have their fun—the
double standard. Women, on the other hand, must carefully stack
the cards, i. e., enough charm and sex to retain interest, but not
enough to be an easy catch or the challenge and the interest might
falter before the knot is securely tied. From this perspective the
nature of the game is for the man to remain free to enjoy life's
experiences, while the woman's game is to catch her man and
secure the proper adult status for a woman. Thus, while the woman is congratulated for catching her man, the man is congratulated
for having fun without being caught. If this is his goal, when he
achieves it he must be happy. Although much of the exploitive
nature of dating/mating is gone, the myth dies hard. There still
is the tendency to assume that since a male has the prerogative
to ask for a date and to propose marriage, if he does not marry it
must be because it is more fun that way.

The Strong Male: Always in Control of his Emotions

The final stereotype to be considered is that of the "strong
male". Males in our society are forced into a role which doesn't
permit the open display of emotions, especially those of pain or
sorrow. For example, males suppress their emotions, and from
the time that they are little boys are told that men don't cry.
This view of men is currently being issued in a message spon-
sored by the Philadelphia Commission on Human Resources.
The star of this skit is Lionel, a member of the "All in The Family" cast. At the age of five he saw his dog run over and was told
by his father that men don't cry. One wonders what type of life
experiences, in a child of five, should prevent him from crying
upon seeing a loved pet killed. Whether male or female, a
five year old who reacts with such little feeling must certainly
have endured a traumatic, frightening childhood. Yet this is
the reaction we sanction as proper from our male children.

First, men *do* cry—often publicly. In the political arena we have seen Nixon, Humphrey, McCarthy, and Muskie weep in public and from history we learn that Abraham Lincoln and Alexander the Great were noted for this habit. The comedian, Flip Wilson, labor leader John L. Lewis, baseball star Mickey Mantle and General George Patton are among the numerous notables who have broken down in public.

For men to act "controlled" and not allow emotions to surface is a cultural trait of American society. Mead clearly shows that what is considered masculine behavior in one society is often feminine behavior in another.[41] Thus the inexpressiveness which is characteristic of many American males is culturally rather than biologically produced. If deep emotions are not vented by tears, other organs weep instead, upsetting glandular balance. When grief, rage, or irritation are repressed, ". . . profound chemical changes occur which result in nervous conditions, crippling migraines, high blood pressure and digestive tract disorders."[42]

Balswick and Peek suggest that the inexpressive male comes in two basic varieties: the cowboy syndrome where the man places women on a pedestal and the playboy or the James Bond syndrome in which a man avoids personal involvement and sees women as consumer objects to be manipulated and exploited.[43] Balswick and Peek further suggest that as American society becomes increasingly mechanized and depersonalized, the family becomes a supportive agency providing affection and companionship. Thus, inexpressiveness on the part of males may be dysfunctional for marital adjustment.

Conclusion

Most of these current stereotypes or myths regarding male roles today have only a kernel of truth. Yet like all stereotypes they tend to persist. Perhaps we are comfortable, especially in times of rapid change, to be able to categorize males and females. However, there is inherent danger both for men and women in allowing these myths to continue unquestioned. When men and women are forced into stereotyped roles, they lose a variety of options which could make life fuller and more rewarding.

Stereotypes are perpetuated by a variety of mechanisms—tradition, media, and social scientist. In our rapidly changing society, with emerging alternative family and sex-roles, these stereotypes are no longer functional. It is time to urge for "a society which allows equal opportunity for the realization of full human potential in all persons . . . in which there are no sex-roles, but only roles determined by one's abilities and interests in which problems of sexual identity will disappear because society will no longer demand that one's identity be founded on one's sex." [44]

MOTHERHOOD, WHO NEEDS IT? *

BETTY ROLLIN

Motherhood is in trouble, and it ought to be. A rude question is long overdue: Who needs it? The answer used to be 1) society and 2) women. But now, with the impending horrors of overpopulation, society desperately doesn't need it. And women don't need it either. Thanks to The Motherhood Myth—the idea that having babies is something that all normal women instinctively want and need and will enjoy doing—they just think they do.

The notion that the maternal wish and the activity of mothering are instinctive or biologically predestined is baloney. Try asking most sociologists, psychologists, psychoanalysts, biologists—many of whom are mothers—about motherhood being instinctive; it's like asking department-store presidents if their Santa Clauses are real. "Motherhood—instinctive?" shouts distinguished sociologist/author Dr. Jessie Bernard. "Biological destiny? Forget biology! If it were biology, people would die from not doing it."

"Women don't need to be mothers any more than they need spaghetti," says Dr. Richard Rabkin, a New York psychiatrist. "But if you're in a world where everyone is eating spaghetti, thinking they need it and want it, you will think so too. Romance has really contaminated science. So-called instincts have to do with stimulation. They are not things that well up inside of you."

"When a woman says with feeling that she craved her baby from within, she is putting into biological language what is psychological," says University of Michigan psychoanalyst and motherhood-researcher Dr. Frederick Wyatt. "There are no instincts," says Dr. William Goode, president-elect of the American Sociological Association. "There are reflexes, like eye-blinking, and drives, like sex. There is no innate drive for children. Otherwise, the enormous cultural pressures that there are to reproduce wouldn't exist. There are no cultural pressures to sell you on getting your hand out of the fire."

There are, to be sure, biologists and others who go on about biological destiny, that is, the innate or instinctive goal of motherhood. (At the turn of the century, even good old capitalism was explained by a theorist as "the instinct of ac-quisitivess.") And many psychoanalysts still hold the Freudian view that women feel so rotten about not having a penis that they are necessarily propelled into the child-wish to replace the missing organ. Psychoanalysts also make much of the psy-chological need to repeat what one's parent of the same sex has done. Since every woman has a mother, it is considered normal to wish to imitate one's mother by being a mother.

There is, surely, a wish to pass on love if one has re-ceived it, but to insist women must pass it on in the same way is like insisting that every man whose father is a gardener has to be a gardener. One dissenting psychoanalyst says, simply, "There is a wish to comply with one's biology, yes, but we needn't and sometimes we shouldn't." (Interestingly, the woman who has been the greatest contributor to child therapy and who has probably given more to children than anyone alive is Dr. Anna Freud, Freud's magnificent daughter, who is not a mother.)

Anyway, what an expert cast of hundreds is telling us, is, simply, that biological possibility and desire are not the same as biological need. Women have childbearing equipment. To choose not to use the equipment is no more blocking what is instinctive than it is for a man who, muscles or no, chooses not to be a weight lifter.

So much for the wish. What about the "instinctive" activity of mothering. One animal study shows that when a young mem-ber of a species is put in a cage, say, with an older mem-ber of the same species, the latter will act in a protective, "ma-ternal" way. But that goes for both males and females who have been "mothered" themselves. And studies indicate that a human baby will also respond to whoever is around playing mother—even if it's father.

Margaret Mead and many others frequently point out that mothering can be a fine occupation, if you want it, for either sex. Another experiment with monkeys who were brought up without mothers found them lacking in maternal behavior toward their own offspring. A similar study showed that monkeys brought up without other monkeys of the opposite sex had no interest in mating—all of which suggests that both mothering and mating behavior are learned, not instinctual. And, to turn the cart (or the baby carriage) around, baby ducks who lovingly follow their mothers seemed, in the mother's absence, to just as lovingly follow wooden ducks or even vacuum cleaners.

If motherhood isn't instinctive, when, and why, then, was The Motherhood Myth born? Until recently, the entire question of maternal motivation was academic. Sex, like it or not, meant babies. Not that there haven't always been a lot of interesting contraceptives tried. But until the creation of the diaphragm in the 1880's, the birth of babies was largely unavoidable. And, generally speaking, nobody really seemed to mind. For one thing, people tend to be sort of good sports about what seems to be inevitable. For another, in the past, the population needed beefing up. Mortality rates were high, and agricultural cultures, particularly, have always needed children to help out. So because it "just happened" and because it was needed, motherhood was assumed to be innate.

Originally, it was the word of God that got the ball rolling with "Be fruitful and multiply," a practical suggestion, since the only people around then were Adam and Eve. But in no time, super-moralists like St. Augustine changed the tone of the message: "Intercourse, even with one's legitimate wife is unlawful and wicked where the conception of the offspring is prevented," he, we assume, thundered. And the Roman Catholic position was thus cemented. So then and now, procreation took on a curious value among people who viewed (and view) the pleasures of sex as sinful. One could partake in the sinful pleasure, but feel vindicated by the ensuing birth. Motherhood cleaned up sex. Also, it cleaned up women, who have always been considered somewhat evil, because of Eve's transgression (". . . but the woman was deceived and became a transgressor. Yet woman will be saved through bearing children . . .", 1 Timothy, 2:14–15) and somewhat dirty because of menstruation.

And so, based on need, inevitability and pragmatic fantasy—the Myth worked, from society's point of view—the Myth grew like corn in Kansas. And society reinforced it with both laws and propaganda—laws that made woman a chattel, denied her education and personal mobility, and madonna propaganda that said she was beautiful and wonderful doing it

and it was beautiful and wonderful to do.   (One rarely sees a
madonna washing dishes.)

In fact, the Myth persisted—breaking some kind of record
for long-lasting fallacies—until something like yesterday.   For
as the truth about the Myth trickled in—as women's rights
increased, as women gradually got the message that it was certainly possible for them to do most things men did, that they live
longer, that their brains were not tinier—then, finally, when
the really big news rolled in, that they could choose whether or
not to be mothers—what happened?   The Motherhood Myth
soared higher than ever.   As Betty Friedan made oh-so-clear
in *The Feminine Mystique,* the 40's and 50's produced a group
of ladies who not only had babies as if they were going out of
style (maybe they were) but, as never before, they turned motherhood into a cult.[1]   First, they wallowed in the aesthetics of it
all—natural childbirth and nursing became maternal musts.
Like heavy-bellied ostriches, they grounded their heads in the
sands of motherhood, only coming up for air to say how
utterly happy and fulfilled they were. But, as Mrs. Friedan says
only too plainly, they weren't.   The Myth galloped on, moreover,
long after making babies had turned from practical asset to lia-
bility for both individual parents and society.   With the average
cost of a middle-class child figured conservatively at $30,000 (not
including college), any parent knows that the only people
who benefit economically from children are manufacturers of
consumer goods.   Hence all those gooey motherhood commer-
cials.   And the Myth gathered momentum long after sheer
numbers, while not yet extinguishing us, have made us intensely
uncomfortable.   Almost all of our societal problems, from minor
discomforts like traffic to major ones like hunger, the population
people keep reminding us, have to do with there being too many
people.   And who suffers most?   The kids who have been
so mindlessly brought into the world, that's who.   They are the
ones who have to cope with all the difficult and dehumanizing
conditions brought on by over-population.   They are the ones
who have to cope with the psychological nausea of feeling un-
needed by society.   That's not the only reason for drugs, but,
surely, it's a leading contender.

Unfortunately, the population curbers are tripped up by a
romantic, stubborn, ideological hurdle.   How can birth-control
programs really be effective as long as the concept of glorious

motherhood remains unchanged? (Even poor old Planned Parenthood has to euphemize—why not Planned Unparenthood?) Particularly among the poor, motherhood is one of the few inherently positive institutions that are accessible. As Berkeley demographer Judith Blake points out, "Poverty-oriented birth control programs do not make sense as a welfare measure . . . as long as existing pronatalist policies . . . encourage mating, pregnancy and the care, support and rearing of children." Or, she might have added, as long as the less-than-idylic child-rearing part of motherhood remains "in small print."

Sure, motherhood gets dumped on sometimes. Philip Wylie's *Momism* [2] got going in the 40's and Philip Roth's *Portnoy's Complaint* [3] did its best to turn rancid the chicken-soup concept of Jewish motherhood. But these are viewed as the sour cries of a a black humorist here, a malcontent there. Everyone shudders, laughs, but it's like the mouse and the elephant joke. Still, the Myth persists. Last April, a Brooklyn woman was indicted on charges of manslaughter and negligent homicide—11 children died in a fire in a building she owned and criminally neglected—"But," sputtered her lawyer, "my client, Mrs. Breslow, is a mother, a grandmother and a great-grandmother!"

Most remarkably, The Motherhood Myth persists in the face of the most overwhelming maternal unhappiness and incompetence. If reproduction were merely superfluous and expensive, if the experience were as rich and rewarding as the cliche would have us believe, if it were a predominantly joyous trip for everyone riding—mother, father, child—then the going everybody-should-have-two-children plan would suffice. Certainly, there are a lot of joyous mothers, and their children and (sometimes, not necessarily) their husbands reflect their joy. But a lot of evidence suggests that for more women than anyone wants to admit, motherhood can be miserable. ("If it weren't" says one psychiatrist wryly, "the world wouldn't be in the mess it's in.")

There is a remarkable statistical finding from a recent study of Dr. Bernard's, comparing the mental illness and unhappiness of married mothers and single women. The latter group, it turned out, was both markedly less sick and overtly more happy. Of course, it's not easy to measure slippery attitudes like happiness. "Many women have achieved a kind of reconciliation—a conformity," says Dr. Bernard, "that they interpret as happiness. Since feminine happiness is supposed to lie in devoting one's life to one's husband and children, they do that; so ipso facto, they assume they are happy. And for many women, untrained for independence and processed for motherhood, they find their state far preferable to the alternatives, which don't really exist." Also, unhappy mothers are often loath to admit it. For one thing, if in society's view not to be a mother is to be a freak, not to be a blissful mother is to be a witch. Besides, unlike a disappointing marriage, disappointing motherhood cannot be terminated by divorce. Of course, none of that stops such a woman from expressing her dissatisfaction in a variety of ways. Again, it is not only she who suffers but her husband and children as well. Enter the harridan housewife, the carping shrew. The realities of motherhood can turn women into terrible people. And, judging from the 50,000 cases of child abuse in the U. S. each year, some are worse than terrible.

In some cases, the unpleasing realities of motherhood begin even before the beginning. In *Her Infinite Variety,* Morton Hunt describes young married women pregnant for the first time as "very likely to be frightened and depressed, masking these feelings in order not to be considered contemptible. The arrival of pregnancy interrupts a pleasant dream of motherhood and awakens them to the realization that they have too little money, or not enough space, or unresolved marital problems. . . ." [4]

The following are random quotes from interviews with some mothers in Ann Arbor, Mich., who described themselves as reasonably happy. They all had positive things to say about their children, although when asked about the best moment of their day, they all confessed it was when the children were in bed. Here is the rest:

"Suddenly I had to devote myself to the child totally. I was under the illusion that the baby was going to fit into my life, and I found that I had to switch my life and my schedule to fit him. You think, 'I'm in love, I'll get married, and we'll have a baby. First there's two, then three, it's simple and romantic. You don't even think about the work' . . . 'You never get away from the responsibility. Even when you leave the children with a sitter, you are not out from under the pressure of the responsibility' . . . 'I hate ironing their pants and doing their underwear, and they never put their clothes in the laundry basket.

. . . As they get older, they make less demands on your time because they're in school, but the demands are greater in forming their values . . . Best moment of the day is when all the children are in bed. . . . The worst time of day is 4 p. m. when you have to get dinner started, the kids are tired, hungry and crabby—everybody wants to talk to you about their day . . . your day is only half over.

"Once a mother, the responsibility and concern for my children became so encompassing . . . It took a great deal of will to keep up other parts of my personality . . . To me, motherhood gets harder as they get older because you have less control . . . In an abstract sense, I'd have several . . . In the non-abstract, I would not have any . . ." "I had anticipated that the baby would sleep and eat, sleep and eat, Instead, the experience was overwhelming. I really had not thought particularly about what motherhood would mean in a realistic sense. I want to do other things, like to become involved in things that are worthwhile—I don't mean women's clubs—but I don't have the physical energy to go out in the evenings. I feel like I'm missing something . . . the experience of being somewhere with people and having them talking about something—something that's going on in the world."

Every grown-up person expects to pay a price for his pleasures, but seldom is the price as vast as the one endured "however happily" by most mothers. We have mentioned the literal cost factor. But what does that mean? For middle-class American women, it means a life-style with severe and usually unimagined limitations; i. e., life in the suburbs, because who can afford three bedrooms in the city? And what do suburbs mean? For women, suburbs mean other women and children and leftover peanut-butter sandwiches and car pools and seldom-seen husbands. Even the Feminine Mystiqueniks—the housewives who finally admitted that their lives behind brooms (OK, electric brooms) were driving them crazy—were loath to trace their predicament to their children. But it is simply a fact that a childless married woman has no child-work and little housework. She can live in a city, or, if she still chooses the suburbs or the country, she can leave on the commuter train with her husband if she wants to. Even the most ardent job-seeking mother will find little in the way of great opportunities in Scarsdale. Besides, by the time she wakes up, she usually lacks both the prep-

aration for the outside world and the self-confidence to get it.
You will say there are plenty of city-dwelling working mothers.
But most of those women do additional-funds-for-the-family kind
of work, not the interesting career kind that takes plugging during "childbearing years."

Nor is it a bed of petunias for the mother who does make it
professionally. Says writer/critic Marya Mannes: "If the creative woman has children, she must pay for this indulgence with
a long burden of guilt, for her life will be split three ways between them and her husband and her work . . . No woman
with any heart can compose a paragraph when her child is in
trouble . . . The creative woman has no wife to protect
her from intrusion. A man at his desk in a room with closed
door is a man at work. A woman at a desk in any room is available."

Speaking of jobs, do remember that mothering, salary or not,
is a job. Even those who can afford nurses to handle the nitty-
gritty still need to put out emotionally. "Well-cared-for" neurotic rich kids are not exactly unknown in our society. One of
the more absurd aspects of the Myth is the underlying assumption that, since most women are biologically equipped to bear
children, they are psychologically, mentally, emotionally and
technically equipped (or interested) to rear them. Never mind
happiness. To assume that such an exacting, consuming and
important task is something almost all women are equipped to do
is far more dangerous and ridiculous than assuming that
everyone with vocal chords should seek a career in the opera.

A major expectation of the Myth is that children make a not-
so-hot marriage hotter, or a hot marriage, hotter still. Yet
almost every available study indicates that childless marriages
are far happier. One of the biggest, of 850 couples, was conducted by Dr. Harold Feldman of Cornell University, who states his
finding in no uncertain terms: "Those couples with children had
a significantly lower level of marital satisfaction than did those
without children." Some of the reasons are obvious. Even the
most adorable children make for additional demands, complica-
tions and hardships in the lives of even the most loving parents.
If a woman feels disappointed and trapped in her mother
role, it is bound to affect her marriage in any number of ways:
she may take out her frustrations directly on her husband,

or she may count on him too heavily for what she feels she is missing in her daily life.

". . . You begin to grow away from your husband," says one of the Michigan ladies. "He's working on his career and you're working on your family. But you both must gear your lives to the children. You do things the children enjoy, more than things you might enjoy." More subtle and possibly more serious is what motherhood may do to a woman's sexuality. Often when the stork flies in, sexuality flies out. Both in the emotional minds of some women *and* in the minds of their husbands, when a woman becomes a mother, she stops being a woman. It's not only that motherhood may destroy her physical attractiveness, but its madonna concept may destroy her *feelings* of sexuality.

And what of the payoff? Usually, even the most self-sacrificing maternal self-sacrificers expect a little something back. Gratified parents are not unknown to the Western world, but there are probably at least just as many who feel, to put it crudely, shortchanged. The experiment mentioned earlier—where the baby ducks followed vacuum cleaners instead of their mothers—indicates that what passes for love from baby to mother is merely a rudimentary kind of object attachment. Without necessarily feeling like a Hoover, a lot of women become disheartened because babies and children are not only not interesting to talk to (not everyone thrills at the wonders of da-da-ma-ma talk) but they are generally not empathetic, considerate people. Even the nicest children are not capable of empathy, surely a major ingredient of love, until they are much older. Sometimes they're never capable of it. Dr. Wyatt says that often, in later years particularly, when most of the "returns" are in, it is the "good mother" who suffers most of all. It is then she must face a reality: The child—the appendage with her genes—is not an appendage, but a separate person. What's more, he or she may be a separate person who doesn't even like her—or whom she doesn't really like.

So if the music is lousy how come everyone's dancing? Because the motherhood minuet is taught free from birth, and whether or not she has rhythm or likes the music every woman is expected to do it. Indeed, she *wants* to do it. Little girls start learning what to want—and what to be—when they are still in their cribs. Dr. Miriam Keiffer, a young social psychologist at Bensalem, The Experimental College of Fordham University, points to studies showing that "at six months of age, mothers are already treating their baby girls and boys quite differently. For instance, mothers have been found to touch, comfort, and talk to their females more. If these differences can be found at such an early stage, it's not surprising that the end product is as different as it is. What is surprising is that men and women are, in so many ways, similar." Some people point to the way little girls play with dolls as proof of their "innate motherliness." But remember, little girls are *given* dolls. When Margaret Mead presented some dolls to New Guinea children, it was the boys, not the girls, who wanted to play with them, which they did by crooning lullabies and rocking them in the most maternal fashion.

By the time they reach adolescence, most girls, unconsciously or not, have learned enough about role definition to qualify for a master's degree. In general, the lesson has been that no matter what kind of career thoughts one may entertain, one must find, first and foremost, be a wife and mother. A girl's mother is usually her first teacher. As Dr. Goode says, "A woman is not only taught by society to have a child; she is taught to have a child who will have a child." A woman who has hung her life on The Motherhood Myth will almost always reinforce her young married daughter's early training by pushing for grandchildren. Prospective grandmothers are not the only ones. Husbands, too, can be effective sellers. After all, they have The Fatherhood Myth to cope with. A married man is *supposed* to have children. Often, particularly among Latins, children are a sign of potency. They help him assure the world—and himself—that he is the big man he is supposed to be. Plus, children give him both immortality (whatever that means) and possibly the chance to become "more" in his lifetime through the accomplishments of his children, particularly his son. (Sometimes it's important, however, for the son to do better, but not *too* much better.)

Friends, too, can be counted on as myth-pushers. Naturally one wants to do what one's friends do. One study, by the way, found an absolute correlation between a woman's fertility and that of her three closest friends. The negative sell comes into play here, too. We have seen what the concept of non-mother means (cold, selfish, unwomanly, abnormal). In practice, particularly in the suburbs, it can mean, simply exclusion—both from child-centered activities (that is, most activities) and child-centered conversations (that is, most conversations). It can also mean being the butt of a lot of unfunny jokes. ("Whaddya waiting for? An immaculate conception? Ha Ha.") Worst of all, it can mean being an object of pity.

In case she's escaped all of those pressures (that is, if she was brought up in a cave), a young married woman often wants a baby just so that she'll 1) have something to do (motherhood is better than clerk/typist, which is often the only kind of job she can get, since little more has been expected of her and, besides, her boss also expects her to leave and be a mother); 2) have something to hug and possess, to be needed by and have power over; and 3) have something to be—e. g., a baby's mother. Motherhood affords an instant identity. First, through wifehood, you are somebody's wife; then you are somebody's mother. Both give not only identity and activity, but status and stardom of a kind. During pregnancy, a woman can look forward to the kind of attention and pampering she may not ever have gotten or may never otherwise get. Some women consider birth the biggest accomplishment of their lives, which may be interpreted as saying not much for the rest of their lives. As Dr. Goode says, "It's like the gambler who may know the roulette wheel is crooked, but it's the only game in town." Also, with motherhood, the feeling of accomplishment is immediate. It is really much faster and easier to make a baby than paint a painting, or write a book, or get to the point of accomplishment in a job. It is also easier in a way to shift focus from self-development to child development—particularly since, for women, self-development is considered selfish. Even unwed mothers may achieve a feeling of this kind. (As we have seen, little thought is given to the aftermath.) And, again, since so many women are underdeveloped as people, they feel that, besides children, they have little else to give—to themselves, their husbands, to their world.

You may ask why then, when the realities do start pouring in, does a woman want to have a second, third, even fourth child? OK, 1) Just because reality is pouring in doesn't mean she wants to *face* it. A new baby can help bring back some of the old illusions. Says psychoanalyst Dr. Natalie Shainess, "She may view each successive child as a knight in armor that will rescue her from being a 'bad/unhappy mother.' " 2) Next on the horror list of having no children, is having one. It suffices to say that only children are not only OK, they even have a high rate of exceptionality. 3) Both parents usually want at least one child of each sex. The husband, for reasons discussed earlier, probably wants a son. 4) The more children one has, the more of an excuse one has not to develop in any other way.

What's the point? A world without children? Of course not. Nothing could be worse or more unlikely. No matter what anyone says in LOOK or anywhere else, motherhood isn't about to go out like a blown bulb, and who says it should? Only the Myth must go out, and now it seems to be dimming.

The younger-generation females who have been reared on the Myth have not rejected it totally, but at least they recognize it can be more loving to children not to have them. And at least they speak of adopting children instead of bearing them. Moreover, since the new non-breeders are "less hung-up" on ownership, they seem to recognize that if you dig loving children, you don't necessarily have to own one. The end of The Motherhood Myth might make available more loving women (and men!) for those children who already exist.

When motherhood is no longer culturally compulsory, there will, certainly, be less of it. Women are now beginning to think and do more about development of self, of their individual resources. Far from being selfish, such development is probably our only hope. That means more alternatives for women. And more alternatives mean more selective, better, happier, motherhood—and childhood and husbandhood (or manhood) and peoplehood. It is not a question of whether or not children are sweet and marvelous to have and rear; the question is, even if that's so, whether or not one wants to pay the price for it. It doesn't make sense any more to pretend that women need babies, when what they really need is themselves. If God were still speaking to us in a voice we could hear, even He would probably say, "Be fruitful. Don't multiply."

WHAT GOES ON IN HIS HEAD
WHEN YOU'RE PREGNANT? *

Tom Congdon

"The trouble with all the books about childbirth," my wife said one evening several months after our first child was born, "is that they tell you everything except how to put up with your husband."

I asked her what she meant.

"Nothing personal," she said. "It's just that your behavior throughout this whole thing was incredible. Not bad, just incredible. Every woman I know who's had her first baby says that husbands turn peculiar during pregnancy. It really makes you wonder what goes on in men's heads."

It wasn't until years later, after much thought and many conversations with other fathers, that I gathered a notion of what does in fact go through men's minds when their wives are bearing. My wife, I might add, was right: women don't have a clue as to what their husbands are feeling. The manuals that expectant mothers read are written from the woman's point of view, never the man's. There is natural childbirth, of course, the system in which husbands take part in the birthing, and it's all very well and good; I went through it myself for our second baby with happy results. But even natural childbirth is a totally female-centered routine, with the husband serving as acolyte and coxswain and spectator while the woman does her unique thing. No expert I know of has paid much attention to the fact that though childbearing is physically a female enterprise, psychologically it is fully 50 percent male.

To begin, let me suggest that for a young new husband, the day his wife tells him she is pregnant is the day it dawns on him that this—and not his wedding day—is really the end of his bachelorhood. Until there is a baby on the way, the foot-loose part of a man can pretend that this isn't a marriage he's got himself involved in, it's just the latest in his string of love affairs. No matter how much he loves his wife and no matter how much, on one level, he desires a baby, there is something in the situation that whispers to him: "Locked in forever."

* © 1970 Thomas B. Congdon Jr.

That "locked-in" feeling can sometimes cause a young husband to resist the new situation. And this, in turn, can be distressing for his wife, who had assumed he would be just as happy about the baby as she.

When my wife first got pregnant we'd been married only three months. When she gave me the news I found myself insisting that we couldn't have a baby. We'd just put all our money— $7,000—into buying a ramshackle townhouse in a terrible slum. We had no choice but to live in the place, I pointed out, and no choice but to do the renovation ourselves. I needed her as a workman, I said; she couldn't quit on me. And how, I asked could we bring a nice new baby into a former tenement that still had rats and rotten walls?

I pressed her so hard that she glumly agreed that we could ask the gynecologist if he would "help" us, if there was anything he could "do." We drove to his office one evening and sat in the car, trying to get up the courage to go in and make our request. But we never did find the courage. We went back home to our slum and went along with the inevitable. My wife managed to keep working with me on the renovation all through her pregnancy (one neighbor, watching my wife burn old paint off the front door, said: "Lady, you're the only pregnant blowtorcher I ever saw"), and by the time the baby came, we had finished some rooms for it and I had thoroughly finished with bachelorhood.

The "locked-in" feeling, however, is a hidden factor, where it exists at all. Perhaps for many men it is at most just a fleeting reaction, quickly controlled and dismissed. And of course there are factors acting in the opposite direction, impelling a man to become a father. The usual ones include the very obvious desire to be a father and to have a child with the woman one loves. Less obvious but almost as strong is a man's desire to confirm his fertility. For a man, on some level of consciousness, the ability to conceive is closely related to his sense of personal power. If he can't make a baby, it reflects on his entire capacity to act. I'm not saying this is a sensible or a wholesome attitude, but I do believe it is a prevalent one.

Fueling this anxiety is a set of sub-anxieties so bizarre as to seem ridiculous to a woman. For example, there is the memory of the time when he was fourteen years old and a baseball hit him in the testicles; the pain was so bad that surely, he half believes, the blow must have sterilized him. And what about that attack of mumps? And there are those Portnoian suspicions that despite the gingerly reassurances offered by the Boy Scout Handbook, masturbation really isn't good for you and may even be bad for you—maybe, he thinks, he used up his sperm quota before he even got married. Or what if . . . (Masters and Johnson, the sex researchers, would understand; they have statistically documented the male's concern about the brevity of his sexual apparatus) . . . what if his penis is too short to effect the transport? When a man and wife learn they are going to have their first child, the husband's first reaction may be joy or panic, but his second reaction is likely to be relief.

The third reaction, somewhat delayed, will be exasperation, because there are few things as exasperating as living with a pregnant woman. In the beginning, she may be sick, and most husbands are no good at coping with a normally sturdy wife who suddenly gives out. A husband tries to be sympathetic, but after a few days he has to fake it. What he really wants is for her to get up off her bed and start making breakfast.

And then when she stops being sick she starts being hyper-healthy. Nature programs her hormones to give her that famous pregnant-woman glow and also to send her off into that little dreamland For Prospective Mothers Only, where no disturbing thought may intrude. But nature doesn't do a thing for the prospective father. Nothing is programming his hormones to make him tranquil, to insulate him from reality. While his wife becomes daily more serene he becomes daily more frantic. He's all alone with the stark thoughts any sane person has when approaching one of life's great confrontations.

Such as, what if the birthing goes wrong? What if the baby is born defective or injured? What if his wife dies? (The statistics on death-in-childbirth suddenly seem menacing.) The possibility that his wife could die as a result of his desire to make love; the fact that she runs the whole risk herself—these are fears that scratch at the edges of consciousness, contributing to that air of unease that distinguishes the prospective father. And there are anxieties of a lesser order. Is it true that having a baby deteriorates a woman's figure—spoils the resiliency of her breasts, slackens the vagina and God knows what else? Not that it matters all that much, except that it does matter to a man.

And what about sex during pregnancy? A man expects certain things of his wife, including a continuous supply of meals, a continuous supply of fresh underwear and fairly continuous supply of sex. Suddenly he is faced with the prospect of a period of abstinence. Even new husbands know that it's all right to make love during pregnancy, but some think that the permissible period is only the first few months. Once the woman's belly begins to swell they grow nervous; and nervousness is the enemy of good sex. In truth, there is something vaguely redundant about making love to a pregnant woman, something akin to carry coals to Newcastle. And there is something about maneuvering around that belly, especially since one is always aware that there's a small person inside it. Hence the strange thoughts that flit through the mind during intercourse. Invariably, though very briefly, it would occur to me that my penis might poke the placenta. Once I confessed this absurdity to another father, and he replied that he was somewhat inhibited during sex with his pregnant wife by the occasional lunatic fantasy that the baby might bite him.

I hasten to add that there are nice things about sex during pregnancy. As is often observed, many women are in some ways more attractive when pregnant. Their skin may be fresher, their coloring higher, their breasts fuller and firmer. And there is the obvious fact that for most new husbands, sex with a pregnant woman is a novelty, and novelty in sex can be pleasant.

The other-women problem is one of the most disturbing for the father-to-be. There comes a point during the nine months when the wife, though technically able to continue to have sex, becomes so deeply absorbed in the coming event, so relentlessly pre-maternal, that she is no longer able to be the same kind of lover to her husband. It is not very appealing to make love to someone who is first and foremost a mother rather than a woman; undiluted maternity turns a man off. And so at about the seventh month the sex diminishes, and the man bravely resigns himself to semi- or total abstinence.

In some simpler, older societies, I am told, this period presents no difficulty. It is quietly expected that the husband, deprived of the services of his wife, will seek satisfaction elsewhere. I myself can recall being shocked, when I was a teenager working summers as a manual laborer, at the what-the-hell attitude of my fellow workmen whose wives were expecting.

I mentioned the aggravation of living with a pregnant woman. It's just the normal aggravation (usually heavily outweighed by manifold pleasures) but intensified a degree or two. Women, that is, become more so during pregnancy, especially, I think, in regard to preliminaries. As natural ritualists, women love preliminaries. A woman dressing and making herself up is savoring preliminaries. A woman in her lover's bed craves preliminaries. And having a baby is, for the expectant mother, a half year or more of sweet preliminaries. There is the buying or borrowing of the maternity clothes, the preparation of the nursery, the gathering of the layette, the swathing of the bassinet. There is the seemingly interminable discussion of the virtues of breast-feeding, followed by the debate over which kind of bottle is better. And of course there is the matter of choosing a name for the baby, a relatively simple task which women endlessly prolong, not so much out of indecision as out of a sense that preliminaries are not to be rushed.

Here again the baby routine is rigged against a man's nature— or at least the "nature" our culture has imbued him with. Men like to dress fast, love fast, decide fast. The little ritual preliminaries that a pregnant woman dotes on and with which she dawdles away her incubation, are fun and touching for the husband too—at least at first. But when she wonders aloud for the nineteenth time whether to gamble on either pink or blue for the color of the baby's blanket or instead to compromise on yellow, her husband may grind his teeth.

A less-noted affliction of the expectant father is Dagwoodphobia. No man with any spirit likes the idea of falling into a cliché, and the weariest of all the domestic clichés is the expectant father bit.

"Oh, my God," a man says to himself upon hearing of his oncoming paternity, "I'm going to have to pace up and down the waiting room like those guys in cartoons and then I'm going to have to buy flowers for my wife." It's like the embarrassment and faint rebelliousness a man feels when it occurs to him that getting married is going to involve a wedding with the rented clothes and the insipid song about cutting the cake and the routine about the bride and groom dancing together alone on the dance floor while everybody else watches. "I'm not going to have to go through all that crap, am I" he asks himself. And all the time he knows full well that, yes, he is going to have to go through all that crap, partly because he himself actually wants to, has in fact been looking forward to going through all that crap and would feel cheated, somehow, if one single absurdity of it were denied him.

As ritualists, women are not put off as easily by life's operational banalities. Upon encountering a cliché, a woman will try to give it her own touch, to make it work for her. She instinctively understands the usefulness of petty ritual in getting a person from the beginning of an experience to its end without undue trauma. A man, however, especially a young man, feels obliged to stamp and roar at clichés, which, as we have seen, is what the whole birth procedure seems to consist of.

A woman should know, therefore, and not be appalled, that as happy as her husband is about the baby, within him there may be a certain amount of stamping and roaring going on.

Of all the clichés that beset the father-to-be, I might add, the hoariest is the one that says all fathers naturally prefer to have a boy. The counter-cliché is when the father-to-be replies that, no, it doesn't matter to him, a boy or a girl, either one will be fine. I, happily, was beset by neither cliché, because I knew from the beginning that, whether I liked it or not, I was going to have a son. I just knew it. What else, after all, could I have? I worried about other things—whether my son would be as rough on me as I sometimes had been on my own father, whether the doctor's knife might slip during the circumcision and with a single stroke carve years of paradise out of the little fellow's life. But as to the gender of the child, I never had a moment's doubt.

And so when at 7:00 A.M. on that notable morning, after my wife had spent all night in labor, Doctor Rugart came into the waiting room and said, "Well, Tom, you're the father of . .," I was already thinking Son, and my chest was already swelling with pride. And when he continued with ". . . a fine baby girl," the hand I had raised to meet his involuntarily sank. I couldn't lift it. I wasn't just disappointed I was thunderstruck. The doctor, who had been through it all before, reached down and shook it, too weary to disguise the fact that he thought me a familiar kind of fool.

The first glimpse of his child is another small ordeal for the father. It is not always love at first sight, as one encounters that miniature stranger. In fact, it can be frightening. Mothers never seem to have much trouble understanding that babies are bound to look odd for a while, having just been squeezed through a knothole, but fathers seem doomed to despair over the pinched and florid little faces. That may be because one of those anxieties that a husband experiences while his wife is being serenely pregnant is that some unfortunate hereditary trait, probably from her side of the family, will reappear in his child. Looking at a newborn, one can believe the worst.

One can also be frightened in other ways. A newborn baby typically looks as if it is angry with you—so angry that you feel guilty instantly, whereas you had thought it would be years before the child found you out. My first response, upon seeing my daughter, was to recall something a friend of my wife's had told me. She said that when she was little, her father had kissed her too warmly, too intimately, and that this had been pleasant but also upsetting and undoubtedly one of the things that had driven her to the psychoanalyst's couch. And so, ridiculously, when my daughter gave me that angry little scowl, something inside me said: "She knows—she knows I'm going to kiss her too warmly."

The point I am making is that for husbands, the birth of the first baby can be an unpredictable, unexpectedly trying time, a time when they may not be quite themselves. I, for one, find it a little embarrassing to think back upon. I remember, for example, my attitude toward the woman who shared the hospital room with my wife. She had just had her eighth child, and whenever a visitor would ask her about it, she would say, "Don't mention that baby! I'm here for a rest." Such a humorless, high-strung state was I in that I found her remark almost irreverent.

The silly behavior reached its climax a few days after the baby was born when the woman at the hospital desk showed me a picture of my child and said I could buy it for five dollars. The photo was extremely overlit, and the child was a ghastly white. Obviously the hospital had let some hack of a photographer go into the nursery, hold a flashgun in my baby's face and fire it off point-blank. I was enraged—I was sure the baby's retinas had been singed, if not her psyche—it must have been like Hiroshima for the child. I'm not the type who complains to strangers, but I yelled at the woman at the desk and actually threatened to bring suit against the hospital and contemplated trying to get a local newspaper to mount a crusade against the practice. Six floors up, in the maternity wing, my wife communed with her unharmed infant.   When they showed her the photo, she loved it.

In due course, the mother and child come home from the hospital and true family life begins, and in the ordinary urgencies of that new life, the anxieties are quickly forgotten.   Now there is an actual new human being for the husband to relate to, not just a lump under a maternity jumper, and there are practical new routines for him to occupy himself with, such as learning to hold his breath while changing diapers.   And by and large his wife is her old self again.   The hormones have eased off, and she is no longer playing Earth Mother, no longer maddeningly remote or ethereal.

Of course the husband may not readjust immediately.   It may take him a while to realize that his wife is no longer Queen of the World and he her footman.   It may be necessary, in fact, for him to be apprised of the new situation by his wife herself—as was a friend of mine an hour after his first child was born.   The maternity-ward nurse had summoned him to his wife's chamber, where she was resting after the delivery.   Her face was pale against the pillow and her eyes were closed, so he tiptoed into the room and stood silent by the bed.   As he gazed down upon her almost worshipfully, her eyes popped open.   "For God's sake, Peter," she said, reaching up and pulling him down for a hearty kiss, "I'm still your wife!"

FLOOD TIDE *

JEANNE LOHMANN

These long nights bring back my pregnancies
With their heavy waiting dreams,
Their loneliness.
So much I wanted to give you then,
And I could not.
I lay awake many times in those years.
The child within me rounded and hardened my belly,
Sustained on my air and food.
I felt my body grow and change.
Bewildered, estranged from myself,
Swept by a great mystery-tide towards birth,
Wanting our child, fearful of the coming,
Trusting and not trusting,
Doing it all alone.
I was whole and not-whole,
Myself and other, certain of my place,
Every cell essential, wondering who I was,
Questioning the new and unseen
Growing inside me,
Growing upon me,
Five times I moved out on those seas,
Adventuring in our name and for us,
Losing treasure,
Bringing treasure safely home.

There were things we did not say
To one another in those years.
I am hungry now for the lost words.
I am afraid to ask.
The tears I have not shared are stored
In a dam behind my throat and eyes;
They threaten flood,
And we may be washed away.

I touch myself now, years later,
In these same wakeful nights.
No baby grows inside.

* Jeanne A. Lohmann, unpublished
manuscript.

My body curves in roundness and responds
With fresh awareness to all our loving.
Why then this heaviness in dreams?
What tides are carrying me,
And toward what shores?
Is there some birth awaits me now
With children grown and gone,
Mystery calling again for surrender?

Will you hold me close, these stranger years,
Listening long in love, accepting for us both
The tears I do not understand?
Stay near me in the wakeful nights
When I am not myself, and lonely-lost,
Questioning who and why I am,
And where I go.

*

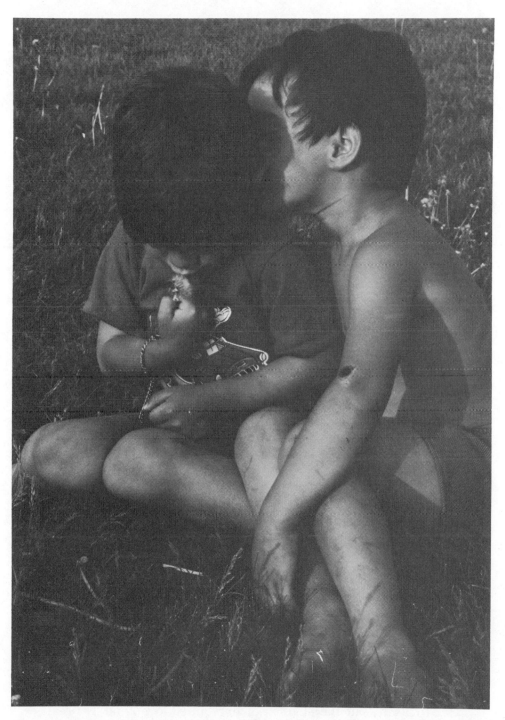

77

INTRODUCTION

Obviously, love is a complex emotion. It involves the giving of self and the receiving from others in a way unique from other relationships. While it is easy to hide parts of self in typical interaction with others, a love with meaning and significance demands a level of honesty and openness about ourselves that may be frightening. This level of intimacy is neither easy to attain nor to maintain. For one thing, stress and anxiety exist in all relationships, even the very best. They may lead us to question the basis of love, ourselves as lovable, others as worth loving, or even whether the feeling is love. In addition, as a relationship develops these questions arise again and again, further complicated by changing bases for relationship and adjustments in feeling. Then, when the romance often experienced early in the relationship may not seem as strong, we wonder whether we are still in love.

The resulting ambiguity in the relationship is hard for us to handle. How do we move from being "in love" to loving? That "irresistible urge" is characteristic of being in love, yet it is not enough to contribute to or sustain a loving relationship. Love grows only through hard work and increasing honesty, toward total revelation of self.

Such honesty must include growing knowledge and self-understanding as well as honesty toward the loved one. An instructive yet rarely asked question, "Why do I love you?" can tell us much about ourselves and clarify what love means to us. Only then does some of the ambiguity of a love relationship disappear, to be replaced by response *as* a real person *to* a real person.

All of this hints at the complexity of love. We want love, yet we often fear it. We need it, yet often avoid it. And when love is established, we often prevent it from flourishing. It is only when we become fully committed to an honest, open relationship that the obstructions to achieving intimacy are removed.

The difficulties inherent in the quest for love and intimacy provide the basis for the readings that follow.

Armour's experience is common enough for many of us, whether the object of first love is one's teacher, the high school football hero, or an older sibling's best friend. Adults often call it "puppy love", but the anguish of unrequited love is no less real to the lover.   At a later age, as suggested by Brokering, the anguish may come from not knowing how the loved one will respond to the first profession of "I love you".

Dahms explores levels of intimacy in relationships, with emotional intimacy the deepest yet most difficult to achieve.   Fear of self-disclosure and the risk of rejection often hinder or prevent us from reaching this most authentic intimate relationship. Jourard suggests that this fear may cheat us of a meaningful experience of love.

The need for possessiveness that may characterize love is challenged by Lohmann, while Gibran's prose-poem "Love" presents one statement of an ideal relationship.   Love as experience, however, often differs from this ideal.   We may expect the flush of romance to be characteristic of marriage in its early years, but Colette suggests there are varied ways by which love is expressed.   The meaning of a gift lies in the eyes and heart of the recipient.

These selections keynote the paradoxical nature of love—it is a desirable emotion yet difficult to understand.   It is possible that a lasting love may depend more on the degree of commitment than it does on the basis of the "emotion".   Maybe love is better described as an experience rather than as an emotion.   In any case, the ultimate solution to making love work for us appears to lie in the old dictum: Know thyself.   As we become more honest with ourselves, we shall have a clearer view of what love means as well as an understanding of why we love others.

MY LIFE WITH WOMEN (EXCERPT) *

RICHARD ARMOUR

Then I fell in love with Miss Webster, and everything changed.

Miss Webster was my third-grade teacher and all I had ever hoped for in a woman. She had a soft, sweet voice. Her eyes crinkled when she smiled. She smelled good. And she could write on the board without making the chalk squeak.

One day when I came home from school, I broke the news to my mother, who was in the kitchen making cookies.

"I'm going to marry Miss Webster," I said.

"That's nice," my mother said, not the least surprised. It was almost as if she already knew. Could Miss Webster have told her? And yet I hadn't told Miss Webster myself.

"And we're going to have two children, both boys," I said.

"That's fine," my mother said. "Now you can scrape the bowl and lick the spoon."

All the time I was scraping the bowl and licking the spoon, I was thinking of Miss Webster. We were going to be very happy together. I would look after her and give her everything she wanted, and she could just stay home and make cookies.

A short time afterward, I disclosed my plans to one of my friends during recess while we were swinging on the monkey bars.

"I'm going to marry Miss Webster," I said.

"So am I," he said.

This came as a surprise to me. I was even more surprised to learn, after a little asking around, that every boy in the class planned to marry Miss Webster. I was not greatly disturbed, however, since I had an advantage over most of the others. We were seated alphabetically, and I sat in the front row. I was much closer to Miss Webster than boys like Jack Williams and Eddy Zorn. Besides, Miss Webster obviously liked me. Who else got to clap erasers twice a week?

* From MY LIFE WITH WOMEN by Richard Armour. Copyright © 1968 by Richard Armour. Used with permission of McGraw-Hill Book Co.

But I had competition more serious than my classmates. One day I saw Miss Webster go by in a sporty car with the top down. She smiled and waved at me. I waved back but I couldn't smile. A man was driving the car, and he had one hand on the steering wheel and the other around Miss Webster. After waving at me, Miss Webster said something to the man, and he turned and looked back at me and laughed.

As the car drove on and disappeared around a corner, I had a feeling that I was losing Miss Webster. For the first time it occurred to me that she might marry someone else, someone who owned a car and was old enough to drive it.

I was right about Miss Webster. Just before the end of the school year, when I should have been excited about summer vacation and being promoted to fourth grade, I got the bad news. Though I had rather expected it, I was pretty depressed for several days.

"I am not going to teach after this year," Miss Webster told our class. "I am getting married." The girls cried, they were so happy, and the boys would have cried too, if they had not been boys. As it was, they just looked miserable.

It was the first time I had ever been beaten out by a rival, and I took it hard. Miss Webster had led me on and then let me down. But she wasn't as much to blame as the man in the car. I hated him. A couple of times I imagined myself fighting a duel with him, the winner to get Miss Webster. One time it was with swords and one time it was with pistols, and I won both times. But I couldn't go on imagining forever, and when I wasn't imagining I knew I had lost Miss Webster for good.

When I came home from school and told my mother Miss Webster was getting married, she sympathized with me.

"I know how you feel," she said. "But I've always thought she was a little old for you."

Then she told me that Miss Webster was twenty-two, and by the time I was twenty-two she would be thirty-six. By the time I was thirty-six she would be fifty.

"A woman can be older than her husband," she said, "but she shouldn't be too much older. I'm three years older than your father, and that's about enough."

"Why?" I asked.

"Well, it just is," she said, and seemed to think this is a satisfactory answer. It was all I could get out of her.

By the time I was eight years old, I had learned a good deal about women. From the girl next door I learned that the ones who are always after you are the ones you don't want. From Miss Webster I learned that the ones you want are always the wrong age or something, and then somebody comes and carries them off anyhow.

LOVE IN MOTION *

HERBERT BROKERING

That's that!
THE MAILBOX LIPS SNAPPED SHUT.
It was on its way.
SHE HURRIED ACROSS THE STREET
TO BEAT THE RED LIGHT.
And her mouth twisted in a tiny smile.
SHE HAD DONE IT.
THE LETTER WAS ON ITS WAY.
There was no way to change it.
IT WAS NOT POSSIBLE TO OPEN THE BOX
OR TO REACH IN.
It was not legal.
IT WAS AGAINST THE LAW TO TAKE IT BACK.

It was now the ruling of the federal government
that the letter go through.
IT WAS THE RULING OF HER MIND.
HER HEART WAS NOT SURE.
She had a feeling of relief, and it was
in the way she ran across the street.
SHE COULD SEE THE LOOK ON HIS FACE,
SHE HAD WAITED LONG TO WRITE;
NOW SHE WOULD WAIT TO HEAR.
It was his turn.
THE RELIEF WAS LIKE THE ROSEBED
BY THE WALK.
Freed from the winter freeze.
SHE HAD SAID HER SENTENCE.
NOW HE MUST SAY HIS.
The conversation was the only one
of its kind in the world.
THE CATEGORY WAS AN OLD ONE.
But this was different.
Absolutely no one had ever had this to say.
IN THIS WAY.

* From *Break Out* by Herbert Brokering, copyright © 1970 by Concordia Publishing House. Used by permission.

They were the only two of their kind
of the 3 billion people or 5 billion.
MULTIPLIED.
THERE IS NO COUNTING THE COMBINATIONS.
And this was like none of those.
She smiled.
SHE HAD JUST CREATED A SENTENCE.
With a new subject and predicate: "I love you."
WHAT HE'D SAY BACK WOULD BE LIKE
NOTHING EVER SAID BEFORE.
Nor again.
"I LOVE YOU," SHE SAID.
No one had ever said it before.
Not this way.

INTIMACY HIERARCHY *

Alan M. Dahms

Intimacy may be one of the most overworked words in our vocabulary. It is used to sell perfume and all manner of artificial self-enhancement materials. It is used to sell magazines, perfume, and automobiles and to purvey the philosophy of the effective social swinger. It strikes fear in the hearts of many who equate it with sexual irresponsibility and promiscuity.

INTIMACY HIERARCHY

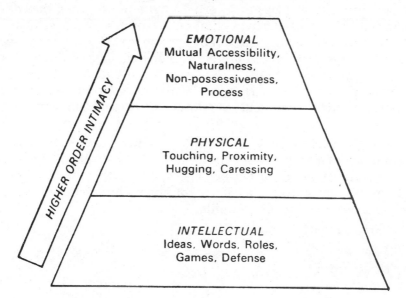

INTELLECTUAL INTIMACY

Though I speak with the tongues of men and of angels, and have not charity, I am become as sounding brass, or a tinkling cymbal.

I CORINTHIANS 13:1

[A8744]

* Reprinted   by   permission   of
SHIELDS PUBLISHING CO., INC.

It may be helpful to conceive of intimacy as a hierarchy of various levels, rather than an either-or proposition. Intimacy can be viewed as a pyramid with three interrelated levels: intellectual, physical, and emotional. In this view all levels are of equal importance, although some seem to be more frequently embraced than others. None should be emphasized to the exclusion of the others, and none should be omitted. It is possible that at birth humans have the potential to fully embrace all levels of intimacy, but in the course of development, many lose their original capacity.

How often we've heard that. How *little* we have believed it! Intellectual intimacy is the intimacy of brass and cymbals. It is the intimacy of ideas and verbal interactions. It is the intimacy of the cocktail party, the selling of the social self, and the strictly intellectual classroom experience. People exchange ideas in ways that tend to protect rather than expose their inner selves. Isolation remains. Everyone stays safe in their emotional aloneness. At parties, we strive to be "cool," to appear unruffled, attractive, and invulnerable (except on our own terms).

Eric Berne, in *Games People Play,* showed how such games help us *avoid* intimacy, not achieve it.[1] *Who's Afraid of Virginia Woolf,*[2] and *Waiting for Godot*[3] also speak to this point. When games are played to the exclusion of honest interaction the cost is enormous. The script is familiar.

"How are you? "

"I am fine."

"How's work? "

"Fine."

"I like you, and have been thinking about you all evening."

"Let's go somewhere where we can be alone."

"My wife doesn't understand me   .   .   ."

Then, *later,* "I'll call you sometime."

"Goodnight."

In Camus' novel, *The Stranger,* the main character, Meursault, refused to play games, to exchange false social verbiage, and to feign affection that did not exist.[4] His various experiences illustrated well how his isolation seemed to be encouraged by his contemporaries through their superficial, script-playing interchanges. Meursault's attempts to simply be himself resulted in his conviction for murder. For example, when he refused to say he was upset over his mother's death and his killing of an Arab in self-defense, he was branded a "not me" by his society.

The John Wayne syndrome that encourages young men to be ruggedly independent and to need no one is one example of intellectual intimacy. The hero of the movie western or detective story who seems to need no one in order to survive is a high prophet of this form of intimacy. The intimacy at this level is mostly verbal and capacities for it are acquired early in the socialization process. This intimacy is extremely role-oriented and one is more concerned with the self one is conveying than with the self one is.

The plethora of books describing how to be popular, how to win friends and influence people, and how to get ahead in the business world all seem to focus on this superficial intellectual intimacy level.

> *When I was a child, I spake as a child, I understood as a child, I thought as a child; but when I became a man, I put away childish things.*

> *I CORINTHIANS 13:11*

This well-known verse is an accurate description of the "fall" from childlike openness and trust to a "mature" style of relating that is characterized by intellectual and defensive behavior.

It may be useful to adopt the premise that at birth the human being is maximally able to experience intimacy at all levels— emotional, physical, and intellectual. As human development progresses, a person may lose the capacity to experience higher levels of intimacy. As soon as the infant is able to manipulate verbal symbols he begins to acquire from others his "looking-glass self," which he will cling to with great tenacity. He literally learns what he is, what he is not, and what he should be from the responses elicited from others in interactions with them. He is especially rewarded for success at intellectual intimacy, for saying and doing socially acceptable things. In short order, his self is shaped by others in ways consistent with society's conception of "right."

The real goal of survival education may be to free persons from past learning in order to acquire survival skills. Educational institutions may need to get about the business of facilitating *unlearning*. It is assumed here that anyone with enough

skill in dealing with verbal symbols to read these printed words
is in *need* of help. He is already *maimed* in terms of full human
survival. However, much of what currently goes on in organized education is exclusively at the intellectual level of intimacy.
The lecture, note-taking, test-taking, competition paradigm best
illustrates intellectual intimacy. Students are allowed to become intellectually intimate with an instructor's ideas, but many
educators either feel obligated to stifle any higher order intimacy or are unable to participate in high levels of interaction.

Jerry Farber, in his little book *The Student As Nigger,* pointed out that the student's role is similar to that of an indentured
servant.[5] They have little influence and are subjected to the
control of teachers and administrators. Their second-class status is overseen by administrators on behalf of the whole society.
Intellectual, often destructive, intimacy interactions are their
lot. As long as they remain deferential and passive they are
accepted. But if they should disagree or ask those frightening
questions that begin with "Why? " they are termed unruly, un-
appreciative, disobedient, difficult, and delinquent. They are
seldom treated as full persons—as colleagues in the survival task
of all men.

The educational system in this country still shows the influence of the Puritans and the clergymen who became the administrators of the early New England colleges. College and
university administrators, representing society's conservative
ruling elite, worry endlessly about how to control student behavior in dormitories. They have been appointed *in loco paren-
tis*—the parent's representatives—so sexual activities, drinking,
and housekeeping are of great concern to them. This is amaz-
ing when one realizes that the student's age mates who went
directly into the world of work after high school are accepted
as responsible. No one polices the halls or living quarters of
the urban apartment houses. Our society guarantees the rights
of working youth. It does *not* guarantee similar rights to the
student-nigger.

In L. Frank Baum's delightful story, *The Wonderful Wizard
of Oz,* written in the year 1900, several characters illustrate how
persons learn and believe in unfounded assumptions about their
personal limitations.[6] Dorothy and her dog Toto want to return
to Kansas, the Scarecrow wants a brain, the Tin Woodman wants
a heart, and the Cowardly Lion wants courage.

The Scarecrow learned he had no brain. An old crow said to him, "If you only had brains in your head you would be as good a man as any of them. Brains are the only things worth having in this world, no matter whether one is a crow or a man."

The Tin Woodman loved a Munchkin girl and was prevented from marrying her by the Wicked Witch of the East. She caused a series of accidents followed by a succession of replacement operations by a tinsmith until the woodman was *all* tin. He was convinced that without a "heart" he couldn't care for anyone.

The Cowardly Lion was convinced that he lacked the courage shown by other lions. He was constantly afraid of everything.

All the characters felt that only the Great Wizard of Oz could solve their problems. They were most distressed when the never-seen wizard was exposed as an impotent charlatan. He said, "I'm just a common man!" In response to their continued insistence he finally gave the Scarecrow a head full of bran and sawdust for a brain, the Tin Woodman a velvet-sawdust heart, and the Cowardly Lion a courage potion to drink. Other versions of the story have him giving the Scarecrow a diploma, the Tin Woodman a small clock "heart" and the Cowardly Lion a medal. The point remains.

When the story is examined it can be seen that throughout the adventures of the characters the Scarecrow was the problem-solver, the Tin Woodman was continually weeping over the plight of a crushed beetle and other misfortunes and was beginning to rust, and the Cowardly Lion was consistently courageous. In short, each possessed those capacities he had been taught, either by others or by experience, that he lacked.

The similarity between Dorothy's friends and many real people is worth noting. We all know people who feel obliged to earn certificates and diplomas (bestowed by wizards) to have proof of their intellectual prowess. Psychologically maimed persons seek out various wizards whom they have enthroned as omnipotent and omniscient. Psychotherapists, professors, teachers, parents, advice-giving columnists, spouses, and friends are all commonly chosen as wizards. When they are revealed sooner or later as "common men," the searcher is disappointed and angry. We need to begin realizing our capacities already exist and no magician is needed to help us unlearn the internally accepted limits, which we have been carefully taught.

It is amusing to think about the need for unlearning and relearning following our mastery of the intellectual intimacy level

in order that we may redevelop capacities for productive physical and emotional intimacy. It could be proposed that a certain
block of courses be experienced by students at all levels in educational structures. Teachers-in-training, who will exert such
a profound influence on children, should certainly be exposed.
The following block of courses may serve to illustrate the point:

> De-educational Psychology
> Philosophy and History of De-education
> Need for De-education
> De-education for What is Real
> Practicum in De-education
> Theories in De-education
> Techniques of De-education
> The De-educator's Role
> Organization and Administration of De-education
> Individual Similarities
> The De-educated Personality (Healthy Personality)
> Personality Dynamics and De-education

Although we like to think that speech is one of the important
ways in which people set up in-depth communication processes,
it is possible that speech is most often used to keep others *away*
by relating in terms of roles. Speech may be one of the most
popular distance tools!

Spoken English (in the U.S.) has some very interesting characteristics. Our language has many words, with various connotations and denotations, to describe hostility. The words seem
to form a continuum:

> I am distressed, troubled, irritated, perturbed, uncom-
> fortable, disgusted, incensed, angry, hostile.

The highest level of hostility is expressed by "I want to *kill* you,"
or "I *hate* you." The English language, as it is commonly used,
however, offers very few words for describing emotional intimacy. Love, tenderness, gentleness, and caring seem to exhaust
the available terms.

English, as it is currently spoken in this country, is a pauper's
language. The Greeks used ten words to refer to the various
qualities of love ranging from agape to eros; modern English
uses one word only—love.

Abraham Maslow, the noted humanistic psychologist who was
deeply concerned with the barriers to full human functioning,
studied the healthy, self-actualized person, and concluded that

the English language was "rotten for good people." He maintained that the vocabulary for the virtues was terribly limited.
He was fond of pointing out that even our word *love* was "all
smeared up" with various connotations and denotations. Our
country's preoccupation with hostility and dissonance seems revealed in the number of terms we have evolved to describe such
activities. Both naivete and inexperience with emotional intimacy are revealed by the *lack* of terms used communicating in
this area. In fact, we seem to delight in the search for nega-
tivity.

PHYSICAL INTIMACY

In discussing physical intimacy, we will examine the dilemma
of the emerging adolescent behavior, women's liberation, prostitution, pornography, sex education, and the ideas of Desmond
Morris as expressed in his book *Intimate Behaviour.*[7] Physical
intimacy is a "loaded" area. The very term draws strong reactions from most people. How can one remain disinterested in
the one area of life perhaps most laden with taboos, "oughts"
and "shoulds," and guilt feelings?

For most people in our culture, physical intimacy is more
frightening than intellectual intimacy because physical intimacy
is marketed as the highest order. Popular magazines, advertising, literature, and films all portray physical intimacy as the
god at whose altar all should worship.

Initial experiences with physical intimacy are often disappointing, especially when all hopes for escape from a state of
isolation are based on such experiences. The taboo against
teachers touching children in the classroom illustrates that the
fear of physical intimacy is inextricably bound to an equally
intense need for it in educational processes.

The American formula for growing up is tied to our worship
at the altar of physical intimacy. Adolescents often complain
of the isolation and sterility of their lives. Holden Caulfield,
the main character in J. D. Salinger's *Catcher in the Rye* set
out on a personal odyssey to discover routes to connectedness.[8]
The poignant story shows the lack of meaningful human ties
in his life and his faltering attempts to find himself. The Beatles
recorded a song describing a young girl who quietly leaves home
"after living alone for so many years."

Very often parents respond to the child's expression of loneliness by saying that adolescence is a time for learning and

achievement and one day their child will be going about his or her daily routine and all at once Prince or Princess Charming will appear. The world will stop, the sun will rotate, and talcum powder will fall from the trees. (If it *is* prince charming, *hopefully* he will be a graduate of an excellent medical school and be of similar ethnic and racial origin.) The American myth continues by demanding an appropriate period of engagement—perhaps six months—and after waiting patiently, the youngster will be rewarded on the wedding night by discovering how close two persons can be. Not all play this drama according to the script! After the junior-senior prom and a little imbibing, some fall from "grace" by experimenting with physical intimacy in the back seat of a station wagon. Whether experienced by the honeymoon couple at the New Beginnings Motel or by the renegades in the station wagon, sexual physical intimacy is often very tremendously disillusioning. Some have discovered that physical intimacy is not the highest form of intimacy and does not guarantee full human sharing. Nevertheless, the myth is still embraced by the majority of young people.

The plight of women in the American way of life has been discussed by the feminist leader Germaine Greer, whose best-selling book *The Female Eunuch* appeared in America in 1971.[9] She feels that women have been relegated to second class citizenship. Their plight is even more unfortunate than the racial minorities because women have, as yet, no sense of unity. Because physical intimacy is a status symbol for a man, women are used for physical pleasure much as a master uses his slave. Greer feels that until both women and men discard the "I'll use you" attitude, no real human emotional intimacy can be evolved. She deplores the *Playboy* philosophy, its pictures of immature girls, and its emphasis on physical intimacy. She goes beyond the hackneyed militaristic style of some of her colleagues in the feminist movement in that she feels it is pointless to blame either sex for the dehumanizing rules controlling human relationships. She prefers to point the finger at historical, political, economic, and psychological factors. She is also very critical of the nuclear family structure in which the mother can be, and often is, controlled by the child. Although she has never lived in a commune, she feels that communal arrangements in some form, will play an important role in the future.

In our culture physical intimacy is very often conditional. The bride-to-be says, "You may touch me only after we are mar-

ried." The segregationist says, "You can come close to me if
you are of my race."

Our society sets very definite limits on physical intimacy.
For example, no one hesitates to allow a physician to touch
them, yet if a man on the street were to take the same liberties
he would be arrested for assault. Our society very carefully certificates those persons allowed to deal in intimacy. Physicians,
psychiatrists, psychologists, dentists, and beauticians are examples.

One of the major areas of social concern with physical intimacy is that of prostitution. This enterprise could be viewed
as a nonsocially sanctioned form of physical intimacy and may
be meeting a need that is caused by the social system as it is
currently structured. Germaine Greer might define the role of
wives in some marriages as a sanctioned form of prostitution!

Pornography may be a substitute form of physical intimacy.
Although we can't even define what it is, many people persist
in feeling it is evil. Despite increasing amounts of evidence to
the contrary, they are convinced that exposure to pornographic
materials will warp young minds.

In *Intimacy, Sensitivity, Sex, and the Art of Love* Allen and
Martin reported that in Denmark, where pornography has recently been legalized, there has been a marked and continuing
diminution of sexual crime.[10] Researchers in America have
found that rapists and child molesters actually received *less*
exposure to pornographic materials during adolescence than
normal heterosexual adults. One study conducted by Dr. Michael
J. Goldstein of the University of California at Los Angeles and
Harold S. Kant, Director of California's Legal and Behavioral
Institute, compared 60 men convicted of or charged with sex
offenses, with 52 regular patrons of pornography shops, and 63
"solid citizens" as a "control." The results revealed that all the
sexual deviates shared one common characteristic; they had
little exposure to erotica when they were adolescents. The normal adults in the sample reported more experience with pornography both as teenagers and adults than did the sex offenders.
There was no evidence to support a connection between sex
crimes and pornography. The researchers concluded that "a
reasonable exposure to erotica, particularly during adolescence,
reflects a high degree of sexual interest and curiosity that cor-
relates with adult patterns of acceptable heterosexual interest
and practice."

According to Allen and Martin, the recent *Report of the Commission on Pornography and Obscenity* compiled by a group of social scientists at the request of the President suggested that our laws governing obscenity were obsolete and that we should follow the Danes' example and make pornography legal, at least for adults.[11] Our collective inability to deal with these matters seems revealed in that the report, which cost two million dollars, has been ignored; perhaps it just doesn't happen to agree with our traditional "oughts" and "shoulds."

Similarly, the recent *Report of the National Commission on Marijuana and Drug Abuse* recommending the abolishment of criminal penalties for the private use of marijuana may be ignored.[12] When traditional rules are challenged many prefer not to examine the old ways, but to ignore the criticism.

Perhaps our traditional "oughts" and "shoulds" concerning physical intimacy encourage us to do violence to our youth in a variety of other areas such as sex education, or perhaps one should say the lack of it. Such programs are intensely controversial and students often receive a watered-down mixture of anatomical and physiological "facts." Almost no attention is paid to the evolvement of full human intimacy.

The most recent additions in the American tradition of how-to-do-it manuals includes *The Sensuous Woman,*[13] *The Sensuous Man,*[14] *The Sensuous Couple,*[15] and *The Sensuous Child!*[16] These books take a plumbing approach to physical intimacy. *The Sensuous Child,* supposedly written by a 13-year-old, tells how to be successful in spying on bathroom activities; *The Sensuous Couple* gives guidelines for undressing! What next? Perhaps the *Sensuous Senior Citizen* and the *Sensuous Neonate!* That should exhaust the age range. Although some of these books were allegedly written as spoofs of the American view of intimacy, it seems that many readers have taken them seriously and feel more liberated for having read them.

Feminists like Germaine Greer would hold up such manuals as evidence of our misguided approach to a misunderstood goal. How can we find the way to intimacy if we have erroneous ideas about it? Such books may actually discourage the development of relationships that contain elements of real human intimacy. Instead, they encourage sexual athletic competition in the highest tradition of intellectual intimacy.

Rules and regulations regarding physical behavior vary from culture to culture. Diplomats going to South American posts are not accustomed to the Latin habit of standing very close to someone even for routine conversation. American servicemen are amazed to see men friends commonly holding hands in certain Asian cultures.

Within the American social system, women are free to hug and caress more intensely and over longer periods of time than are men. Two men holding hands would attract attention while two women would not.

The fear of intimacy in marriage can be best illustrated by the fable of the freezing porcupines. The two animals were huddled together for warmth, but were repelled by the sting of each other's quills. Each time the need for warmth brought them together, their mutual irritation began anew. The porcupines were continually being driven together and forced apart because of their need for intimacy. One would be hard-pressed to find a better description of the neurotic interaction in some marriages. Deeply felt needs for intimacy draw partners together while the interaction of carefully taught inhibitions drives them apart.

In his most recent book, *Intimate Behaviour,* the famous zoologist Desmond Morris described his observations of physical intimacy processes among humans.[17] His comments extend the work on infant monkeys done by Harry Harlow into the human context. Morris feels that intimacy in a full sense cannot occur *without* bodily contact and that such intimacy is a matter of survival. This was certainly the case with Harlow's infant monkeys who, when deprived of bodily contact with mothers and peers, often showed mental and physical impairment in later years.

According to Morris, human intimate contact can range from the first glance to casual touching to the mating act. He divided the usual human sequence of contact between men and women into twelve stages; (1) eye to body, (2) eye to eye, (3) voice to voice, (4) hand to hand, (5) arm to shoulder, (6) arm to waist, (7) mouth to mouth, (8) hand to head, (9) hand to body, (10) mouth to breast, (11) hand to genitals, and (12) genitals to genitals.[18] Progression through these stages, in some fashion or other, is seen as a useful screening device en route to an intimate "bonding." The sex act itself strongly influences depth bonding, except, of course, in the case of rape, which is characterized by an omission of the intermediate stages in the usual human contact sequence. The matter of human bonding is a serious business, for once the bond is established, emotional disengagement from the bond may be difficult. People who have experienced an unfortunate bonding may be haunted by regret or may be unable to stop caring. They may say, "I'm still thinking of him (her) all the time!"

According to Morris, when true bond-mates are unavailable, humans turn to a variety of culturally accepted substitute sources for physical intimacy. Doctor's offices, beauty parlors, barber shops, cigarettes, pets, and even one's own body are used. Clutching oneself in times of stress illustrates this last substitute.

Physical intimacy is a matter of survival and full human intimacy includes it as an important component along with the intellectual and emotional levels.

EMOTIONAL INTIMACY

The highest level of intimacy is viewed here as emotional intimacy. Emotional intimacy is the level for which we are least equipped in terms of past experiences. Emotional intimacy has four characteristics that are important to this discussion: mutual accessibility, naturalness, nonpossessiveness, and process.

Mutual Accessibility

Persons enjoying an emotionally intimate relationship, as a couple or as a group, tend to see each other as *mutually accessible*. Each person feels he has complete access to the other—free of criticism. The emphasis here is upon *mutual* accessibility. Traditional psychotherapy is not mutual; it could be viewed as one-way accessibility in which the client pays the therapist to enter the client's world. The client is accessible. The therapist and his inner world are not.

Accessibility in emotional intimacy could also be viewed as a continuum including "no way" accessibility, "one way" accessibility, and "mutual" accessibility. Different schools of thought on human behavior could be ranked along this continuum. Recent developments in the science of behavior modification based on stimulus-response psychology contend that no accessibility, in terms of the internal worlds of therapist and client, is required in order for positive gains to be made. Through a system of reward and punishment, the client can change or eliminate undesirable behavior. Many psychoanalytically oriented therapists, drawing upon the classic Freudian model, advance the merits of a one-way communication system wherein the therapist remains a closed system to the client. The most strict advocates of this theory place the therapist outside of the client's field of vision during the sessions. Many perceptual, humanistically oriented psychologists believe deeply in the mutually accessible relationship. Although they certainly do not feel that a therapist should unburden himself to a client, they do hold that the therapist should reveal himself to those he helps. If the therapist is tired or angry, he feels it is his responsibility not to hide his feelings.

Accessibility must be seen in terms of a specific relationship, but it has universal implications. The healthy self-actualized person is comfortable in both offering and taking advantage of accessibility. Experienced therapists of various schools of thought often report that as a client learns to function fully he tends to see the therapist as a colleague rather than an all-knowing wizard. The therapist is gradually "demoted" from wizard status to colleague. The relationship begins to show more mutual accessibility, naturalness, less role orientation, and more process orientation.

Persons who advertise an accessibility they will not or cannot deliver may exert a negative influence on prospective aid-seekers. Instructors, therapists, and others may indicate, verbally or otherwise, "I am available to you whenever you need me." Yet, in fact, they are often not available. This hypocrisy may cause cynicism on the part of prospective helpees. Instructors who claim availability, but who haven't enough time and energy for all students are often guilty of this cue versus practice gap. They lose credibility and are discounted by students to the extent that such a gap is discovered.

Authenticity and honesty can prevent a breakdown in credibility. In short, an honest non-available person may exert a much more positive influence than a person claiming a nonexistent availability. The latter is soon found out.

Ideally, an instructor should be available at all times to all students. But limited time and energy prohibit such a broad range of availability for many faculty members. Honest exposure of such limits seems the only educationally sound approach to this dilemma.

The concept of accessibility in human relationships is critical in view of the developing construction of emotional intimacy. What are the necessary and sufficient conditions that enable one person to view another person as intellectually, physically, and emotionally accessible?

In a recent study that the author carried out at a large midwestern university, student preferences for sources of help were studied. Thirty hypothetical crisis situations were presented to 633 students; they were asked where they would turn for help with the problems. Nearly 19,000 responses were examined. Helping professionals in university counseling centers and on residence hall staffs claim that they are perceived as accessible. The student responses showed otherwise. Seventy percent of all student problems would be taken to other students, faculty members, or others *rather* than to professional helpers. In fact, as many students chose peers *only* as chose professional personnel. This is especially significant since the crises were severe. Some of the 30 hypothetical crisis situations were: "I think I am pregnant." "I think a girl is pregnant because of me." "I'm so depressed and tired—I don't really care what happens anymore!"

The accessibility of the helper must be perceived by needful persons, or, in a real sense, it doesn't exist. The results of this university study also support the development of the peer-helper concept. In this type of program students who have been given some orientation to the task and their limitations are involved in helping their peers. Careful planning can result in a highly effective and nonthreatening referral system for serious difficulties.

HELPER (person wanting to help another)

The establishment of the helping relationship seems to be facilitated by a continuum of cues which the helper furnishes to enable the helpee to see him as accessible. The cues are both verbal and nonverbal.

Verbalization is probably the most often used and least demanding method. Cues that are ranked above this purely intellectual form may involve more activity on the part of the helper—leaving his office door open, receiving clients warmly, and even pursuing ambivalent clients. Such verbal and nonverbal conditions of accessibility, as furnished by a helper, could be measured on a behavioral dimension. Research studies could then explore the conditions of availability furnished, the style of their provision, and their influence on needful persons.

The effective helper seems capable of offering intellectual, physical, and emotional intimacy to people who seek him out for help. He especially furnishes the conditions of emotional intimacy. Such a helper encourages accessibility, naturalness, and nonpossessiveness and he acts on his commitment to the therapeutic process by directing his expertise toward its evolvement. The conditions of accessibility discussed here in terms of the helper-helpee relationship apply equally to all human relationships at all social levels.

HELPEE (person wanting help from another)

Certain conditions must exist within the helpee if he is to perceive another as accessible. He must feel a push to reach out and must perceive the possible helper as palatable, nonthreatening, and in possession of some survival benefits. No matter how effective the helper could be once the relationship is established, if he is not perceived as accessible there will be no relationship.

At various times in our relationships, we all adopt either the helper or helpee roles. One purpose of this book is to furnish a psychological rationale for our reaching out when we need human warmth and for our furnishing accessibility to those who need us. We must realize such accessibility is a matter of psychological survival.

The abrupt loss of an emotionally intimate accessible relationship can cause severe difficulty for all of us. The loss of a life partner is commonly followed by a period of listlessness, grief, apathy, and depression. It is only after a lengthy period in which attempts are made to establish new relationships that such persons regain a feeling of stability and report a renewed feeling about the meaning in life.

Even though a marriage may have lacked positive features, the emotionally tumultuous time following a divorce can literally incapacitate men and women. The passage of time is seldom enough to help someone regain their emotional footing. It is only when new relationships—either romantic or platonic—are established that persons resume their momentum in coping with life.

In our culture, aging is often accompanied by increased alienation from the mainstream of society. Many people see aging as alien to the self and tend to repress their feelings of distaste and anxiety. Old people are looked upon as "not me" because it is too unpleasant to think of oneself as aged. There is very little accessibility between the young and the old.

Retirement communities should provide the aged with the opportunity to establish new relationships and evolve new ways of coping with the problems of aging. Unfortunately, all too often, a highly structured regimen is imposed on senior citizens. After a lifetime of being told what to do—in childhood, in elementary, secondary, and college environments, and on the job for 30 years— the hoary-headed residents are often subjected to more rules and planned activities. It is sad to see the aged conform to schedules —breakfast at 8:00, shuffleboard at 9:30, lunch at 1:00—or obediently answering the cry of the recreational therapist, *"It's volley ball time!"*

The recent movie *Kotch* reveals the basic human revulsion with the programmed community death programs. *Kotch* shows middle class values and morality as confused and the mature man who is sensitive to this prejudice and misunderstanding. He is completely aware of the limited value in retirement corrals and he is not ready to surrender to family pressures. Instead, he takes a Greyhound trip and delivers a baby in a service station restroom.

Naturalness

The emotionally intimate relationship is *natural* in the sense that the Greek Stoics used the word. Persons are accepted as they are, not for their ability to change themselves to meet another's requirements or to play a role assigned to them by others. The conditions for facilitating human interaction (genuineness, unconditional positive regard, warmth, and acceptance) as defined by Carl Rogers, Charles Truax, and Robert Carkhuff are included in this concept of a natural, role-free interaction. People are free to be themselves, to expose their frailities and strengths. Hopefully, they are mutually empathetic in that they can see the world as the other person sees it. Lastly, there should be nonconditional acceptance of the other's natural way of being in the world. Persons are accepted although their behavior may not always be condoned.

The emotionally intimate relationship is an interaction between *human beings*, not *roles*. It is a case of person "A" relating to person "B," not a teacher relating to a student, a therapist to a client, or a superior individual to an inferior one. The emphasis is upon human similarities not human differences.

To set out to attain emotional intimacy as an "assignment" may be self-defeating. If we desire the relationship too highly, we may attempt to change ourselves and become unnatural in order to meet our idea of what the other person will approve. By changing ourselves we have destroyed all chance for a person-to-person relationship, for we are now playing a *role*.

The expressions of young people—"let it be," "don't be other directed"—are indications of their desire for natural relationships. We all want to have feelings of self-worth that are not wholly derived from others. Frederick Perls, the founder of Gestalt therapy, has expressed these sentiments in a poetic statement which is now used on the posters so popular with students:

I do my thing, and you do your thing.
I am not in this world to live up to your expectations and
    you are not in this world to live up to mine.
You are you and I am I,
and if by chance we find each other, it's beautiful.
If not, it can't be helped .   .   .

                              —FREDERICK S. PERLS

In natural relationships, feelings are of ultimate importance and are highly respected. When we choose to or are forced to hide our real selves—our feelings—we begin to "leave" psychologically. Anyone who has attended a meeting and begun to feel angry without feeling free to express the anger has experienced this. We begin to be bored and restless, and we start thinking of other things. Our unexpressed feelings cause us to pull out psychologically, much as a train pulls out of a station. Contrary to our expectations, however, when we do express such feelings in a meeting we often find others share our perceptions, and real communication begins again. When we remain silent we usually think, "If only I would have said something! Next time I will!"

Mainstream society often requires that disadvantaged and disenfranchised groups transform themselves and subdue their feelings as a condition of acceptance into the social order. Relationships with such disenfranchised persons are conditional upon their adoption of a life style palatable to the existing social structure. This requirement may be the cause of our difficulties with minority groups.

The experiences of Meursault, Camus' main character in *The Stranger,* a classic story of alienation, illustrate that being natural in unnatural surroundings can be dangerous.[19] Meursault refused to lie about his feelings concerning the death of his aging mother. He related events unemotionally and refused to inflate his feelings. Immediately, society felt menaced. They asked him, for example, to say that he regretted murdering an Arab in self-defense. He replied that what he felt about the matter was more akin to *ennui* (vexation, annoyance, chagrin, boredom) than to regret. This nuance condemned him. According to the foreword that Camus wrote to one English transaction of his work, Meursault was motivated by a passion for the absolute and for truth, especially in the area of human relationships. In a real sense, Meursault accepts "dying for the truth." It is interesting that many readers of *The Stranger* see Meursault as ill, strange, or monster-life (a creature-feature character?) when Camus' intent was to portray a *natural* man!

Challenging the "oughts" and "shoulds" that demand unnatural behavior forms the central theme of a literary style that is called black humor. In Joseph Heller's novel *Catch 22*, the main character Yossarian, lives by a sane, natural code in an insane world.[20] He questions the morality of war after watching the slaughter of his friends, and adopts the logic of survival. He reasons that if he is psychologically ill, he isn't fit for combat. But Catch 22 is invoked against him. Catch 22 is the loophole the authorities can use to revoke one's rights whenever it suits them. Yossarian's superiors reason that since he realizes he is not well, he must be sane and fit for combat. He was not allowed to be natural. He was forced to adapt to an insane world.

Nonpossessiveness

The third characteristic of emotional intimacy is nonpossessiveness. Intimacy cannot be based on "I'll love you if you love me too!" Caring on the highest level delights in the independence of others, not in the possession of them.

A truly emotionally intimate relationship cannot exist between "superior" and "inferior" individuals. The treatment of children as little persons who are smaller in stature but just as sacred as adults meets this requirement. Treating children as chattel does not.

Parents often find it difficult to see their children as individuals. Researchers of the "battered child syndrome" have found that many parents who beat their children do so because they see in the child certain aspects of their own personality that they cannot tolerate. Their actions are a mixture of self-hate and the desire to rid the child of the undesirable attribute. Insecure, rigid parents often batter their children to death, ostensibly for the child's own good!

The highest order intimacy, emotional, exists when we are nonpossessive. Many marriages flounder when one party attempts to possess the other. This smothering eventually destroys an intimate relationship which otherwise might have flourished.

When we view life as an unfolding process it is easier to be nonpossessive. To the extent we see our roles as prescribed (father, husband, daughter), we will attempt to possess others in order to fulfill our assigned role.

To share but not to possess is a large order. Even some psychotherapists lose their effectiveness because they are unable to see that they should be freeing, not possessing, their clients in a dependent relationship.

The turmoil in families often associated with the child's struggle for independence and autonomy also illustrates that for most of us the capacity for intimacy of a nonpossessive nature needs to be learned the hard way.

Process

Lastly, the attainment and maintenance of emotional intimacy is a *process* that requires *constant attention*. When time and energy are not expended to maintain this process, entropy sets in and the relationship deteriorates. It seems clear that emotional intimacy as an experience is a higher order capacity for human beings, and includes both intellectual and physical components.

The "state" of emotional intimacy is one that is never attained once and for all. It is evolved, maintained, and enhanced only by constant effort which leads to total consciousness.

Divorce could be viewed as the failure to evolve and/or maintain emotional intimacy. After emotional intimacy disappears, physical intimacy follows, soon only the chatter about daily routine (intellectual intimacy) remains.

Apart from its religious significance, a marriage ceremony could be seen as a simple verbal and nonverbal statement by two persons: "We have agreed to put some extra effort into our attempt at evolving higher order intimacy with each other. We intend to invest time and energy in the process of intimacy over an extended period of time."

One client commented movingly on the breakdown of her marriage; early in a series of sessions she said, "We don't share as

openly as we once did. He withholds things from me. He is
distant from me." Perhaps this signalled the loss of emotional
intimacy. She reported some weeks later, "He comes home,
takes a shower, runs to the bedroom and shouts, 'Come in here!'
Sex is just a duty for me now!" Evidently, only the physical and
intellectual levels were still present. One month later she reported, "I have been *relieved* of my duties! We just sit around
trying to maintain polite small talk about the yard, car, and our
social calendar." Evidently, all that remained at this point was
the intellectual level. In this case, since neither spouse valued
the relationship highly (did not choose to attend to process) a
divorce, perhaps in the best interests of both parties, quickly
followed.

We would conclude that if people really embraced the need
they have for intimacy almost any two persons could establish
and maintain such a relationship. Some of the science-fiction
movies that depict the last two survivors of a holocaust may
indicate this. If two persons really needed each other for survival, they *would* invest the time and energy required to establish some form of higher order intimacy as a life-support system. Small requirements of personal taste would soon be drop-
ped and the large benefits of the relationship would be paramount.

The following statement by Henry Ford seems to capture the
idea that we must "attend" to relationships as a part of effectively working together:

> *Coming together is a beginning; keeping to-*
> *gether is progress, working together is success.*
>
> *—HENRY FORD*
> *as quoted by S. M. Basta*
> *University of Nevada*

The expenditure of time and energy on the process does *not*
mean we must work to change ourselves. The real work is in
pushing back the thundering chorus of traditional "oughts" and
"shoulds" which advises us *not* to be intellectually, physically, or
emotionally intimate. It is a full-time task to break through
these "no-nos." Especially at the emotional intimacy level, much
of what we have been taught leads us to resist accessibility, naturalness, and non-possessiveness. Lastly, and perhaps most importantly, we fail to realize the process is worth it! The task of
freeing ourselves from the "oughts" and "shoulds" which endanger our individual and collective welfare is demanding and
never ending. It is also crucial to our survival.

THE FEAR THAT CHEATS US OF LOVE *

SIDNEY M. JOURARD WITH ARDIS WHITMAN

If we want to be loved, we must disclose ourselves. If we want to love someone, he must permit us to know him. This would seem to be obvious. Yet most of us spend a great part of our lives thinking up ways to avoid becoming known.

Indeed, much of human life is best described as impersonation. We are role players, every one of us. We say that we feel things we do not feel. We say that we did things we did not do. We say that we believe things we do not believe. We pretend that we are loving when we are full of hostility. We pretend that we are calm and indifferent when we actually are trembling with anxiety and fear.

We not only conceal ourselves; we also usually assume that the other person is in hiding. We are wary of him because we take it for granted that he too will frequently misrepresent his real feelings, his intentions or his past, since we so often are guilty of doing those very things ourselves.

As a therapist and research psychologist I often meet people who believe that their troubles are caused by things outside themselves—by another person, bad luck or some obscure malaise—when in fact they are in trouble because they are trying to be loved and seeking human response without letting others know them. For example, a husband and wife may come to me with a problem they think is purely sexual in origin but instead it turns out to be a frustration that has arisen because these two people can't communicate with each other.

Of course we cannot tell even the people we know and love everything we think or feel. But our mistakes are nearly always in the other direction. Even in families—good families—people wear masks a great deal of the time. Children don't know their parents, parents don't know their children. Husbands and wives are often strangers to each other.

One has only to think of the astronomical rate of divorce and of the contemporary conflict between parents and children, one has only to hear the anxiety and pain expressed in the therapist's

* Reprinted from Redbook Magazine,
October 1971. Copyright © 1971 by
The McCall Publishing Co.

office when these closest of all relationships are touched upon, to know that it is possible to be involved in a family for years, playing one's role nicely and never getting to know the other members of the family—who also are playing roles.

A few years ago a colleague and I devised a questionnaire with which we sought to find out what people were willing to disclose to others. We discovered that even with those they cared about most, people shared little of their true feelings, or their most profound longings and beliefs; revealed little of what they really thought on such touchy subjects as sex, self-image, religion.

Why is this so? For a great variety of reasons, some obvious, some not; some sensible, some profoundly harmful. But the most important reason springs from the very nature of the human enterprise itself. Paradoxically, we fail to disclose ourselves to other people because we want so much to be loved.

Because we feel that way, we present ourselves as someone we think can be loved and accepted, and we conceal whatever would mar that image. If we need to believe that we are without hostile impulses, that we are morally superior to other people, we won't give anything away that spoils that image.

Another reason we hide is to protect ourselves from change. Change is frightening to most people. Here is a young bride, for example, who returns from her honeymoon still lost in the romantic haze of being in love, blissfully happy and convinced that this is the way it is always going to be. But what happens?

One day her husband comes home, troubled over some problem at work, and broods in silence or snaps at her irritably. She in turn finds that getting meals and cleaning house—even when they're done for the chosen beloved—are not all that satisfying. Her feelings are changing. But instead of facing the fact that nothing in life stands still, she tries to pretend, to herself and to her husband, that she feels exactly as she did before.

The truth is that we want to think of ourselves as constant. Once we have formed our image of who and what we are, we proceed to behave as if that were all we ever could be. We "freeze," as though we had taken a pledge to ourselves that even if we did change, we'd try not to notice it.

And we don't want the other person to change either. Once he is labeled husband or child or father or unselfish friend, we have no wish to disturb that image. If something is happening inside him that may make him behave differently toward us, we don't want to hear about it.

Still another reason we don't disclose ourselves is that we were never taught how. On the contrary, unless we were very lucky as children, we were taught more about how to conceal ourselves from other people than about how to disclose ourselves. And we are still playing roles that we adopted almost before we can remember.

As small children we are and we act our real selves. We say what we think; we scream for what we want; we tell what we did. Then quite early we learn to disguise certain facts about ourselves because of the painful consequences to which they lead.

In fact, our own self-deceptions, painfully acquired, are among the strongest factors in our inability to reveal ourselves.

Personal ambition and economic pressures also give us powerful reasons for concealing what we really are. We grow up in a world where it is important to get ahead, and you can't do that without competing with other people. To put it bluntly, we want the job the other person wants, so of course we aren't going to be talking to him very candidly. Nor are we going to be honest with our professional superiors if being so reflects to our discredit. Our society itself exerts pressures on a person to suppress all but those characteristics that are considered acceptable.

All of us hide behind the iron curtain of our public selves. And with our "intimates" we again fail to disclose ourselves because we are so vulnerable to those we love. Under special pressures we might tell the stranger on the train about our longings and lusts and frailties, but how can we talk about them to those we love, who might be hurt by such revelations?

And of course it is true that we should not gratuitously hurt those we love. In the intimacy of daily life we *must* at times hide our feelings. But it is fatally easy to assume from this that we must never tell the truth when it will hurt. Every therapist, for example, is familiar with the man who, because his marriage is profoundly dissatisfying to him, is carrying on an affair. His involvement with another woman may break up his marriage; yet he says that he cannot talk abut his basic dissatisfactions with his wife "because it will hurt her"!

Finally, we are uncertain about our roles as men and women, and this uncertainty confuses us about how to communicate with those we love. What is it to be a good husband, a good wife, a good father, a good mother? What is it to be a man, a woman?

If people find it too difficult to impersonate the ideal version of "masculine" and "feminine" current in their time, they will hide their deviant attitudes. I've noticed recently, for example, that women who come for therapy tend to withhold whatever is spontaneous and authentic about themselves if those characteristics do not fit the social role they've been led to believe is appropriate. They try not to sound aggressive, strong, ambitious. They're afraid that even the therapist will reject them.

Men, on the other hand, hide what prevents them from seeming strong and masculine. Our researches showed that in general men tend to disclose considerably less than women do—and are told less. Often fathers seem to be the last to know anything subjective about their children; they talk a lot less about themselves to their sons and daughters than mothers do. All this may be changing for the young; but males 30 and over have been brought up in a world in which they have been taught to hide their feelings of weakness, their fears and their hurts, in order to appear tough, achieving, unsentimental.

If we have such good reasons not to disclose ourselves, why should we? Admittedly there are times when telling everything is unwise and hurtful. Neither can we always avoid playing roles. Often they are inescapable; they must be played or else the social system will not work. We *are* teachers and businessmen, housewives and mothers; and as responsible people we often must discipline ourselves to these roles.

Moreover, each person is entitled to be a "self" and entitled to keep that self private when he feels that he is not yet ready to disclose it. Healthy personalities aren't always fully visible. Chronic self-revelation may be idolatrous or even destructive in certain circumstances.

What matters is that we should be able to be private when we wish, when that's meaningful, and to be quite open and transparent when that's appropriate. That is all we should be trying for; but that is a great deal. We are warm, live, human, growing creatures; and when we suppress our identities completely, serious consequences follow.

For there is a limit to intuitive understanding. If we must spend much time together, if our lives are bound together, if we must collaborate for common ends, we are in trouble if we cannot communicate.

Thus a wife who finds her husband silent and preoccupied may believe that there is another woman in his life; a husband who finds his wife unresponsive in bed may blame himself for a problem that is really hers. When our loved ones do disclose themselves, we find all our preconceptions altered, one after another, by the facts as they come forth, since our previous ideas were based on insufficient evidence.

Another reason disclosure is so important is that without it we really cannot know ourselves. Or to put it another way, we learn to deceive ourselves while we are trying to deceive others. For example, if I never express my sorrow, my love, my joy, I'll smother those feelings in myself until I almost forget that they were once part of me.

What is the truth about ourselves? Often we ourselves don't know. But if I feel so safe in your presence that I am willing to try to disclose myself to you I'll find out about myself just by talking about how I feel and what I need and whether my needs are defensible.

When we cannot communicate we not only fail to have access to our inner selves but we also are under psychic and bodily stress. It's hard work trying not to be known and it brings a lot of patients to doctors and therapists.

Perhaps the most important reason for self-disclosure is that without it we cannot truly love. How can I love a person I don't know? How can the other person love me if he doesn't know me?

IN OPPOSITION *

JEANNE LOHMANN

I cannot put my loving you on call,
And in a cage, well groomed, content to wait
For times you make a choice to come, and set
The creature loose for daily walks and air.
It is no docile pet to call for romp,
Or chase the sticks, and follow where you will;
My loving you is more than animal,
And cannot walk obedient by your side,
Be mirror to your need, or glove to pride.

Nor will I make a chain of words for you
As amulet to keep the hurt away;
When love and freedom cross and disagree
There is no magic that can ease the strain
Till stubborn will begins to find a place
Of trust that guards and keepers never know,
Where tears are safe and anger right to flow.
But that the work is easy no one claims;
It asks a harder thing than cage or chains.

* Jeanne A. Lohmann, unpublished manuscript.

THE PROPHET (EXCERPT) *

KAHLIL GIBRAN

Then Almitra spoke again and said,
And what of Marriage, master?

And he answered saying:

You were born together, and together
you shall be forevermore.

You shall be together when the white
wings of death scatter your days.

Aye, you shall be together even in the
silent memory of God.

But let there be spaces in your together-
ness,

And let the winds of the heavens dance
between you.

Love one another, but make not a bond
of love:

Let it rather be a moving sea between
the shores of your souls.

Fill each other's cup but drink not from
one cup.

Give one another of your bread but eat
not from the same loaf.

Sing and dance together and be joyous,
but let each one of you be alone,

Even as the strings of a lute are alone
though they quiver with the same music.

Give your hearts, but not into each
other's keeping.

For only the hand of Life can contain
your hearts.

* From THE PROPHET, by Kahlil Gibran, copyright © 1923, by Kahlil Gibran. Reprinted by permission of Alfred A. Knopf, Inc.

And stand together yet not too near together:

For the pillars of the temple stand
apart,

And the oak tree and the cypress grow
not in each other's shadow.

MY MOTHER'S HOUSE (EXCERPT) *

SIDONIE COLETTE

She was eighteen years old when, in about 1853, he carried her off from her family, consisting of two brothers only, French journalists married and settled in Belgium, and from her friends —painters, musicians and poets—an entire Bohemia of young French and Belgian artists. A fair-haired girl, not particularly pretty, but attractive, with a wide mouth, a pointed chin and humorous gray eyes, and her hair gathered into a precarious knot slipping from its hairpins at the nape of her neck. An emancipated girl, accustomed to the frank companionship of boys, her brothers and their friends. A dowerless young woman, without trousseau or jewels, but with a slender supple body above her voluminous skirts: a young woman with a neat waist and softly rounded shoulders, small and sturdy.

The Savage saw her on a summer's day while she was spending a few weeks with her peasant foster-mother on a visit from Belgium to France, and when he was visiting his neighboring estates on horseback. Accustomed to his servant-girls, easy conquests as easily forsaken, his mind dwelled upon this unself-conscious young woman who had returned his glance, unsmiling and unabashed. The passing vision of this man on his strawberry roan, with his youthful black beard and romantic pallor, was not unpleasing to the young woman, but by the time he had learned her name she had already forgotten him. He was told that they called her "Sido," short for Sidonie. A stickler for formalities, as are so many "savages," he resorted to lawyers and relations, and her family in Belgium were informed that this scion of gentlemen glass-blowers possessed farms and forest land, and a country house with a garden, and ready money enough. Sido listened, scared and silent, rolling her fair curls around her fingers. But when a young girl is without fortune or profession, and is, moreover, entirely dependent on her brothers, what can she do but hold her tongue, accept what is offered and thank God for it?

So she quitted the warm Belgian house and the vaulted kitchen that smelled of gas, new bread and coffee; she left behind the

---

piano, the violin, the big Salvator Rosa inherited from her father, the tobacco jar and the long slender clay pipes, the coke braziers, the open books and crumpled newspapers, and, as a young bride, she entered the country house isolated during the hard winters in that forest land.

There she discovered an unexpected drawing room, all white and gold, on the ground floor, but an upper story barely rough-cast and as deserted as a loft. In the stables a pair of good horses and a couple of cows ate their fill of hay and corn; butter was churned and cheeses manufactured in the outbuildings; but the bedrooms were icy and suggested neither love nor sweet sleep.

Family silver engraved with a goat rampant, cut glass, and wine were there in abundance. In the evenings, by candlelight, shadowy old women sat spinning in the kitchen, stripping and winding flax grown on the estate to make heavy cold linen, impossible to wear out, for beds and household use. The shrill cackle of truculent kitchenmaids rose and fell, depending on their master's approach or departure; bearded old witches cast malign glances upon the young bride, and a handsome laundrymaid, discarded by the squire, leaned against the well, filling the air with noisy lamentations whenever the Savage was out hunting.

The Savage—a well-intentioned fellow in the main—began by being kind to his civilized little bride. But Sido, who longed for friends, for innocent and cheerful company, encountered in her own home no one but servants, cautious farmers, and gamekeepers reeking of wine and the blood of hares, who left a smell of wolves behind them. To these the Savage spoke seldom and always with arrogance. Descendant of a once noble family, he had inherited their disdain, their courtesy, their brutality, and their taste for the society of inferiors. His nickname referred exclusively to his unsociable habit of riding alone, of hunting without dog or companion, and to his taciturnity. Sido was a lover of conversation, of persiflage, of variety, of despotic and loving kindness and of all gentleness. She filled the great house with flowers, whitewashed the dark kitchen, personally superintended the cooking of Flemish dishes, baked rich plum cakes and longed for the birth of her first child. The Savage would put in a brief appearance between two excursions, smile at her and be gone once more. He would be off to his vineyards, to his swampy forests, loitering long at the wayside inns where, except for one tall candle, all is dark: the rafters, the smoke-blackened walls, the rye bread and the metal tankards filled with wine.

Having come to the end of her epicurean recipes, her furniture polish and her patience, Sido, wasted by loneliness, wept; and the Savage perceived the traces of tears that she denied. He realized confusedly that she was bored, that she was feeling the lack of some kind of comfort and luxury alien to his melancholy. What could it be?

One morning he set off on horseback, trotted forty miles to the county town, swooped down upon its shops and returned the following night carrying, with a fine air of awkward ostentation, two surprising objects destined for the delight and delectation of his young wife: a little mortar of rarest marble, for pounding almonds and sweetmeats, and a cashmere shawl.

I can if I like still make almond paste with sugar and lemon peel in the now cracked and dingy mortar, but I reproach myself for having cut up the cherry-colored shawl to make cushion covers and vanity bags. For my mother, who had been in her youth the unloving and uncomplaining Sido of her first and saturnine husband, cherished both shawl and mortar with sentimental care.

"You see," she would say to me, "the Savage, who had never known how to give, did bring them to me. He took a lot of trouble to bring them to me, tied to the saddle of his mare, Mustapha. He stood before me holding them in his arms, as proud and clumsy as a big dog with a small slipper in his mouth. And I realized there and then that in his eyes his presents were not just a mortar and a shawl. They were 'Presents,' rare and costly things that he had gone a long way to find; it was his first unselfish effort—and his last, poor soul—to amuse and comfort a lonely young exile who was weeping."

INTRODUCTION

A persistent concern of our humanness is the identification and then the expression of our feelings toward others. Further, our feelings change over time and we devise different forms of expressions for those changed feelings.

For most of us, our interest in the "other" sex goes back to earliest memories. The reasons for our feelings are rather vague, but we know whether or not we like the little boy or girl who sits behind us in school. Not knowing how to express the liking without rejection or ridicule, we try to gain attention by showing off, teasing, furtive kisses on the playground, or even knocking them down, all the while denying our interest in that other person.

Despite our denial of interest, rejection hurts just as much as it does when we are older. Perhaps this hurt may explain why we fall in love with an older person during the preteen years. A person who seems truly interested in our needs and problems, who is accepting of our awkwardness, becomes our first secret love—a teacher, the new minister, or the woman across the street even though she is 32.

To this point, our interest in the opposite sex and our sexual behavior seldom includes the sexual act. Self-exploration, playing "doctor", or fondling each other may arise from simple interest in the unknown or from enjoyable feelings of physical contact. Soon, however, our desires and feelings toward others become more physically oriented. Social and behavioral scientists disagree as to why this happens. Some argue that sexual behavior is instinctive to the human creature and inevitably emerges. Others suggest that the elements of society, (movies, books, TV, discussion with friends, etc.), teach us to express our interest in the opposite sex in a very physical manner. We need not resolve in this book whether sexual behavior is innate or learned. The end product of either is that desires for physical intimacy become very strong and may give confusing signals. What does sex have to do with love or with emotional intimacy? What restraints should there be on sexual expressions? Should we wait until marriage or until we know we're in love? Is sexual involvement an indication we are loved? Is sex the ultimate expression of love or are sex and love separate experiences? We resolve these questions in light of our culture and our values, but the issues will arise again.

The manner in which we express emotional and sexual feelings and the balance between them are dilemmas that continue throughout our lives. Varied experiences may change our attitudes and values so that what is appropriate behavior at one time may be unsatisfying at another. And, not only are there different strokes for different folks, but the strokes I want at 25 may be very different from those desired at 50. For these reasons, there are dangers in many of the current "how to" books. First they often make the assumption that their prescription for sexual "freedom" and for satisfaction is right for all persons. Second they emphasize performance and technique as the criteria for whether sexual expression is meaningful to the participants.

The selections presented here explore some of these issues. Granted the reading on masturbation is many years old but a goodly number of persons still harbor intense guilt feelings about masturbating and the resulting pleasure.

Then there is the interrelationship of the sexual act and love: does love justify and/or demand sexual intercourse? What happens when the question arises after the fact? There are many voices today which say that sex and love do not need to be co-existent, that sex can and should be enjoyed for its pleasure, in and of itself alone. Huxley would suggest that sometimes, however, sex without love can be used as a weapon in a relationship, and that the interrelatedness of the two may not be a mutual decision agreed upon by both participants.

Either years ahead of his time or with tongue in cheek, Twain portrays the difficult situation of women with regard to sexual expression. Whichever interpretation is placed on Twain's essay, the research by Blazer indicates a surprisingly large number of married women have never experienced a full sexual expression within their marriage relationship.

To close this section, Vincent presents some guidelines for determining the interrelationship of sex and intimacy, aware that the expression of sexual feeling differs at different times in our lives. He challenges us to explore our value structures to clarify some of the uncertainty about our nature as sexual beings.

PERFECT WOMANHOOD (EXCERPT) *

MARY MELENDY

Go Teach Your Boy

I say to you, mother, and oh, so earnestly: "Go teach your boy that which you may never be ashamed to do, about these organs that make him specially a boy."

Teach him they are called sexual organs, that they are not impure, but of special importance, and made by God for a definite purpose.

Teach him that there are impurities taken from the system in fluid form called urine, and that it passes through the sexual organs, but that nature takes care of that.

Teach him that these organs are given as a sacred trust, that in maturer years he may be the means of giving life to those who shall live forever.

Impress upon him that if these organs are abused, or if they are put to any use besides that for which God made them—and He did not intend they should be used at all until man is fully grown—they will bring disease and ruin upon those who abuse and disobey those laws which God has made to govern them.

If he has ever learned to handle his sexual organs, or to touch them in any way except to keep them clean, not to do it again. If he does, he will not grow up happy, healthy and strong.

Teach him that when he handles or excites the sexual organs, all parts of the body suffer, because they are connected by nerves that run throughout the system, this is why it is called "self-abuse." The whole body is abused when this part of the body is handled or excited in any manner whatever.

Teach them to shun all children who indulge in this loathsome habit, or all children who talk about these things. The sin is terrible, and is, in fact, worse than lying or stealing! For, although these are wicked and will ruin their soul, yet this habit of self-abuse will ruin both soul and body.

If the sexual organs are handled it brings too much blood to these parts, and this produces a diseased condition; it also causes

---

disease in other organs of the body, because they are left with a less amount of blood than they ought to have. The sexual organs, too, are very closely connected with the spine and the brain by means of the nerves, and if they are handled, or if you keep thinking about them, these nerves get excited and become exhausted, and this makes the back ache, the brain heavy and the whole body weak.

It lays the foundation for consumption, paralysis and heart disease. It weakens the memory, makes a boy careless, negligent and listless.

It even makes many lose their minds; others, when grown, commit suicide.

How often mothers see their little boys handling themselves, and let it pass, because they think the boy will outgrow the habit, and do not realize the strong hold it has upon them! I say to you, who love your boys—"Watch!"

Don't think it does no harm to your boy because he does not suffer now, for the effects of this vice come on so slowly that the victim is often very near death before you realize that he has done himself harm.

The boy with no knowledge of the consequences, and with no one to warn him, finds momentary pleasure in its practice, and so contracts a habit which grows upon him, undermining his health, poisoning his mind, arresting this development, and laying the foundation for future misery.

SELF-ABUSE AND ITS EVILS

As in the boy, so in the girl, self-abuse causes an undue amount of blood to flow to those organs, thus depriving other parts of the body of its nourishment, the weakest part first showing the effect of want of sustenance. All that has been said upon this loathsome subject in the chapter for boys might well be repeated here, but space forbids.

Read that chapter again, and know that the same signs which betray the boy, will make known the girl addicted to this vice. The bloodless lips, the dull, heavy eye surrounded with dark rings, the nerveless hand, the blanched cheek, the short breath, the old faded look, the weakened memory, and silly irritability tell the story all too plainly. The same evil result follows, ending perhaps in death, or worse, in insanity. Aside from the injury the girl does to herself by yielding to this habit, there is one other reason which appeals to the conscience, and that is, self-abuse is an offense against moral law—it is putting to a vile, selfish use the organs which were given only for a high, sacred purpose.

Let them alone, except to care for them when care is needed, and they may prove the greatest blessing you have ever known. They were given you that you might become a mother, the highest office to which God has ever called one of His creatures. Do not debase yourself and become lower than the beasts of the field.

If this habit has fastened itself upon any one of our readers, stop it now. Do not allow yourself to think about it; give up evil associations, seek pure companions, and go to your mother, older sister, or physician for advice.

And you, mother, knowing the danger that besets your daughters at this critical point, are you justified in keeping silent? Can you be held guiltless if your daughter ruins body and mind because you were too modest to tell her the laws of her being? There is no love that is dearer to your daughter than yours, no advice that is more respected than yours, no one whose warning would be more potent. Fail not in your duty. As motherhood has been your sweetest joy, so help your daughter to make it hers.

I LOVED HER *

NORMAN HABEL

I had always dreamed
that making love to a lovely girl
would be like
bouncing slowly from a diving board
and then floating slowly
through the gentle air
until my body was surrounded
by the swirling crystal waters.

But it wasn't like that at all.
Something went wrong, very wrong.
It took a long time
before we agreed to go all the way.
We said we loved each other
and wanted to show that love.

It took a long time
before we said yes.

Then suddenly it was over.
Just like that, it was over,
and we lay there
saying nothing.

I was spent
and she was almost crying.
It was no fun for her,
not really.

And now I hate myself.
It wasn't worth it
and I hate myself for it.

It didn't help us
to grow closer,
it didn't help at all.
In fact, we're further apart.
We're like strangers.

* Reprinted by permission of Fortress
Press.

RED RIDING HOOD UNEXPURGATED *
(or Love Under Solomon's Apple Tree)

ANONYMOUS

One day, as reported in the Song of Solomon, Red Riding Hood went down to the nut orchard, to see whether the vines had budded, whether the pomegranates were in bloom. All of a sudden a wolf appeared.

"Your eyes are pools in Heshbon, by the gates of Bathrabbim," he said.

"All the better to see you," the quick-thinking lass replied.

"Your nose is like a tower of Lebanon, overlooking Damascas."

"All the better to smell you, Wolfie."

"Your rounded thighs are like jewels."

"All the better to catch the roving eye of my beloved prince."

"Your lips are like a scarlet thread," the wolf continued, moving closer.

"All the better to kiss my prince," Red Riding Hood teased.

"Your two breasts are like two fawns, twins of a gazelle," breathed the wolf.

"All the better to tempt the mammary obsession of my prince," she smiled coyly.

"How graceful are your feet in sandals, O queenly maiden," cried the panting wolf and made a grab for Red Riding Hood.

"All the better to run like a gazelle," she shouted, and took off through the nut orchard. But under an apple tree the wolf caught her. Knowing the dangers of resisting ravishment, she let him have his way. And when the wolf's lips touched her ivory neck, he turned into her beloved prince.

"O loved one, O delectable maiden," the prince moaned. And Red Riding Hood sighed, too: "Under the apple tree I awakened you. As an apple tree among the trees of the wood, so is my beloved among young men. Refresh me with apples, for I am sick with love."

* Reprinted with permission of En-
gage/Social Action, 100 Maryland
Ave., NE, Washington, DC 20002.

POINT COUNTER POINT (EXCERPT) *

ALDOUS HUXLEY

"Do you love me?" he asked her one night. He knew she didn't. But perversely he wanted to have his knowledge confirmed, made explicit.

"I think you're a darling," said Lucy. She smiled up at him. But Walter's eyes remained unansweringly sombre and despairing.

"But do you *love* me?" he insisted. Propped on his elbow, he hung over her almost menacingly. Lucy was lying on her back, her hands clasped under her head, her flat breasts lifted by the pull of the stretched muscles. He looked down at her; under his fingers was the curved elastic warmth of the body he had so completely and utterly possessed. But the owner of the body smiled up at him through half-closed eyelids, remote and unattained. "Do you *love* me?"

"You're enchanting." Something like mockery shone between the dark lashes.

"But that isn't an answer to my question. Do you love me?"

Lucy shrugged up her shoulders and made a little grimace. "Love?" she repeated. "It's rather a big word, isn't it?" Disengaging one of her hands from under her head, she raised it to give a little tug to the lock of brown hair that had fallen across Walter's forehead. "Your hair's too long," she said.

"Then why did you have me?" Walter insisted.

"If you knew how absurd you looked with your solemn face and your hair in your eyes!" She laughed. "Like a constipated sheep dog."

Walter brushed back the drooping lock. "I want to be answered," he went on obstinately. "Why did you have me?"

"Why? Because it amused me. Because I wanted to. Isn't that fairly obvious?"

"Without loving?"

"Why must you always bring in love?" she asked impatiently.

"Why?" he repeated. "But how can you leave it out?"

"But if I can have what I want without it, why should I put it in? And, besides, one doesn't put it in. It happens to one. How rarely! Or perhaps it never happens; I don't know. Anyhow, what's one to do in the intervals?" She took him again by the forelock and pulled his face down toward her own. "In the intervals, Walter darling, there's you."

His mouth was within an inch or two of hers. He stiffened his neck and would not let himself be pulled down any farther. "Not to mention all the others," he said.

Lucy tugged harder at his hair. "Idiot!" she said frowning. "Instead of being grateful for what you've got."

"But what *have* I got?" Her body curved away, silky and warm, under his hand; but he was looking into her mocking eyes. "What *have* I got?"

Lucy still frowned. "Why don't you kiss me?" she demanded, as though she were delivering an ultimatum. Walter did not answer, did not stir. "Oh, very well." She pushed him away. "Two can play at that game."

Repelled, Walter anxiously bent down to kiss her. Her voice had been hard with menace; he was terrified of losing her. "I'm not a fool," he said.

"You are." Lucy averted her face.

"I'm sorry."

But she would not make peace. "No, no," she said, and when, with a hand under her cheek, he tried to turn her face back toward his kisses, she made a quick fierce movement and bit him in the ball of the thumb. Full of hatred and desire, he took her by force.

LETTERS FROM THE EARTH (EXCERPT) *

MARK TWAIN

It is as I have said: every statute in the Bible and in the law-books is an attempt to defeat a law of God—in other words an unalterable and indestructible law of nature. These people's God has shown them by a million acts that he respects none of the Bible's statutes. He breaks every one of them himself, adultery and all.

The law of God, as quite plainly expressed in woman's construction is this: There shall be no limit put upon your intercourse with the other sex sexually, at any time of life.

The law of God, as quite plainly expressed in man's construction, is this: During your entire life you shall be under inflexible limits and restrictions, sexually.

During twenty-three days in every month (in the absence of pregnancy) from the time a woman is seven years old till she dies of old age, she is ready for action, and *competent*. As competent as the candlestick is to receive the candle. Competent every day, competent every night. Also, she *wants* that candle—yearns for it, longs for it, hankers after it, as commanded by the law of God in her heart.

But man is only briefly competent; and only then in the moderate measure applicable to the word in *his* sex's case. He is competent from the age of sixteen or seventeen thenceforward for thirty-five years. After fifty his performance is of poor quality, the intervals between are wide, and its satisfactions of no great value to either party; whereas his great-grandmother is as good as new. There is nothing the matter with her plant. Her candlestick is as firm as ever, whereas his candle is increasingly softened and weakened by the weather of age, as the years go by, until at last it can no longer stand, and is mournfully laid to rest in the hope of a blessed resurrection which is never to come.

By the woman's make, her plant has to be out of service three days in the month and during a part of her pregnancy. These are times of discomfort, often of suffering. For fair and just

* Excerpt from MARK TWAIN LETTERS FROM THE EARTH edited by Bernard De Voto copyright © 1962 by The Mark Twain Co. Reprinted by permission of Harper & Row, Publishers, Inc.

compensation she has the high privilege of unlimited adultery all the other days of her life.

That is the law of God, as revealed in her make. What becomes of this high privilege? Does she live in the free enjoyment of it? No. Nowhere in the whole world. She is robbed of it everywhere.

Who does this? Man. Man's statutes—if the Bible *is* the Word of God.

Now there you have a sample of man's "reasoning powers," as he calls them. He observes certain facts. For instance, that in all his life he never sees the day that he can satisfy one woman; also, that no woman ever sees the day that she can't overwork, and defeat, and put out of commission any ten masculine plants that can be put to bed to her.* He puts those strikingly suggestive and luminous facts together, and from them draws this astonishing conclusion: The Creator intended the woman to be restricted to one man.

So he concretes that singular conclusion into a *law,* for good and all.

And he does it without consulting the woman, although she has a thousand times more at stake in the matter than he has. His procreative competency is limited to an average of a hundred exercises per year for fifty years, hers is good for three thousand a year for that whole time—and as many years longer as she may live. Thus his life interest in the matter is five thousand refreshments, while hers is a hundred and fifty thousand; yet instead of fairly and honorably leaving the making of the law to the person who has an overwhelming interest at stake in it, this immeasurable hog, who has nothing at stake in it worth considering, makes it himself!

You have heretofore found out, by my teachings, that man is a fool; you are now aware that woman is a damned fool.

Now if you or any other really intelligent person were arranging the fairnesses and justices between man and woman, you

* In the Sandwich Islands in 1866 a buxom royal princess died. Occupying a place of distinguished honor at her funeral were thirty-six splendidly built young native men. In a laudatory song which celebrated the various merits, achievements and accomplishments of the late princess those thirty-six stallions were called her *harem,* and the song said it had been her pride and boast that she kept the whole of them busy, and that several times it had happened that more than one of them had been able to charge overtime. [M.T.]

would give the man a one-fiftieth interest in one woman, and
the woman a harem. Now wouldn't you? Necessarily. I give
you my word, this creature with the decrepit candle has arranged
it exactly the other way. Solomon, who was one of the Deity's
favorites, had a copulation cabinet composed of seven hundred
wives and three hundred concubines. To save his life he could
not have kept two of those young creatures satisfactorily refresh-
ed, even if he had had fifteen experts to help him. Necessarily
almost the entire thousand had to go hungry years and years
on a stretch. Conceive of a man hardhearted enough to look
daily upon all that suffering and not be moved to mitigate it.
He even wantonly added a sharp pang to that pathetic misery;
for he kept within those women's sight, always, stalwart watch-
men whose splendid masculine forms made the poor lassies'
mouths water but who hadn't anything to solace a candlestick
with, these gentry being eunuchs. A eunuch is a person whose
candle has been put out. By art.

From time to time, as I go along, I will take up a Biblical statute and show you that it always violates a law of God, and then
is imported into the lawbooks of the nations, where it continues
its violations. But those things will keep; there is no hurry.

MARRIED VIRGINS—A STUDY OF UNCONSUMMATED MARRIAGES *

John A. Blazer

Why some women remain virgins after marriage is not clear in the professional literature. Although Friedman [1] reports the first comprehensive study of the problem, he does not offer adequate classfications for the numerous variables operating in unconsummated marriages. Nor does he report any substitute sexual behavior of the couples. The present study was designed to determine the reasons underlying persistent virginity in marriage ("virginity" meaning that, as far as can be determined, there has been no entry of a penis into the vagina) and to explore some of the interrelations of the variables.

One thousand American females of the Caucasian race were used as the sample. The sample was chosen from replies received from newspaper advertisements, personal appeals to men's and women's clubs, notices on college bulletin boards, clients appealing to a state psychological agency for assistance, leads from marriage counselors, and leads from gynecologists.

Ages in the sample ranged from 17 to 47 with a mean of 29 years, compared to a range from 18 to 55 with a mean of 27 reported in the Friedman study. Length of marriage (and period of nonconsummation) ranged from one to 21 years with a mean of eight years, compared to a range of less than a month to 17 years reported by Friedman. Length of marriage for 98 per cent had been more than three years, compared to 43 per cent who had been married this long in the Friedman study. Marriage took place between the ages of 20–29 for 76 per cent of the current sample, compared to 74 per cent reported by Friedman.

Each subject in the present study was subjected to an examination by a gynecologist. In some cases (432), little or no physical evidence (hymen) substantiated the subject's claim to virginity. In such instances, the gynecologist was asked to render a medical opinion as to the virginity of the subject. In cases of doubt or suspicion, the subject was removed from the sample.

* Reprinted from *Journal of Marriage and the Family*, May, 1964, pp. 213–214, by permission of the author and the National Council on Family Relations.

The gynecologist also rendered a medical opinion regarding the physical capability of the subject to experience intercourse. Vaginismus was diagnosed in 476 cases, but the entire sample was considered physically capable of experiencing intercourse.

Each subject remaining in the sample was interviewed by the author and asked a standard question: "Why are you still a virgin?" The subjects were prompted to speak until all details were revealed. All interviews were recorded on tape, and three licensed psychologists reviewed the tapes and agreed on the reasons as categorized. When the psychologists disagreed on categorization of a subject, the subject was removed from the sample.

To verify the gynecologist's opinion and to verify the wives' reasons for virginity, the husbands were interviewed separately. In almost all cases, the husbands supported the wives' statements.

RESULTS

All the "reasons" for abstinence were subsumed under 15 general categories, which are listed below in descending order of prevalence in the sample.

1. *Fear of pain in the initial intercourse* was expressed by 203 (20.3%) of the sample. Mutual masturbation to orgasm was practiced by 108 of these couples. The remaining 95 couples admitted to total abstinence.

2. The sex act was considered to be *nasty or wicked* and a disgust for sexuality was expressed by 178 (17.8%) of the sample. All of these couples denied mutual masturbation, but 63 husbands practiced self-stimulation.

3. *Impotent husbands* were blamed by 117 (11.7%) of the wives. Mutual masturbation was engaged in by 38 couples, and self-stimulation was practiced by 49 wives. Friedman reported 35 cases of impotence in his study.[2]

4. *Fear of pregnancy or childbirth* was expressed by 102 (10.2%) of the wives. The husbands agreed, and in 12 cases, the husbands admitted to being more afraid than their wives. Mutual masturbation was practiced by 42 of these couples.

5. *Small size of the vagina* was reported to prohibit intercourse by 82 (8.2%) of the subjects. On examination, neither partner was considered to be beyond the range of normality in size. Mutual masturbation was practiced by 38 of these couples.

6. *Ignorance regarding the exact location of their organs* and, to avoid embarrassment and mistakes, avoidance of intercourse was reported by 52 (5.2%) of the wives. All of these couples denied mutual masturbation, but 18 husbands admitted self-stimulation. This is the same category as Friedman's "Sleeping Beauty."

7. *Preference for a female partner* was stated by 52 (5.2%) as the excuse for denying their husbands. These couples denied mutual masturbation, but 12 husbands admitted self-stimulation.

8. *Extreme dislike for the penis* was expressed by 46 (4.6%). The couples denied mutual masturbation, but 29 husbands admitted self-stimulation.

9. *Intense dislike for intercourse without pregnancy* was expressed by 39 (3.9%). The couples agreed that pregnancy was completely undesirable up to the time of the study and expressed no intense dislike for intercourse *per se*. Twelve couples admitted mutual masturbation.

10. *Dislike of contraceptives* was indicated by 33 (3.3%). The couples agreed that intercourse could not be accomplished without contraceptives in their case because of fear of pregnancy. Twelve of these couples admitted mutual masturbation.

11. *Belief that submission implies inferiority* was expressed by 31 (3.1%). These couples denied mutual masturbation, but 12 husbands and three wives admitted self-stimulation. This is the same category as Friedman's "Brunhild."

12. *General dislike of men* was expressed by 30 (3%). The subjects stated other reasons for their marriage ("the thing to do," "fear of being an 'old maid,'" "security," "dislike living alone," etc.). These couples denied mutual masturbation, but 11 husbands and two wives admitted self-stimulation.

13. *Desire to "mother" their husbands only* was indicated by 14 (1.4%), and such behavior did not include sexual intercourse. The couples denied mutual masturbation. Six husbands and two wives admitted self-stimulation.

14. *Fear of damaging the husband's penis* was expressed by 12 (1.2%). The couples denied mutual masturbation. Three husbands and two wives admitted self-stimulation. One subject in Friedman's study revealed such fear.[3]

15. *Fear of semen* was mentioned by nine (.9%) subjects. Three couples admitted mutual masturbation without discharge

for the husband. Three husbands and two wives admitted self-stimulation.

DISCUSSION

Due to the manner of selecting the sample, no estimates of the prevalence of virginity in marriage within the general population can be made. However, the relative importance (as perceived by the wife) of 15 factors in the etiology of married virginity has been revealed. Moreover, the results of this study suggest that married women are ignorant of sexual matters. None of the factors reported in this study (with the possible exception of number 7 and, perhaps, 3) would destroy or distort the sexual relationship of the woman and her husband *if the woman had scientific knowledge of sex at her disposal.* Hence, each category is a facet of the underlying disruptive cause—ignorance.

It is obvious that more general knowledge of sex imparted at an earlier age, especially to females, might prevent later behavior of the type categorized here. Similarly, where such a sexual relationship has already appeared, the wife can be given scientific instruction about sex. Friedman reports [4] that early treatment of this type was successful in 71 per cent of the cases.

PREREQUISITES FOR MARITAL AND SEXUAL COMMUNICATION *

Clark E. Vincent

The Problem of Identity

We have a strange way of revering revolutionaries from the perspective of history. To prove my point, let us take a two-minute historical tour and go back to the time of one of the earlier hippies—not one as early as John the Baptist, but just to the French Revolution, to the time of Jean Jacques Rousseau. Rousseau was a man who said in no uncertain terms, "Down with the establishment," a radical statement for the time. Medieval Europe, remember, had a plurality of social institutions: the family, the Church, the community, and the work guilds.[1] In effect, a person had little or no identity apart from these organizations, which had literal life-and-death control over him. No one asked in those days, "Who am I?" Everyone knew who he was. Grandfather was a smithy and father was a smithy, and so your name was Smith and you were a smithy. Rousseau and others wrote that these social institutions, by binding men, had corrupted them. Their thesis was that the natural man is good and should be set free. Their writings, the legislation following the Revolution, and other factors contributed to freeing the individual from many of the controls formerly exercised by the family, Church, and guild.

This brief tour of history precludes other than noting that the increased freedom of the individual from the control of social institutions was accompanied by the rise of the increasingly powerful State ("State" in the amorphous sense meaning the federal government, state government, county and city governments). The family no longer tells you if and when you must go to war, as it once did when there was a war to fight; but the State does. The family no longer decides whom and when you marry, but the State does. It also tells you what you have to do beforehand. These are only two of the many areas in which the "State" now has assumed the authority and control over the individual that were once exercised by other social institutions.

Another source of control and authority over the individual is the mass media of communication and advertising. Women may protest the expense of adopting new styles, but not very successfully. If the designers agree on dropping skirts halfway between the knee and the ankle, down they will go. Men too are finding they have less individual control over the width of their ties, the style of their suits, and the design of their cars.

The relevance of all this to the problem of identity is that the "State" is much too large and amorphous to identify with, and our horizontal and vertical mobility encourages only a tenuous identity with community, Church, and family. As a result, we are increasingly thrown back on ourselves for the achievement rather than ascription of our identity.

It is this quest for individual identity that has been the most persistent theme in the novels, the plays, the poems, and the philosophic essays during our lifetime. The theme is much older than we, of course; Job struggled with it, as did the Romans and the Greek tragedians. But for us it has an intenseness born of individualness. Job focused on what is man in relation to God. We are more likely to ask, "Who am I, in relation to me?" In between we find a Dostoevski, a Kafka, a Kierkegaard, and many others deserving at least a semester's seminar to consider their various portrayals of man's search for individual identity in relation to the State, his fellowman, or his environment.

The mass media of communication aid and abet our current tendency to be faddish not only about clothing styles and cars, but also in the choice of concepts and key phrases used to discuss the problem of identity. The concept of "outer directed-people in lonely crowds," à la Riesman, had its day, as did "the organization man," "men in gray flannel suits," "conformity," "anomie," "alienation," "the disenchanted," and the "disenfranchised." Also up for a turn were Eliot's "Hollow Men," Wilson's "Outsiders," Miller's "Misfits," Lindner's "Rebels Without a Cause," and Kerouac's "Beat Generation." And now we have the "Drop-Offs"—those professional and business leaders who drop off the career-promotion ladder to "have their thing," by accepting a financial, professional, or managerial plateau in lieu of further upward mobility and ever increasing responsibility.

Arthur Miller, in *Death of a Salesman,* provides a very poignant example of an individual searching for identity. Willy Loman had the capacity to change colors, depending on the potential client.   If the client was a Republican, he could talk Republican;   if a Democrat, he could talk Democratic.   This kind of constantly changing, other-directed identity did not work too well for Willy, and he committed suicide.   You will remember that, at his graveside, one of his sons comments to the other, "Poor Dad—he never really knew who he was."

This search for identity is a central theme in *The Graduate* and is meaningfully portrayed in the first few minutes of the film.   The young boy just home from college is seeking to further his identity as a college graduate and adult through a meaningful conversation with other adults.   The first evening at home he encounters various people who are there for a cocktail party, and he tries to get them to relate, to converse with him as a person.   Unsuccessful, and in despair, he goes up to his room.   Several weeks later, after sleeping with the older woman several times (still calling her "Mrs.") he finally says in despair, "Couldn't we just talk—you know, have a conversation?"   He is still groping to establish his identity as a person in the relationship with this woman, and he hasn't succeeded.   All the way through the film, not one of the four parents had anything to offer the boy in the way of a meaningful relationship.   It is interesting to compare *The Graduate* with *Tea and Sympathy,* a play that created a similar stir some twenty years ago.   In that play the boy feared he was homosexual, and the older woman slept with him in an effort to help him establish his heterosexual identity.   It was a meaningful kind of identity relationship, in contrast to that in *The Graduate.*

THE NEED FOR SELF-LOVE

The foregoing is the historical context for my comments about self-love—a lifetime process inseparable from the quest for identity.   The most difficult lifetime task we have is to love self.   With all of our Freudian sophistication and our knowledge of the terminology of ego psychology, we are not always able to perceive the simple truth that "I must love myself."   Part of this difficulty results from our religious heritage, which has taught us that it is not right to love self—that to love self is to be selfish, self-centered;   we are supposed to love other people.

Erich Fromm, among others, has for several decades tried to get across the idea that, in order to love others, we must first love self.   Before Fromm, the Danish philosopher, Kierkegaard, pointed out that the idea was at least as old as the Old Testa-

ment commandment, "Thou shalt love thy neighbor as thyself."
Kierkegaard's thesis was that the only way you can make any
sense out of that commandment is to start with the premise
that you first love self deeply, wisely, and well; then give that
same quality of love to neighbor. If I do not love self wisely
and well it is an ill-advised commandment, because my neighbor is going to be better off without my feeling toward him as
I feel toward myself. All of us know a few people whose neighbors have cause to hope they will never follow that commandment, because of their self-degradation, self-disparagement, self-
distrust.

Only to the degree that a person loves and respects self can
he love and respect anyone else. What happens when a person
has insufficient self-love? (1) If I do not love and respect self,
then I do not believe anyone else can possibly love and respect
me. (2) Fearing that others will reject or not accept and love
the me I do not love creates more anxiety than I can safely tolerate. (3) The law of self-preservation comes into play, and
the law of psychic preservation is as viable as that of physiologic
self-preservation. (4) Our psychic self-preservation involves a
wide selection of defenses which we employ to keep people from
seeing the "me," the person I do not love. In effect, the defenses
work as follows: "Okay, I don't love me and I know you won't.
So I won't let you see me, and if you can't see the real me, you
can't reject me and I am protected." We all do this—even normal people with normal, garden-variety kinds of defenses. People who are neurotic or psychotic employ the same sort of defense mechanism, but carry it to a greater extreme. Here, however, we are dealing with "normal" people who are functioning
adequately and are on their feet emotionally.

DEFENSES USED TO PROTECT SELF

Consider a boy in elementary school who is so ashamed of his
family's poverty that he has little love and respect for himself.
He is afraid the other kids will reject him because he is poor.
What is his defense? He tells them about how much money his
dad has, their 50-foot yacht, their trip to Europe. The other
kids are turned away by his bragging more than by his poverty.
The defense ill serves him. They do not see it for what it is—
a sign that says, "This boy does not love self enough."

Or imagine yourself in a small gathering of people who have
been, perhaps for two hours, discussing sixteenth-century art.

Two hours is a long time to listen without being able to contribute anything (if you don't know any more about sixteenth-century art than I do). In order to enter the conversation without exposing your ignorance of sixteenth-century art, what do you do? You change the subject. You say, "Have you seen So-and-So's painting?"—naming the work of a twentieth-century artist, because you happen to be up on twentieth-century art., All of us at times engage in changing the conversation so as to hide our ignorance of topic "A" and exhibit our knowledge of topic "B." (It is easy to change the conversation to sex because most people are interested and you do not have to know very much about sex to talk about it.)

Perhaps the most universal form of defense is criticism. In a way, we each have barometers built in. There are days when everything goes like clockwork: you get the mid-term paper in on time; you get a few compliments; you feel well physically. Your own self-love, self-image—call it what you will—is high. If you observe yourself closely on those days, rare as they are, you will realize that you love the whole world. It's good to be alive. It takes a great deal to make you angry, because you are pleased with yourself. There are other days—and sometimes they stretch into weeks—when you might do better to have remained in bed. Your professors comment only on the inadequacies of your term paper; you have missed a deadline; your roommate has a few uncomplimentary remarks for you; and you have not satisfied your own work standards. Your self-image goes down, down, down. If you will observe yourself, you will notice that on these days you are hypercritical of everyone. Why? As a defense it is a way of thinking, not necessarily consciously, "Okay, I'm not much, but you're worse." And to defend and protect our own low self-esteem, we have a barrage of criticisms —of professors, classmates, the government, the driver of the car ahead of us, and our spouse.

Criticism of others is a neon sign flashing the message, "He who excessively criticizes others loves self not too much but too little." We ignore or even misinterpret such a sign in the case of the person who appears selfish and self-centered. Such an individual has all too little love, respect, and appreciation of self. To love and respect ourselves sufficiently is to be able to forget self, and think about and do for others. Without self-love we spend an inordinate amount of time and energy trying to draw attention to ourselves, to prove to ourselves and others that we are worthwhile.

Lack of Self-Love as a Source of Marital Discord

Interpreting someone's defenses (bragging, changing the subject, withdrawal into silence, criticism of others) as a sign that the individual needs more love and understanding from us, to enable them to love self, is much easier said than done in the marital arena. For example, it is on those days when your self-image has gone down, down, down that you as a husband come home and are able to find six things your wife has done that *you* think she ought not to have done, or vice versa. So, either bluntly and directly or in a termitish fashion, you proceed to point out what she should have done, did not do, or did inadequately—most of which you would have overlooked on a day when your own self-esteem was high. But on days when you are down, your psyche comes to your defense almost without your awareness to reassure you, "Okay, I'm not much, but you're not either, because you did or didn't do this, this, and this."

How should the wife respond to this berating, fault-finding, belittling, and scolding of her? In practice, she is *supposed* to say, "Ah ha! This poor guy needs more love. I will give him more love and that will stop his fault-finding." In theory, that is the way to stop his criticisms by giving him enough love and reassurance that he no longer needs the defense of criticism. But the theory is seldom put into practice. Chances are that his wife's own self-image is not at its peak that day—perhaps because their children have had a down day at school and have already given mother self-doubts about her adequacy as a mother. So before the husband gets very far in criticizing her, she has a few counter comments about what is wrong with him. And much of what passes for marital communication is in reality two simultaneous monologues—each partner defensively concentrating on vulnerable areas, defending his own and probing for those of the spouse. Who listens? Each is too busy defending and justifying self to heed the cues of insufficient self-love in the other.

The beauty of marital arguments is that you will never run out of ammunition. If you start the argument about what happened last night and exhaust that subject, one of you is sure to bring up what happened last week, the last time you went out to dinner, the last time you went to a movie—and then there is the year before that, and the year before that. If you exhaust five, ten, fifteen years of marital material, you can bring in what happened during courtship. Then, as a last resort, you have her parents to criticize and she has yours. Again, no one is really listening because each is too busy defending, recalling the other's mistakes and shortcomings.

It takes considerable practice to be able to recognize defense mechanisms for what they are. Your partner's unlovable behavior is telling you loud and clear, "I love myself not enough. That's why I'm being obstreperous, ornery, bragging, or critical." Unfortunately, we do not often listen to this message. Our natural tendency is to return criticism for criticism, boast for boast, argument for argument, tit for tat. And effective communication is blocked.

The foregoing is a considerable oversimplification of only one aspect of what the therapist accomplishes when, by what he does or does not do, what he says or does not say, he keeps communicating to the patient or client, "I accept *you*, with or without your defenses." Gradually the troubled person feels that, because *someone* accepts him, he can accept himself; accepting self, he has less need of defenses—many of which may have ill-served him. (As is true of many concepts in therapy, this one is implicit in the Old Testament comment, "We love God because He first loved us." Awareness of His love and acceptance—and most often this awareness comes initially through the love of a parent or friend—makes us feel that we are worth loving and therefore can love ourselves; and by loving self we are then able to love others, including God.)

SEX DIFFERENCES IN THE SOURCES OF SELF-LOVE

Our competitive, comparative society makes it difficult to develop and maintain intelligent self-love. The emphasis is too much on proving that we are worth loving. The manner and means of proving are quite different for males and females. One difference can be illustrated in the context of two very broad generalizations: (1) We love girls because they exist and attract attention. (2) We love boys for what they will become, what they will accomplish. Observe a girl six or eight years of age come into the living room when guests are present; she need do nothing to arouse admiration other than look attractive and behave in a feminine way. If she has on a clean dress, if her hair is combed, and if she smiles sweetly, she will receive compliments, be told that she "looks lovely." But a boy the same age has already learned, in some mysterious way, that it is not enough for him to be dressed in clean jeans and have his hair combed. If given half an opportunity he will state or ask: "Feel my muscle. You know how fast I can run? Did you ever see me jump? Would you like to see what I made?" Already he has learned that he must offer proof, evidence that he is worthwhile. I'm not sure how we inculcate this orientation, but we do so at a very young age.

These two differential sources of self-love continue to influence us throughout our lifetime. All during childhood, adolescence, and courtship, the girl is literally brainwashed (with the aid of a multibillion dollar cosmetic and clothing industry) with the idea that the affirmation of her worth as a woman is inseparable from her ability to use her appearance to attract the attention of women and men—but most especially the *right* men. During courtship, this difference works reasonably well, because the male is trying to prove his masculinity by winning her and she is using herself, her appearance to attract him. These two efforts complement each other nicely. He is trying to prove he can date her, kiss her, woo her into courtship, bed, and/or marriage. Once they are married, however, many men feel that they have proved their ability to win a wife and they can then forget about the courtship aspect of their lives. Such a man, from the time he is married, will spend most of his productive hours, his creative energy continuing to prove himself financially, in his profession or occupation, in the neighborhood, in the church, in his political party.

Unfortunately, no one ever told the girl he married about the pressures, expectations, and stimuli confronting the male constantly to prove himself. She interprets this personally as unique to her husband and therefore wonders, "What's wrong with me? Why has my husband stopped loving me?" What is happening to her self-image? Having been brought up to believe that, if she is worth her salt, she can attract and hold any man, she finds that as wife of a student she cannot even compete with a mid-term exam.

As for the husband, he is in a competitive society from the day he enters kindergarten. In school he competes for the highest grades, for a place on the first-string team, for first seat in the band, for acceptance in a good college, and then in the graduate school of his choice. After graduation, he competes for a good job or a good opening in a partnership. Regardless of how much money he is making this year, he is supposed to make more next year; these days, in fact, he has to, just to stay in place. If he writes one book, he is supposed to write two—because someone else has. Having been taught as a boy and bombarded daily as a man by the stimuli *to prove his worthwhileness by what he does and achieves,* he has little awareness or understanding of his wife's childhood and adult orientation to *affirm her self-worth by being able to* attract and maintain his daily attention, compliments, and creative thoughts, as she did during courtship.

The burden of proving is so basic to the male that it is built into his anatomy. Every time a man wants to make love, he has to prove his potency first; he has to provide the evidence of an erection. No wonder that the male in his forties or fifties is traumatized by the thought of impotence! Failure to get an erection is inseparable from fear of failure in all the areas in which a man feels he must constantly prove his worth.

It will not be easy to change this difference in the sources of self-love for the two sexes, but at least we can help young married couples to realize that it exists, so that they do not personalize it. The wife who feels that she is not able to attract her husband's time and attention is in a very vulnerable position. She is not able to come right out and say, "Honey, love me; I need love." That would make her still more vulnerable; furthermore, women were not taught to be direct. So what does she do? Because her self-love is threatened, she defends herself by criticizing her husband: "Why do you have to spend so much time doing this? Why don't we do this? Why don't we do that?" And he responds defensively. "Woman, get off my back!" How different it would be if her self-love were sufficient for her to say, "Honey, love me! I need your love." Sometimes she does ask, "Do you still love me?" But his possible reply, "Of course, I told you last night, last week. Don't you see how hard I work, how well I provide for you?" reflects that the male's idea of evidence of love is not the same as the female's. Having been taught to emphasize tangible evidence or proof of things done or accomplished, the male overlooks or minimizes the degree to which the female needs compliments and assurances of her attractability as a daily diet. She was brought up this way; her husband gave her this kind of nourishment when they were courting.

IMPRESSIONS AS REALITY

Another problem that adds to the difficulty of communication in marriage, as well as in other relationships, is the fact that interaction between two people is based on their *impressions* of self and of each other. I have discussed this concept in some detail elsewhere,[2] and in the interest of time will review it only briefly here. If we were to give a husband and wife each a complete battery of psychological tests and had the agreement of several psychometrists as to the test results, this husband and wife would not necessarily perceive themselves as measured to be. Moreover, the husband will interact on the basis of his impression of himself, and the wife is going to interact on the basis of her impression of herself.

As an example, suppose that everybody in the neighborhood says, "This gal is beautiful." If she herself believes that she is unattractive (perhaps on the basis of her husband's failure to express admiration and love), this is reality for her and she runs scared. As another example, take the guy who thinks he is the best violinist in town. Perhaps he is really the tenth best, but for him his impression is reality, and he is going to be miffed at the seating arrangement in the civic symphony.

Second (to go back to the marital partners), this husband is not going to interact with his wife on the basis of her impression of herself, nor on the basis of what she was measured to be; he is going to interact with her on the basis of *his* impression of her (HIW)—what he thinks she is like. And she is going to be interacting with him on the basis of her impression of him (WIH). How many times have you met someone whose name you did not hear and with whom you were not at all impressed? Chances are that you did not converse with him or her for very long. Suppose you discovered later that this was a very important, influential person. You think, "What did I say? What did I do?" Of course the person was the same person at the time you met him that he is when you learn his true identity. You were not interacting with him, but with your *impression* of him.

Now back to the marital partners again, and to the bottom line of the accompanying diagram. Does the husband interact with his wife on the basis of her impression of herself (WIW) or her impression of him (WIH)? No. He interacts on the

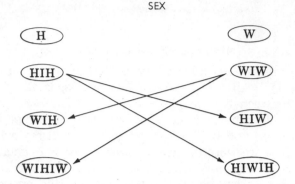

basis of his impression of her impression of him (HIWIH). And the wife interacts on the basis of her impression of his impression of her (WIHIW). For example, within the last day or two you probably have gone up openly, warmly, to someone because you think that person thinks highly of you. (Perhaps it is a good thing you do not know what he really thinks of you!) Or you have stayed away from someone because you think that person thinks negatively of you. Perhaps he does not at all— *but reality for you is what you think he thinks of you.*

Consider for a moment some examples occuring during dating and courtship. The male thinks the female thinks (MIFIM) he should make an approach—or he thinks the girl will think he is not masculine unless he does. The girl thinks he thinks (FIMIF) that unless she responds enthusiastically to the approach he is not likely to date her again. Thus they may end up going to football games neither of them enjoy or climbing into bed before either is ready.

WHO IS RIGHT? WHO IS WRONG?

The foregoing can be summarized by saying that we do not interact with people, but rather with our impressions of people and with our impressions of their impressions of us. Although the difference between "HIW" and "WIW" in the foregoing diagram might be enormous, the impression each has of the wife *represents reality* for that spouse. Although this differential reality is implied, its implications for communication are rarely examined in discussions of the selectivity of individual perception. It is doubtful, for example, that the "same" experience, movie, book, or event is ever experienced, seen, read, or witnessed in precisely identical ways by any two individuals.

Chemically treated paper can be used to demonstrate the selectivity of taste, as related to genetic differences in taste buds.

Some tasters will report that the paper tastes "sweet"; others, that it is "bitter"; and still others, that the taste is "neutral." In this case we do not ask, "Which taster is right?" or "Which taste is real?" We know that each taster is "right" within the context of his or her own taste buds. Moreover, we say that the question of "right" and "wrong" is, in this case, irrelevant.

Almost inevitably husband-wife communication bogs down when each denies the reality of different individual impressions and seeks fruitlessly to establish who is right and who is wrong. If you can understand and accept the fact that an identical piece of chemically treated paper has different tastes to different people, then you can begin to appreciate how extremely difficult it is for you and your spouse (fiancee)—each with a unique physiologic, mental, spiritual, familial, and social background—to have identical recall or impressions of any experience, event, or conversation. Without this understanding, your courtship and marital arguments will usually consist of a dialogue which, as illustrated in the following excerpt, erroneously assumes that if you argue long and successfully one can be proven right and the other wrong.

> *Wife:*   "I said . . .!"
> *Husband:* "No you didn't! You said . . .!"

This classic spousal dialogue (at times becoming a monologue) will frequently reflect not only each person's impressions but their impressions of the other person's impressions.

> *Wife:*   "You said . . .   and furthermore you said it because . . .!"
> *Husband:* "I did not! I said . . .! I didn't even know . . .!"
> *Wife:*   "Yes you did. I know what you think about me. You think . . .!"
> *Husband:* "You're wrong! That's not what I think at all. You think that . . .!"

If it is impossible for two people with genetic differences in their taste buds to derive the same taste from a simple thing like a piece of chemically treated paper, how much more difficult it is for two people to remember, or even to hear and perceive, the same thing in identical ways, particularly when we consider the uniqueness of our total physiological, mental, spiritual, and historical backgrounds. Selective perception and re-

membering are influenced not only by our different backgrounds
but also by our changing needs. Two men go into a restaurant.
One is hungry; the other, thirsty. Half an hour later the man
who was hungry can tell you about the foods on the menu; the
man who was thirsty will remember more about the beverages.
We bring *needs of the moment* to our selectivity. Yet in our
society we do not want to allow others or even ourselves the
freedom of differential impressions.

Husband and wife go to a play; they come home and begin
to talk about what the playwright had in mind, and the wife says,
"I thought it was very interesting; he was getting across such-
and-such a point." The husband replies, "My gosh, Honey, you
weren't even at the same play I was. You missed the whole
point!" (Meaning, your impression was wrong; now listen to
the right impression, mine.) And so the argument—the unset-
tleable argument—starts. If the wife could listen uncritically to
the husband's impression of the play and the husband could listen with interest to the wife's impression of the play, they could
get *two plays for the price of one*. But we cannot tolerate this
kind of abundant life, because we are afraid of differences of
opinion, differential impressions that are real.

ALLOWING OTHERS THE FREEDOM TO BE DIFFERENT

Our efforts to change the behavior, ideas, and attitudes of the
people we are closest to and love the most reflect all too frequently our unsureness of the worth of what we are, do, and
think. Couples say to a marriage counselor, "We can't possibly
make a go of this marriage; we're too different." Their problem
is not so much that they are different as it is that they lack the
freedom to be different.

Your fiancee or wife enjoys the music of Glen Campbell; you
prefer Beethoven. You can enjoy her enjoyment of Campbell
while she enjoys your enjoyment of Beethoven. Her impression
that Campbell's music is enjoyable *is as real* for her as your
impression of Beethoven's works is for you; not right or wrong,
good or bad, highbrow or lowbrow. To accept and grant the
validity of her impression is neither to agree nor to disagree
with her impression; she does not need your agreement or disagreement. What she needs (and you need as well) is the ongoing affirmation that her impressions, recall, views have as
much validity, realness, for her as yours do for you.

Keep in mind, however, that I am not saying that anything anybody does is all right; I am not saying that there *is* no right or wrong; I am not talking about behavior. I am talking only about impressions, which are the bases for communication. If we will learn to accept the other person's impressions as real for that person, not as right or wrong, we can listen without having to agree or disagree. Then the communication lines begin to open up. It is surprising how many husbands and wives, after years of marriage, have not the foggiest notion what their spouse thinks, really thinks and feels. All they know is what *they think* the spouse thinks.

The need to win an argument and prove oneself right is deeply instilled. It can lead all the way to the divorce court, where a plaintiff and a defendant each seeks to prove that he (or she) is right and the other one is wrong. The judge (except in California where the concept of an adversary has been revised) rewards the "right" one and punishes the "wrong" one.

In your dating, courting, and subsequent marital communications you will find it takes considerable practice to implement the freedom to have and respect differential impressions as real. Most of us are well indoctrinated to polarize differences into who is right and who is wrong. We grew up in families in which mother-father, parent-child, and sibling arguments had but one goal—to establish who was right. Communication, conversation, or dialogue, all assume that someone is listening. How can you listen if all you hear is that your impressions are wrong? It is not surprising that all too many wives lament, "He never listens to me. He thinks I haven't a brain in my head. He always wins the argument even when I know I'm right."

The husbands of such wives (or the wives of such husbands) fail to see the degree to which their "need to always be right" (1) erodes the self-image, the self-love of the wife, and (2) reflects the insufficient self-love of the husband. The more adequate our self-love, the more likely we are to listen to and respect as real for them the quite different impressions of others.

SEXUAL COMMUNICATION HANG-UPS

The concepts of "self-love" and "impressions as reality" are useful theoretical schemas for discussing and illustrating some of the communication difficulties adults experience as a result of the sex "education" received during childhood. One example

*   *   *   had to do with what Gagnon [3] has called the "nonlabeling phenomenon."

VOCABULARY AND PERSPECTIVE. Couples sometimes ask me, "Do you think it is all right for a husband and wife to masturbate each other?" The way they ask the question and use the word "masturbation" makes one feel that they surely must be doing something very wrong. My usual reply is in the form of a question: "Do you think it is all right for a husband and wife to *caress* each other?" And they say, "Well, of course; but what's that got to do with it?" Is not that what we are talking about—caressing each other? Unfortunately a perfectly normal means of expressing marital love has become associated with a "loaded" word that throws us out of kilter.

Whether it be a married couple or a single college student, the word "masturbation" still conveys many negative connotations. Generally, it refers to the act or process of giving self sexual pleasure by stimulation of the genitalia, usually alone and perhaps most frequently by hand. Some perspective may be gained if we consider other kinds of "masturbation." Consider the husband at one o'clock in the morning, down in the kitchen all alone, the refrigerator door is open, and by hand he is giving himself gastronomic pleasure. It would not occur to his wife to appear at the door and say, "Henry, are you masturbating again?" He is "gastronomically masturbating." Or suppose you are alone and have an itch; it gives you epidermal pleasure to scratch the itch by hand. We can call this "epidermal masturbation." There are many ways and areas in which, by hand alone, we give ourselves pleasure—eating, drinking, exercising, scratching, even reading a book and turning the pages by hand. Why the hangup only about giving ourselves sexual pleasure? In part, we are still victims of the "mental illness" bugaboo concerning sexual masturbation. To be sure one can give self too much pleasure in any area—scratching until you have a bleeding sore, eating until you are fifty pounds overweight, and so on. My point is simply that we need to place the giving of pleasure to self sexually in perspective—see it as but one area of life in which we do on occasion, and not exclusively or to excess, give ourselves pleasure alone and by hand.

EQUATING MASCULINITY WITH EXPERTISE IN SEX. Why is it so difficult for wives to tell their husband what gives them sexual satisfaction? If a wife asks her husband to scratch her back and he complies, she does not hesitate to give him instructions: "Not so hard; now over to the left, under the shoulder blade; slow down . . . easier; over to the center . . . *there*." She can give her husband ten or twelve sets of instructions and it does not bother him. Why? Because no one ever told him that expertise in back-scratching has anything to do with masculinity. There is no threat to his male ego, and she can give as many instructions as she wants. Now suppose this same wife is trying to derive some sexual pleasure from intercourse. Do you think she can give twelve instructions to her husband as to how to give her sexual pleasure? She is lucky if he will accept two. This is because males in our society learn at a very young age to equate "masculinity" with "knowing all about sex." In elementary school you can hear two or three boys talking: "Jimmy is a sissy; he doesn't know anything about sex." To be a real boy, to be masculine, is to know all about sex.

This indoctrination puts the adult American male in a box and keeps him from learning about female sexuality. To learn something about a subject, you have to admit you do not already know everything there is to know—but for the male to admit there is something about sex he does not know is for him to question his own masculinity. This is why he ignores (at least while she is observing him) the magazine article opened up and put beside his favorite chair at home. Why? Because his impression of his wife's impression of him (HIWIH) is: "She thinks I'm not a man."

For the same reason, the second or third suggestion she tries to make as to how he might help her have some pleasure in their love-making threatens his self-image, his self-love, and he becomes defensive: "Well, if you were a normal woman, you'd probably be there by now." His remark threatens her self-image, and she puts up her defenses: "Well, forget about it; it isn't worth it." In such a case each partner needs to appreciate the price they are paying for the fact that the male is taught to equate masculinity with knowing all about sex, and thereby finds it difficult to learn how complex the female is—sexually as well as in other areas.

SEX DIFFERENCES AS THE BASIS FOR PROBLEMS IN SEXUAL ADJUSTMENT. I've been interested over the years in phrases couples use to initiate love-making in marriage. One couple that I counseled will serve to illustrate how standardized are the male's phrases, and how great is the variety of the female's responses. In response to the husband's standard verbal approach, "Honey, how about it?" she and he recalled seven different responses she might give, ranging from enthusiastic to negative:

1. "It's about time!"
2. "I'd love to!"
3. "Why aren't you more artful?" (Meaning, "You spoil it by asking; just go ahead, man.")
4. "How about what?" (Obviously she knows what, so this is teasing, playing, or hostility.)
5. "Let's go out for dinner." (Bargaining.)
6. "It's only been two days."
7. "I've a splitting headache."

Now consider the plight of the poor male. In his occupational life if he makes a sale by using a certain approach, he sticks with that approach because he has learned that it works. But his wife keeps changing, and what worked last night will not work tonight; what worked last week will not work this week. During courtship he had the patience and curiosity to try different approaches and techniques. After he is married, however, he does not want to take the time to try to figure out her mood. He may not even realize that women have an infinite variety of moods, and that this may be one of the reasons he loves her.

The male has the capacity for a large range of moods, but in adult life he tends to become increasingly goal-oriented and involved in proving himself as discussed earlier; for him, getting through the woods is more important than enjoying the walk. On a family vacation, he will pick out a city 300 to 500 miles down the road and direct his efforts all day toward reaching that goal by evening. His wife and children, however, have retained more of their capacity to *da sein* ("to be there") and to enjoy things as they come; they will want to stop here and there and see this and that—much to his frustration.

This predominant focus of the male's energies upon reaching a goal previously set is consistent with his work pattern of meeting deadlines and being bombarded by stimuli for goal achievement throughout each working day. It is not easy for the husband, particularly if he is in business or one of the professions, to be spontaneous and impulsive, whether on a walk, a vacation, or in bed. His direct attack on achieving the goal of orgasm and getting to sleep in preparation for the next day's work means that he seldom thinks of giving more than five to fifteen minutes to love-making. To the wife this represents a very poor substitute for the two to three hours he was willing to spend in amorous approaches during courtship, and, as discussed earlier, undermines her confidence in her ability to attract. Awareness of her feeling may help the husband to understand why she sometimes seems less than enthusiastic about his approaches to coition, and why she attempts to restore a Gestalt orientation to marital coition and to be reassured that her total self is more important to her husband than the objective of an orgasm.

Another general sex difference is that men can be "down," depressed, low in self-love, and yet be very interested in coition— as a way of escalating their ego. To the wife who needs to feel she is attractive, complimented, and self-confident in order to respond sexually, her husband's interest in sex when he is discouraged or depressed may seem to her to be "physical therapy" or only an interest in "my body." She fails to perceive how pervasive is his task of proving himself and now inseparable is this proof in his sexual, financial, and occupational worlds. He fails to perceive her indoctrination to attract attention to herself as a test of her worthwhileness, and that with such an indoctrination his interest in sex to reaffirm himself is to her "using her."

COMPARTMENTALIZED THINKING. Twenty years ago I was more likely to see in my office husbands complaining of sexually unresponsive wives. Within the past several years this pattern has nearly reversed; now it is more likely to be wives lamenting about husbands who do not satisfy them sexually. Some of these wives are married two months, others for twenty years. The publicity given the Masters and Johnson research [4] has made it more acceptable and respectable for wives to seek the sexual pleasure that they may have gone without for many years.

One reason for the failure of wives to experience sexual pleasure with their husbands relates to the general difference in the premarital sexual experience of many males and females—a difference that may be not as applicable to the present generation. The male often starts self-caressing very early; he is goal-oriented and his purpose is to achieve orgasm. A female, at ten or eleven years of age, begins to hold a boy's hand and gets her first kiss. During several years of dating in junior and senior high school and in college, she is increasingly stimulated by sexual contacts and often reaches the "plateau stage" described by Masters and Johnson.[5] Society says, "This is as far as you're supposed to go"—so by the time she gets married or sleeps with a male for the first time, she may have had anywhere from five to ten years of training herself to get excited and then say, "That's far enough."

Experiencing an orgasm is something like learning a new word: a synaptic connection has to be made. By the time you have heard the word twelve times, you have a nice groove. The male comes to marriage with a beautiful groove for the synaptic connection of an orgasm. The female, on the other hand, may never have had this synaptic connection—and to make such a connection more difficult, she has built in a physiological dam. This is why Mark Twain purportedly observed that Niagara Falls was the *second* greatest disappointment to honeymooners. Most young husbands have spent years training themselves to reach orgasm quickly, and they do not know what a plateau is. A good wife can help her husband, over a period of years, to develop a very pleasurable plateau; but he has to learn it. When he is first married, the sexual stimulation provided by the sight and touch of his wife causes him to reach the point of orgasm even faster than before—and it is a case of "Wham, bam, thank you, ma'am." His bride is lucky if she can even get up on the plateau.

Some of the couples that come to me have been married ten, twenty, and even thirty years, and the wife has not yet achieved orgasm. The mass media have taught her that this is something women have a right to—and now this is one more area in which her husband must prove himself adequate.

In working with such a couple, I ask them first whether she desires sexual pleasure. She may say that she does but she does not know whether she will ever achieve any, because she has sort of lost interest. During the first months of marriage—maybe even for the first year or two—marital love-making was exciting because she felt just like she did when they were courting. After a while, however, she begins to feel she is only getting excited and then being frustrated. If you will accept the analogy, her experience has been to be teased with a succulent beefsteak, but, each time she starts to partake, it is taken away. Time and time again she has been excited, then frustrated; excited, frustrated; excited, frustrated. Gradually she learns that the only way to keep from getting frustrated is not to get excited. Finally intercourse becomes actually distasteful to her. Why? Because she not only fails to get the beefsteak, she has to be present and watch her husband enjoy it. No wonder she hates sex after a while! For what it is worth, the analogy may help some of you appreciate if not understand why many women of your mother's and grandmother's generations have quite negative attitudes regarding marital sex.

Returning to the couple desiring sexual enjoyment for the wife who has never experienced an orgasm, I try to explain the physiological conditioning that may account for her being unable to go beyond the plateau. The person who can help her most is a husband who is loving, considerate, and compassionate enough to forget temporarily about his own orgasm and concentrate on the pleasure that comes from giving his wife pleasure. This may include a discussion of his caressing of the clitoral area if his caressing previously has been too limited in time and area. He may be unaware of how general the "clitoral nerve area" is. She, of course, will need to communicate verbally and nonverbally to him what feels good, what feels blah, what is irritating. And the husband needs encouragement to try not to be defensive because she is telling him this.

At first the couple may feel that discussing and thinking about techniques in love-making give it an aura of being contrived, mechanistic, and awkward. It is. The first time you tried to keep your elbow straight in learning to play golf, it was awkward and mechanistic too; that is part of the learning process—but you get through that phase. Couples who assume that their love-making must always be automatic, impulsive, spontaneous, and romantic have forgotten that "skillful" dancing, piano playing, painting, or golfing can come only after considerable practice and many "mechanical movements" in the early stages of learning.

The compartmentalized, and even upside-down, nature of our thinking about sex is frequently reflected when the couple talk or ask about caressing the genitalia with the mouth or tongue. The wife may desire and enjoy her husband's oral caressing of the clitoral area, but will state that her enjoyment is accompanied by feelings that it is "dirty" or "unnatural." It is, of course, quite unsanitary—primarily because of the high bacteria count in the mouth. With normal hygiene practices, the genitalia are the cleanest parts of the body. It is the mouth which is unclean, yet this rarely stops couples from osculation, or oral kissing. And they rarely think of this as unclean. Nor do many females think it unclean for a male to kiss their hand which (I would hope) has handled some money which a few hundred other people with various diseases have handled.

The notion that mouth-genital caressing is "unnatural" reflects the lack of logic in our compartmentalized thinking about human sexuality. In the areas of food, wine, and the arts, for example, we compliment people who enjoy a wide range of variety. We consider them gourmets or connoisseurs. We compliment the person who enjoys a variety of foods prepared in various combinations. In fact, the greater the capacity to enjoy variety in color, in food, in music, and in the decorative arts generally, the more we are likely to compliment the person as having developed and utilized all of his or her God-given senses. In the sexual area, however, we turn this upside down—when we regard it as "unnatural" to appeal to the senses and to utilize a variety of means to afford pleasure. (This does not imply that I am condoning a variety of sexual partners, any more than my being in favor of enjoying a variety of foods or paintings implies justification for taking food or works of art which belong to someone else.)

Wives who spend hours preparing a meal to appeal to the senses of smell and sight, as well as to the sense of taste, may rarely think about the normalcy of appealing to the same God-given senses in the sexual area. Many of the extramarital affairs that take place in this country would never begin if more married couples learned to tap the potential for creative sex in their own relationship. It takes years and years to explore the creative potential in this area, and many couples never know it is there. Fortunate couples in their sixties will tell you that their sexual relationship gets better every year—and I suggest that no one under thirty really believes this statement. We tend to think in terms of *quantity* (how many times a week?), just as we measure the success of a meeting in terms of attendance. People in their sixties and seventies are talking about the *quality* of the sexual relationship.

PREMARITAL SEX

Now I should like to consider very briefly the need for bench marks in decision-making, and use for illustrative purposes the age-old question: "Is premarital sexual intercourse right or wrong, good or bad?" I consistently refuse to honor the question in that form, for the same reason that a physician would not attempt to honor the question, "Is surgery good or bad, right or wrong?" He would want to know the conditions: surgery for whom, performed by whom, for what purpose, where? Yet most adults, when asked the same sort of question concerning one of life's most complex relationships, rush right in, usually with a negative answer. To do so is to support the notion that human sexuality is simple, that it requires little thought, only yes or no answers.

One guideline or bench mark for decision-making in this area is to recognize that *all facts are conditional.* Is a given wall solid? When you try to walk through it, it is pretty solid. The fact that two plus two equals four remains a fact only so long as someone does not add another condition, like minus one.

Now what are the conditions involved in premarital sex? There is a whole set of conditions, factual information, involving one partner, and another set involving the other. This is why no one has the right to make this decision for those involved. Nor does one have the right to "buckpass" the decision and responsibility onto someone else. One of the conditions involves the value system that has been built into a person by all his past experiences. All too frequently we underestimate the values that are so much a part of us as to be unrecognized. One example concerns the oversimplified account of an American student in Europe who is attending a meeting where there are a hundred people, ten of whom are also from the United States. The student wishes to identify these ten. To do so he requests the *maître d'* to serve pie for dessert. The pie will be served by placing it with what we regard as the "backside" or large part of the wedge facing the diner. The ten Americans will turn the pie around in order to start eating it from the small part of the wedge, and they are thereby identified. This is "culture," an ingrained way of eating pie. If you think this a simple thing, try eating your next piece of pie by starting on the large part or "backside" of the wedge. I have tried it this way, and it never tastes quite the same as when starting at the small point of the wedge.

Such an example can be multiplied by scores of habits, attitudes, and values we have but either fail to recognize or underestimate. For you to assess what premarital or nonmarital coition will mean to you will involve considerable self-understanding and awareness of what your attitudes and values are. What we need is more creative thought given to ways in which you can become aware of precisely what are your attitudes, values, goals—all of which are conditions to be taken into account in deciding about premarital and nonmarital coition.

REALITY TESTING. The decision-making should also involve some reality testing and planning for contingencies. You did this in driver education, planning what to do in case of an accident, a slippery road—just in case this might happen. You planned for contingencies in the case of college—applying not to one but to several, just in case. So, if as a female you think you are ready to engage in coition with a male, may I suggest a way to reality test, a method of planning for contingencies: type up an affidavit reading, "I, John Green, had intercourse with Jane Doe on the evening of March 13, 1969." Then have a place for his signature and ask that he sign the affidavit *before* coition with you.

This procedure may seem preposterous or even childish, but I have suggested it only as an example of how one might reality test. On some college campuses where I have made this suggestion, the girls laughed at first but after discussing it with their boyfriends found they could reverse the arguments the boys have been using with them.

Female: "You've been telling me that I won't get pregnant, that nobody gets pregnant with the pill; so go ahead and sign it—no problem."

Male: "No, it's silly. Don't you trust me?"

Female: "You've been telling me it's normal, it's natural. You've said everybody is doing it and that it's wholesome and nothing to be ashamed of. So sign it!"

Male: "No! I won't and don't intend to!"

Some high school and college girls have told me that after trying the affidavit idea they have discontinued coition because they realized they did not know either themselves or the boy as well as they thought they did. In some cases the girls realized they were not willing to sign such an affidavit, and some of the boys apparently found that being unwilling to put their name on the dotted line did not quite square up with their notions about premarital or nonmarital coition being very normal and acceptable.

This suggestion about an affidavit is obviously not offered as a panacea for all the problems involved in deciding whether to have sexual intercourse apart from marriage; it is only one means of reality testing in this area. My major point is that we need to focus on guidelines for decision-making, and thereby, we would hope, provide you with some help in making a very complex decision that is yours to make.

My final comment on the subject of premarital sex is this: Whatever your sexual behavior and activity, remember to keep it in context. Do not look back later and judge yourself, with the wisdom you have at twenty-seven, for what you did at seventeen. It is unfair to say to yourself, "How could I possibly have believed it was love?" Those of you who have been married five or ten years and are aware of how your love grows can look back and wonder how in the world you had the audacity to get married when you did. At that point in time, however, you thought your love was full-grown and mature. I repeat, therefore, whatever your activity in the past, maintain the context in which it happened and do not let yourself or anyone else take it out of that context. This is not to whitewash or condone mistakes; rather, it is to admit mistakes when they do occur and go on from there with the mistake kept in the context of the maturity and wisdom you had at that time.

My final comment brings me full circle to the concept of self-love, and involves a paraphrasing of Gibran's observation in *The Prophet*. We need to be more oriented as is the myrtle in our doing and giving. The myrtle gives of its fragrance without striving to be elected best bush or tree of the year. For the myrtle, to give of its fragrance is to live, to be fulfilled. If we could do more of what we do—not just in the area of sex and marriage, but in every area of life—because it gives us fulfillment and not because we are trying to prove our worth, we would have a much better orientation for communication, for making decisions, and for enjoying the quest for meaningful relationships—sexual and otherwise.

CONFLICT

159

INTRODUCTION

Most people think it is just not nice to fight. We seem to feel that anger, hostility or conflict point to a faulty interpersonal relationship or to personal inadequacies. As a result, we often let things slide by without bringing important and vital issues into open discussion or else we become defensive. For each of us, our personal needs become so central that we do not respond to the other. Do we compromise? Maybe. But although we might want a mutually acceptable solution, we simply do not know how to reach one, and the relationship deteriorates or terminates.

A troubled relationship is often rationalized by saying it was not really meaningful—a typical form of the "we never meant to get serious" argument. Or to the amazement of ourselves and others, the fragileness of the relationship comes as a shock. It is in the latter situation, the one in which individuals felt they had something going for them, that the most pain and suffering is experienced.

How did all this happen? In the first place, conflict should be considered a fact of life and reality at all stages of relationships. No matter how similar our backgrounds, we each bring different needs and expectations to the relationship. This keynotes the double-edged sword of the giving and taking of love: the more you give of yourself, the more you stand to lose as well as gain. The more you invest in the relationship, the more you expect from the one you love. Conflict may simply be a perceived violation of these expectations.

Typically, conflicts arise in one of two areas: *over* possible goal options or *within* an established goal framework. The young unmarried couple, experiencing difficulty in constructing sexual guidelines, offers a case of conflict over goals. On the other hand, conflict within already established goals is exemplified by the wife who will not consent to her husband taking a second job, although they are in desperate financial straits. The persistence of a relationship in itself can compound the potential problems in both of these areas as individuals change in their needs and expectations over time.

It may well be that the most stable and harmonious relationships are those in which the parties have learned to cope with conflict in a satisfying manner. If this is the case, the more we care about a relationship, the more concern we should have for handling the inevitability of conflict. Then when conflict situations do occur, they will be less disruptive.

But situations arise where the "resolution" of conflict is never entirely possible. The key in these instances lies in the process of negotiating the problem so that it becomes manageable. The issue may not be put to rest for good for it can easily appear again the next week or the next year, in the same or different form. Conflict management achieved by the process of negotiation, however, is a constructive approach to the problems of intimacy. The parties are really saying to one another: "I care enough about what you mean to me that I am willing to sacrifice some of my own desires to get this problem out of the way."

Negotiation is neither a simple nor quick task. Each person may define the situation as involving a "problem" of different magnitude. Furthermore, during the negotiations other problems may emerge which extend the scope of the conflict. Irrespective of the number, type or degree of conflicts, several vital questions are always raised, at least implicitly: How do I handle this fight? How much am I really willing to give up for the relationship? What *do* I want? These questions must also be faced by the other person.

The selections that follow speak in some way to one or more of the issues raised above. The theme elaborated by the writers is that conflict does not necessarily have to be destructive, but that it *is* a reality which arises frequently throughout the interaction of people. The problem becomes one of making it work for us, not against us. Particular attention should be given to such questions as: Why does conflict arise? How does conflict usually emerge in relationships? How can we constructively manage conflict? How can we avoid unnecessary conflict situations?

Crosby would first have us be aware that conflict may arise within a person or within a relationship. Some conflicts between people may be of "intrapsychic" origin in that conflicting values and needs within one of the persons surfaces to complicate the relationship.

The self-administered questionnaire in "Double Cross" helps us clarify some opposing expectations since unconsciously held ambiguities often lead to dissension in a relationship.

Further light on unrealistic expectations is provided by Bach and Wyden. Not only do we dream of a beautiful, conflict-free engagement, but we are so concerned with presenting an attractive image of ourselves that the relationship becomes a masquerade in which neither person communicates with honesty.

A second excerpt from Shulman gives a glimpse of just such a masquerade for Sasha, both in her job and in relation to her husband. Inadequate and/or dishonest communication complicated their lives fully as much as it did in the fictional presentation by Westlake. When the "right" questions are not asked nor complete information given, even an apparently successful marriage can turn sour and be destroyed.

Had either of these couples been able to confront the issues openly and honestly, Charny would suggest the negotiation could have contributed to a growing relationship and the marriage would have been solidified.

One alternative to the stagnation or to conflict within marriage is proposed by the O'Neills. They submit a useful formula for movement from the traditional to an "open" relationship, in which a high degree of self-fulfillment is available to each of the married couples. The potential for increasing intimacy and mutual understanding may minimize conflict in some areas of relationship.

In sum, the readings frame an idealistic but not unrealistic goal: Accept the fact of conflict, learn how to deal with it, and you will learn to love more completely.

CONFLICT RESOLUTION: AN ENTRÉE INTO THE SELF *

JOHN F. CROSBY

There is a popular societal taboo against conflict, particularly marital conflict. The taboo is not explicit; it is implicit. The word *conflict* conjures up negative connotations due to our historical view that conflict is morally wrong.

CONFLICT AS A FACT OF LIFE

Marital interaction, parental interaction with children and teenagers, sibling interaction, three-generational familial interaction, as well as all other interpersonal relationships are potentially conflict-laden. A cultural tradition which, for whatever historically conditioned reasons, considers conflict morally wrong will encourage the suppression and repression of conflict, thus laying a foundation for misunderstanding, resentment, anger, hostility, bitterness, hatred, and misplaced aggression.

Although many cultures as well as our own endow conflict with moral or immoral connotations, we shall take the position that conflict itself is amoral—that is, without moral value. In other words, we see conflict as a neutral phenomenon; it is how one looks upon conflict and how one handles it that gives it a positive or negative value. If, for example, a married couple is socialized to believe that argument is wrong, that the voicing of disagreement is to be avoided, and that the essence of marriage is to create and maintain harmony at any price, then not only will this couple probably claim that neither of them ever remembers an unkind word between their parents, but they will feel guilt that their own marital relationship is not beautiful or perfect. They will probably feel conflict and sense their underlying hostility, but they will not be able to do anything about it except be miserable, for, after all, conflict implies fighting and fighting is wrong! Isn't it?

* From ILLUSION AND DISILLUSION: THE SELF IN LOVE AND MARRIAGE by John F. Crosby. © 1973 by Wadsworth Publishing Company, Inc., Belmont, California 94002. Reprinted by permission of the publisher.

Perhaps the most unfortunate result of this kind of socialization is the fact that the children of this couple will now in turn be deprived of any viable models of how to face and deal with conflict in a creative, growth-producing, love-filling way.

The root of this negative attitude toward conflict is the popular assumption that love is the polar opposite of hate. At times it may be. At other times, the line between love and hate is a very fine line, and until the negative feelings are allowed expression there is a diminution of the positive feelings as well. This state of affairs leads many couples to conclude: "We feel nothing toward each other, neither love nor hate." Naturally, for when the negative is repressed so will be the positive. "Our love has died," is an expression often heard by marriage counselors and psychotherapists. Why not, for the experience of "dying love" is in part the experience of the denial of feelings, first the negative, and then as a consequence, the positive. Rollo May has described this dynamic:

> A curious thing which never fails to surprise persons in therapy is that after admitting their anger, animosity, and even hatred for a spouse and berating him or her during the hour, they end up with feelings of love toward this partner. A patient may have come in smoldering with negative feelings but resolved, partly unconsciously, to keep these, as a good gentleman does, to himself; but he finds that he represses the love for the partner at the same time as he suppresses his aggression . . . the positive cannot come out until the negative does also. . . . Hate and love are not polar opposites; they go together, particularly in transitional ages like ours.[1]

The following case study illustrates more concretely the effects of forbidding oneself negative feelings.

Case Study 1

Kathy and John have been married for four years. They have come to the counselor only after Kathy has insisted that they do so.

John: I am afraid I don't love Kathy. I don't know how or why but the feelings I used to have are gone. I try to recreate them but . . . well, it just doesn't work. Sometimes I force myself to be loving but then it seems . . . like . . . pow! . . . she turns around and does something to really turn me off! One of these days I'm afraid I'm really going to unload on Kathy.

Kathy: Unload what?

John: Well, just . . . Oh forget it!

Kathy: No! *Unload what?* I suppose you think I'm just feeling good about you all the time. Well, I'm not! You've got me so mixed up and confused I don't know how I feel or what I think. Lately, you just make me sick—acting like a hurt little boy if you don't get everything your way, clamming up, pouting and sulking.

John: You sure put your finger on it. How else am I supposed to feel when you put me down? You're the one who seems to have to get her own way. You act like no one can handle the money as well as you . . . You insist on doing things with *your* friends. You act like sex is a bore and you parcel it out like it was rationed. You undermine everything I try to do with the kids. The fact is, I think sometimes your judgment in handling them stinks . . .

Kathy: I suppose you're an expert!

John: I think you're too easy on them.

And here we go with gunnysacking—the unloading of past grievances. At best, gunnysacking provides a release of pent-up feelings, an unleashing of the negative feelings which have been put down into the gunnysack for safekeeping, but which end up being used as ammunition at some later time. At worst, gunnysacking provides a decoy to get negative feelings out in the open, even if they are not the real cause of the present impasse. If Kathy and John are encouraged to unload on each other on deeper levels, they may succeed in getting at some of their real resentments. And these negative feelings have been dammed up so long that the positive "love" feelings have correspondingly diminished. No therapist would be surprised if at one of the next counseling sessions John would say: "I'm beginning to feel love for Kathy again. I don't seem to have as much resentment . . . and I'm not even trying to make myself be loving."

George R. Bach, who has written *The Intimate Enemy* (sub-titled "How to fight fair in love and marriage") has called at-tention to dirty fighters, sick fighters, fighting for intimacy, and training lovers to be fighters. Bach says:

> Contrary to folklore, the existence of hostility and conflict is not necessarily a sign that love is waning. As often as not, an upsurge of hate may signal a deep-ening of true intimacy; it is when neither love nor hate can move a partner that a relationship is deteriorating. Typically, one partner then gives up the other as a "lost cause" or shrugs him off ("I couldn't care less"). In-difference to a partner's anger and hate is a surer sign of a deteriorating relationship than is indifference to love.[2]

Thus, it is more correct to say that indifference is the polar opposite of both love and hate. Outright rejection is often easier to accept than being ignored or treated indifferently as though one were not there!

Seen in this light, it is clear that the creative facing of con-flict is an absolute necessity in marital relations. In fact, con-sidering that previous generations embraced the ethical and moral concept of "honesty," we may wonder how honest our ancestors were as they avoided conflict like the plague. This is dishonest! Perhaps their dishonesty may be excused in that they were thoroughly conditioned in the belief that conflict was an evil thing. Nevertheless, the avoidance of conflict is, at heart, a dishonest stance in interpersonal relationships.

For lessons in "how to fight fair in love and marriage," as Bach puts it, the reader is referred to his book. Our concern here is to examine the nature of intrapsychic and interpsychic conflict and then to outline a system of **transactional analysis** * which will, hopefully, enable the reader to understand the nature of his own intrapersonal and interpersonal communica-tions. Our premise is that only as a person understands the nature of his inner conflicts is he able to deal creatively with his interpersonal conflicts. To this end, transactional analysis will be used as an entrée into the self.

---

* **Transactional analysis.** A type of psychotherapy based on the study and analysis of the communication metacommunication, and symbolic communication (transactions) be-tween two people.

INTRAPSYCHIC AND INTERPSYCHIC CONFLICT

Intrapsychic conflict is that conflict within the self which arises from our drives, instincts, and values pulling against each other. Classical psychoanalysis (Freud) posits the fundamental conflict as one between the id and the superego. Psychoanalytical and **neopsychoanalytical theory**** since Freud has stressed the centrality of intrapsychic conflict as the essential dynamic of neurotic behavior. Intrapsychic conflict is one of the precursors of interpsychic conflict. These two terms do not refer to phenomena existing within the self but are symbolic references to libidinous (instinctual) energy and the internalized voice of parents and society (conscience). Ideally, the ego is sufficiently strong enough to be the arbiter between the id (seeking pleasure) and the superego (demanding perfection). The ego takes account of the reality of the core self of the person; the degree of strength and maturity of the ego determines the degree of control the superego is allowed to exercise over the instinctual libidinous drives. Frankl has pointed out that there is another kind of conflict besides this conflict of drives and instincts (which result in what he terms "psychogenic neurosis"). He suggests that anxiety ("noogenic neurosis") also arises from "conflicts between various values; in other words, from moral conflicts or, to speak in a more general way, from spiritual problems." [3]

An internal conflict can focus on anything that encounters resistance when attempts are made to incorporate it or make it acceptable to the self. Since facing conflict creates unpleasant feelings of tension and anxiety, individuals develop conscious or unconscious methods of handling conflict. One method is to suppress it—that is, to consciously put it in the back of one's mind and deliberately decide not to deal with it. Repression, on the other hand, is an unconscious process of blocking out the conflict so that it doesn't come out into the open, into consciousness. However, material repressed in the unconscious still exerts a powerful influence on us, for repression can cause conflict to be disguised in the form of compulsions, obsessions, anxiety, and depression.

** **Neopsychoanalytical theory.** Expansion and reinterpretation of Freud's discoveries based on new empirical and clinical evidence. Especially refers to the theories of Karen Horney, Harry Stack Sullivan and Erich Fromm.

If a person is torn within, consciously or unconsciously, he will be unable to deal with conflicts on the interpersonal (interpsychic) level. People who have dealt successfully with their inner conflicts are able to address themselves to interpersonal conflict in a reasonably creative, autonomous, and spontaneous manner. Let us caution, however, that to experience internal conflict is to be human. There can be no counsel of perfection about our inner conflicts; our humanity is such that we are capable of emotionality *and* rationality. We experience drives, desires, feelings, and pleasures; we also experience meaning and meaninglessness, value and worthlessness, intelligence and stupidity. Our intellect can serve us in conflict avoidance as well as in conflict resolution. For example, through *rationalization* one can refer to plausible reasons for his behavior to avoid facing the real reasons; or a person can unconsciously *project* his own traits on another person so that he won't have to see them in himself; or through *transference* an individual might transfer his feelings toward a significant person in his life (particularly parents) to another person. All of these are conflict-avoidance games we play with ourselves.

Case Study 2

George and Betty have been going together for almost a year. Their relationship has been a deep and rewarding experience for both of them. Lately, however, George has become picky, hypercritical, and sensitive to things Betty says and does. George has decided to talk to a counselor about his relationship with Betty.

"I don't know what it is, but everything she does bugs me. I get angry when she tries to plan an evening or a weekend. Then when she doesn't offer her opinions about what we're going to do I feel she doesn't care. We're saving money for our marriage and then she comes up with expensive ideas on how to spend it. Lately, no matter what it is, I react negatively. The other day for instance . . . we were going for a walk downtown and she started window shopping—you know, saying how much she'd like this dress or that coat. I found myself getting critical and hostile. I felt like . . . well, like here was a person who was going to try to manipulate me. (Pause) A couple of weeks ago I wanted her to make over me a little. I had seen some girl really pouring a lot of love onto a guy and it struck me that Betty never makes over me that way. So when I saw her I noted her reactions. She sure was a loser compared to that girl I had seen. And we argue a lot—no matter what we are discussing I end up disagreeing with her. You know—like if she says it's a groovy flick I'll take the opposite approach. If she thinks Vietnam is stupid, I find myself defending our commitment. . . . Yet I love her. I still want to marry her! Why do I keep reacting to her the way I do?

There is, of course, no simple answer to George's question, "Why do I keep reacting to her the way I do?" Every couple needs to work through their interpersonal reactions, and no relationship is entirely free of personality quirks or idiosyncrasies. Basically, however, it may be that George's basic conflict is intrapsychic, or inside himself. He reveals some contradictory tendencies. On the one hand, he fears being manipulated, but he is not altogether sure what constitutes manipulation by Betty. He wants to be made over; yet the result is that he creates a "test" for Betty as if he says to himself, "I'll watch her every move and see how unsatisfyingly she responds." Of course, under these conditions, Betty can't do anything but lose. She doesn't know the name of the game George is playing. George finds himself opposing Betty no matter what the issue. I would suggest that the main conflict is in George himself, not in his relationship with Betty. George has some deeply hidden anxiety and hostility. He is not nearly as autonomous and self-directing as he probably pictures himself. One possible explanation is that George is using transference; he is interacting with and responding to Betty as if he were still fighting his mother. George appears to be easily threatened by Betty and yet, at the same time, he looks to her for reassurance and overt displays of affection. (Why can't you be like her?) Thus, George's problem is intrapsychic, a function of his personal development and environmental conditioning. How and to what extent George sees through and handles his intrapsychic problems will determine the kind and quality of relationship he has with Betty or any other prospective mate.

Interpsychic or interpersonal conflict is the more obvious kind of conflict in that it occurs between two people. It is this kind

of conflict that has been regarded as taboo within marriage.   According to this view, a husband and wife should not have conflict, even though familial conflict between parents and children
is considered normal and acceptable.   Even this conflict is not
very comfortable for society; witness the labeling of intergen-
erational conflict as the "generation gap."   Could it be that the
term "gap" is a way to avoid calling it "conflict"?   And if it is
a conflict, is it a conflict of drives and instincts, or is it a conflict of values, meanings, and purpose?   One may suspect that
a great deal of what is called "campus unrest" today is
none other than youth in conflict with a value system which
they no longer sense as viable.

Interpersonal conflict may focus on trivial, inconsequential
things or it may focus on major issues.   Within marriage, the
little inconsequential things may serve as decoys for the actual
source of conflict.   Much of the pent-up hostility of marital partners is expressed in passive ways or is displaced to inappropriate
objects.   Hence the designation, "passive-aggressive personality"
is given to those who aggress passively, perhaps by being unduly
critical, by faultfinding, or by "nit-picking."   When aggressive, hostile feelings are displaced, we recognize it as a form of
"scapegoating."   There is a well-defined pecking order in our
society which designates in no uncertain terms who may be the
legitimate object of our displaced hostility feelings.   The unfortunate fact is that neither displacement nor passive-aggres-
siveness need be operative if we could take seriously the reality
of conflict and learn how to deal with it maturely and creatively.

Let us turn from our discussion of intrapsychic and interpsychic conflict to a consideration of a method of self-study which
may serve as a "handle" for creatively working through conflict.   The underlying assumption is, of course, that conflict
is a human reality, and as such amoral, and that as we become
proficient in understanding and handling the intrapsychic conflicts, we will be free to become equally proficient at understanding and working through our interpsychic conflicts.

THE DOUBLE CROSS *

GEORGE ROLEDER

Why do many of those beautiful courtships go sour in marriage? One answer is that they run into a "double cross." That is, some of the wonderful traits which attract mates to each other actually become the source of marital problems!

It seems incredible (and unfair) that this should be, that attractions before marriage could lead to stress after marriage. That's why they are called a "double cross." It is terribly ironic. Which may explain why many couples can't pin down the true source of their conflict even when they try. Who would suspect attractions?

The questionnaires which follow are an attempt to help you predict whether you and your mate (or future mate) are in danger of experiencing one or more "double crosses." Follow the directions in filling them out. Then study the discussion of the scoring which follows. Sample solutions are also offered. Of course, the application to each marriage must be much more specific. In fact it will be necessary for some couples to enlist the help of a marriage counselor to explore their needed adjustments more carefully. The survey is intended merely to alert you to potential areas of conflict, not to guarantee success or failure in your marriage.

PART 1—WHAT YOU LIKE

DIRECTIONS: Circle one of the three adjectives in parentheses (*very, somewhat, not at all*) which best describes your preferred *date* or *mate,* in each of the six items listed below.

I am attracted to a date (or mate) who is:

1. (very, somewhat, not at all) cute, good-looking, attractive to most members of the opposite sex.

2. (very, somewhat, not at all) independent of the advice or help of others.

3. (very, somewhat, not at all) careful with money.

* From MARRIAGE MEANS ENCOUNTER (Dubuque, Iowa: Wm. C. Brown Company Publishers, 1973) adapted from the author's FAMLAB–FAMILY LABORATORY (Dubuque, Iowa: Kendall/Hunt Publishing Co., 1970), by permission of the author and publishers.

4. Males answer here:
    (very much, somewhat, not at all)   the typical feminine female, clothes-conscious, concerned about manners, etiquette, and home life.

4. Females answer here:
    (very much, somewhat, not at all)   the typical masculine male, he-man, outdoor type.

5. (very, somewhat, not at all)   fond of social life and social functions.

6. (very, somewhat, not at all)   ambitious and interested in a career outside the home.

PART 2—WHAT YOU'RE LIKE

Listed below are six samples of personality and behavior. Rate *yourself* by circling one of the three appropriate adjectives in parentheses (*very, somewhat, not at all*) to describe what you're like.

1. I am (very much, somewhat, not at all)   the jealous type.

2. I am (very, somewhat, not at all)   desirous of helping others, pleased to be needed for advice or helpful tasks.

3. I am (very, somewhat, not at all)   impulsive in the use of money, hesitant to save it up.

4. I am (very, somewhat, not at all)   desirous to have my mate accept and appreciate my outlook on life, my idea of fun and what is essential for me to spend money on.

5. I am (very much, somewhat, not at all)   the stay-at-home type who can do without crowds and parties.

6. I am (very, somewhat, not at all)   desirous of having my mate put me and our marriage first, before a successful career.

Now let's put the two surveys together and see if you are destined for marital bliss or a marital "double cross."

ITEM 1

Suppose you circled *very* for item #1 on both parts of the survey. In other words, you really go for a cute partner (Part 1). But you are also the jealous type (Part 2). You want your date or mate all to yourself. You expect exclusiveness. You worry when you hear that things are getting cozy at the office. In fact you worry even before you hear it! You simmer with anger (fear?) when there's an office party for your mate but you're not invited. Why worry? Well, you tell yourself, you were attracted to that cute number, so why shouldn't others fall the same way you did? That's why your worry seems realistic to you. If your fear spills over into your conversations, you may even resort to false accusations and thus ruin some of the mutual trust on which marriages depend.

Before that happens confront your mate with your worry-dilemma. This will give your (probably surprised) mate a chance to reassure you directly and often. Ask your mate to stay in touch more than would be expected by a non-jealous partner. Telephone calls when the other is away, brief notes and explanations will help keep your imagination under control.

If you marked *somewhat* for either part, the risk of a "double cross" is still present, just not as great. If you marked *not at all* on either of the two parts, this item is not a potential problem area for you.

ITEM 2

A *very* or *somewhat* in either Part 1 or Part 2 on this trait spells trouble. In Part 1, for example, it means that you are attracted to the independent type. That's the type who is self-reliant and gets along quite well without the advice or help of others. Nice American ideal, wouldn't you say? Of course. No wonder you and many others are attracted to that sort. However, a *very* or *somewhat* on Part 2 would suggest that you enjoy being helpful to others. But unfortunately, your independent mate won't need much help! You enjoy the feeling of being needed. Sorry, you'll have to do your helping somewhere else. Your mate is self-sufficient, remember. And save your advice. Your mate may have tolerated it during courtship (when romance dictated polite manners). In marriage, however, the truth comes out. Your pearls of wisdom fall on bored ears. You'll say, "My mate doesn't seem to need me anymore." You may begin to wonder if it means a loss of love. Useless to your competent mate, you may also feel resentment about the inferior position in which this places and keeps you.

Solutions for this "double cross" include the reminder that your mate hasn't changed since you met. Fact is, your help was never needed as much as you thought. So remember you must have been desired by your mate for other reasons. You must have other attributes. Explore those and concentrate on them. Keep yourself attractive that way and forget the big helper routine. On the other hand, no mate is competent in all areas. Discover the gaps in that independence. Make your help more selective. The increased responsibilities of marriage and family life should provide some new needs in which your help could count.

A *not at all* for either survey means no trouble; the proper combination exists between what attracts you and what you are like.

ITEM 3

A *very* or *somewhat* on either or both parts of Item #3 calls attention to the contrast between your thrifty, penny-saving date or mate, and your own carefree attitude toward money. During courtship you may have liked that in your date because it suggested a secure, bills-paid future. But in marriage that same penny-*saver* comes across as a penny-*pincher*. Especially if that mate controls most of the spending and doesn't agree with your idea of "essential" spending.

If you get caught in this "double cross", you may have to engineer a budget which allows you spending money of your own, a personal allowance. You can squander it as you like without answering to your tight-fisted partner, and without ruining the family finances. Or consider earning money of your own. You may need a "his" and "hers" budget system to keep money squabbles out of your romance.

Suppose you are an impulsive *male* matched to a thrifty wife. You're lucky. Your "double cross" is not as threatening to your happiness. You can more easily indulge your whims in the good ole' double-standard, male-chauvinistic U.S.A. After all, it's your money. You'll have no problems until the income gets shorter than the bills. Or until your worried mate explodes in self-pity over her enormous role (she feels) of budget-saver. In the interest of marital peace, do some compromising as recommended above. Agree to a monthly amount which each of you can "blow" or "save" to suit your unique life styles. Make the amount large enough to satisfy your marriage-compromised need, but not so great as to endanger the family budget or the sanity of your mate, whichever is closer to the breaking point!

Relax! There's no future "double cross" if you marked a *not at all* on either survey.

ITEM 4

This item alerts you to the problems created by mixing the sexes in marriage. Not that I believe, as some do, that the sexes must inevitably be at odds. I believe that friendship and companionship are most responsible for the pleasures of married life. And yet this item unnerves me. Take any combination of *very's* or *somewhat's* and you have a potentially go-nowhere marriage. That would be the matching of the typical male and female. The stereotypes. That was fine in a traditional America when men had to be tough, outdoor he-men. That's what it took to cope with the work and danger. Transportation, for example, required manual taming of wind, wave, or wild horse. Brawn made sense. Wives were busy enough with an indoor world of sewing and baking to leave the man's world to him. It is true that in public they were expected to act refined, quiet, and submissive. However, understanding of each other's worlds was kept alive, because much of the planting, raising, harvesting, and preserving of crops was a partnership venture. Family members watched each other at work and at play, more than many moderns realize.

In today's money-economy approach to family life, a wedge has unintentionally been driven between the sexes. Money comes from some foreign, mysterious source—through Dad or Mom. It is spent by the younger males for their world; by females for theirs. Unfortunately, each sex knows little about the personal money-world of the other—not until their two worlds collide in marriage. Thus "feminine" females are good to look at, but they have difficulty accepting the importance of male essentials: tires for cars, costs of baseball tickets, gun club magazines, beer, liquor, and nude centerfolds. "Won't he ever grow up and do without his *toys?*" complains the surprised wife.

Likewise, "masculine" males of Marlboro fame may keep alive an American dream, but there are few cattle to rope in suburban backyards. The muscled, outdoor type is fun to admire on the beach and football field, but he has generally learned little about the high cost of carrots, cosmetics, and baby diapers. When he is asked to *pay* for them, he'll have no sympathy for such "unnecessary" items. When he starts saying things like, "Spending our money for such foolishness" or "All women seem to think about are the latest styles and hair colors," then his "double cross" has begun.

Misunderstanding, harsh words, and the resulting shaky marriage must be saved by deliberate male-female appreciation. Identify your first rumbles for what they really are: symptoms of mixed sexes. Not selfishness or stupidity, just the result of living in single sex compartments for eighteen years. You might try the following: Males, repeat after me, "Her things are as important to her as mine are to me. My things are as silly to her as hers are to me." Gals, repeat after me, "His things are as important to him as mine are to me. My essentials are as silly to him as his are to me."

Until the differences make sense to both, you could ease the spending strain by splitting the budget into "sex" compartments, agree to a general price tag for each and thus maintain a temporary armed truce.

Not at all appearing in either survey saves these traits from becoming future irritants.

ITEM 5

How did you fare on Item #5? Are you strangely attracted to the type who is fond of social life, even though you prefer to find your own entertainment at home? If your *very* or *somewhat* appeared on either part, the conflict will be obvious to you. Or will it? For many this difference doesn't become a source of irritation until after marriage. Why not? Why isn't this "double cross" exposed during dating and courtship?

Several reasons account for the surprising conflict remaining hidden before marriage. For one thing, until you are actually married you can each visit your same-sex friends as much as you like. Neither of you feels trapped. So you don't *feel* the difference between you. Secondly, during courtship each may curb his natural trait and stretch himself toward the other's life style. Thus the introvert will endure enough social life to hang on to the beloved. Likewise, the social bug will consent (and act content) when kept in. The payoff for the grounded partner may be in the form of intimate necking, petting, and whatnot. So who'd complain? Not even the extrovert!

There's a third reason. Let's imagine that you are the stay-at-home type. During courtship you enjoy your socially experienced friend because of the "social security" provided. You can go places you've always been curious about but afraid to tackle alone. Your date keeps an eye on you. That is also what makes dating fun—being the center of your companion's attention. So you like it. It's not until after marriage that you discover how much your partner's social pace is not your own. You're getting enough marital companionship at home. Why go out? You settle back into your introvert pattern.

What does your crowd-loving mate do after marriage? Chafes under the confinement. Itches to get out. Can't understand what happened to you. So you are asked: "Is it okay to go out without you? To evening activities? At the church? At a nightclub? To parties where couples will be present?"

Do you get the picture? At the stay-at-home end of this relationship you might very well become upset over your mate's desire and ability to achieve public recognition through (too many!) social, church, or civic "duties." Such a mate won't easily say "No" to requests for club work. You will spend time alone with the children. It will be hard to complain about that because your mate invited you to go along (you'll be reminded). Furthermore, those social activities are all "worthwhile." So you'll probably suffer in silence, sleep alone, and have dreams of setting dynamite under enemy bridges.

What might ease the strain? Showing your true self earlier during courtship would alert your partner to the need for adjustment. That would create less future shock. After marriage, your half of the compromise style would include pushing yourself out more often with your mate. Encourage participation without you. Invite friends in more than you really prefer, especially if you wonder what goes on when you're not around. Does this sound like hard work? Compromise usually is.

Notice that on Item #5 you can pick up the "double cross" in reverse. That is, if your preferred date is *not at all* fond of social activities (Part 1), but you are *not at all* the stay-at-home type (Part 2), that's the same problem but with you grounded instead. Work toward the compromise described above. And remember that your home-body mate will respond better to social *invitations* than to *bullying* or *threatening*.

A *not at all* in combination with a *very* or *somewhat* will not produce the "double cross."

ITEM 6

This final item seems ridiculous! What could possibly be dangerous about falling in love with someone who is ambitious? Isn't this what a majority of females list as very important in their choice of mate? In a male, isn't this the trait which makes him a steady provider? Doesn't ambition in a female give her incentive to develop as a person, find a career, keep her brain active, and make her an interesting companion (not to mention the money her career adds to the family finances)? Right! It is a wonderful attribute. And it won't cause irritation in your marriage unless you also happen to expect that ambitious mate to put you and the marriage first. In other words, if you also circled that you are *very* or *somewhat* desirous of having your mate put you and the marriage before a successful career, you are inviting a "double cross."

Think about it! Getting to the top is almost impossible in a competitive society like ours unless it is placed first in one's efforts. That also takes time—time away from home. So if by "first" you mean where and on what your mate spends the most time and effort, you're creating a conflict in which you can't win.

So you will wait at home with cold food, or in vain at the department store meeting place when your ambitious mate forgets to call about working late. You will be expected to forgive the forgetfulness because of the "importance" of the work. How can you object when the extra effort is "for the future of the marriage"? If you also suffer from jealousy you will even add suspicion to your festering resentment.

Solutions? Remember, first of all, that your mate was already like this when you married. It wasn't *because* of you or the marriage that this type became ambitious. It was already part of the personality. Marriage only supplied an additional reason to stay absorbed in work. Remind yourself, secondly, that your mate knows you were attracted by that ambitious streak. Now it's a matter of holding your attraction. You may have to convince your mate that you can settle for a little less ambition, that you're willing to wait a few years for a new home. Try to turn the ambition away from economic success and toward projects within the family.

Perhaps you're also trying to feel successful through your mate. In that case you ought to try working toward a career yourself. As you try to hold home and career together, you will also understand your mate's conflict better.

A *not at all* in either Part 1 or Part 2 means there is no potential conflict on this item.

A Final Word

It may be that your choices fit the categories of a "double cross," but you haven't noticed any problems in your marriage adjustment. Fine! Let's not create problems where none exist. Perhaps you made the switch quickly and maturely. Or perhaps the degree of the traits is milder in reality than the labels of this questionnaire indicated for you. On the other hand, the events which create tensions may still lie in a future stage of your family life cycle.

The aim of the survey is not to condemn you to an irreversible mismatch but to alert you to possibilities and likelihoods of conflict. That's so you can identify your problem and start your switch in thinking early in the marital game. If you uncover very much of, or even somewhat of, a "double cross" while you're still in the dating stage, great! The fewer surprises after marriage, the better.

THE DREAM: COURTSHIP FIGHTS *

George F. Bach and Peter Wyden

It all starts with the dating-mating game, a notorious confused and confusing time and place. The moment two strangers are attracted toward one another across the crowded room, each begins to create a set of three mental images that describe his feelings about the other. There is a *you* image of what the attractive stranger will turn out to be like upon closer acquaintance. There is a *me* self-image that determines how I decide to present myself to the new person and how I expect him or her to see me. The mutual attraction generates a *we* image of what it would be like to become emotionally involved with the stranger.

Each potential intimate enters courtship with such a set of three images. They are related like panels on a three-way tailor's mirror, but unfortunately they show not the real person but only biased, wishful reflections of him. Even more inconveniently, the pictures in each panel overlap portions of the other two. Fights over each of these disparate images—and especially over what constitutes a "fair" image—are inevitable.

The sooner these fights begin and the more realistically the courtship fighters level with each other, the better off they will be. But prospective intimates almost never see courtship in this way. As a result, they often carry along vague or distorted *you*, *me*, and *we* images into their marriages. Disillusionment and pain are the natural consequences.

To meet a prospective intimate is every bit as exciting as it should be. Then, slowly, the *you*, *me*, and *we* images are fleshed out as the new friends gather random pieces of information about each other. Some of this data is objective, like "This girl has nice legs" or "This man has been married before." But much of it is highly subjective and purely emotional, like "See what a handsome couple we make" or "At last someone appreciates the real me!" These facts and feelings combine to produce the overwhelming sense of excitement and anticipation that can be stirred by a fresh encounter with a new and interesting person.

But even among the most sincere and upright people, camouflaging and faking usually begin at once. She may say to herself, "He might not like me. If I'm going to attract him. I better not be too sexy." He may feel like telling her, "I like you." Instead, his expression of interest may be articulated as, "I don't like the way you do your hair." No wonder new acquaintances so often manage to fool—and quickly lose—each other.

Sometimes a spiral of misunderstandings begins in the most innocent way when a man asks himself, "What does she like about me?" The spiral widens when he gives himself the wrong answer and *then* decides to make the most of his supposed advantage. Listen to the following very early courtship fight between two college students:

FIRST ROUND

SHE: What kind of wheels do you have?

HE: Why?

SHE: I just wondered.

SECOND ROUND

HE: Do you like the Beatles?

SHE: Do you?

HE: I asked you first.

THIRD ROUND

HE: I still want to know why you're so anxious to know what kind of car I have. (*Unspoken: She may not like convertibles.*)

SHE: Because I am. (*Unspoken: I hope he doesn't have a convertible. It'll ruin my hair.*)

FOURTH ROUND

HE: I'll give you a ride home.

SHE (*seeing convertible*): Oh!

HE: Don't you like convertibles?

SHE: What makes you say that?

HE: (*Unspoken: Hallelujah, she loves convertibles!*)

FIFTH ROUND (*They're in the convertible.*)

HE: Great night, isn't it?

SHE: (*Unspoken: I like him, but I don't want the top down be-cause it would spoil my hair. On the other hand, if I don't agree it's a nice night he'll think I'm stupid.* She says nothing, but snuggles up to him.)

This romance has barely begun and is already off on several wrong feet all at once. The young man is now entitled to think that she like convertibles. The young lady is entitled to think that he likes a display of affection in his car. The truth is she can't abide convertibles while he relishes his command of the convertible so much that he likes best to drive with one hand, the top down, one arm casually leaning against the left door, his attention focused on a discussion of his latest athletic triumphs. He likes his snuggling later.

Two lessons can be learned from this classic convertible fight; first, it's a lot of extra trouble to start a romance under the cover of camouflage; second, decoding a partner's signals is hard work. Even experts often can't unmask all the dissembling that goes with the spiral of I-think-that-she-thinks-that-I-think and the geometric escalation of misunderstandings that follow. The couple in the convertible will be lucky if their evening manages to end in the following frustrating fight for optimal distance:

HE: See you tomorrow!

SHE: No, I don't think so.

HE: Why not?

SHE: Oh, I've got something on.

If he is leveling by that time, which is unlikely, he would come right out and say, "Hey, I don't like that!" More likely, he'll say, "But I can call you, can't I?" Or, if he is naïve, he may try, "Can't I come along?"

The poignant truth is that it is not easy for men or women to gain a secure place in each other's hearts. The gregarious-ness of people who present themselves most congenially to each other, and are "easy to meet," can be a front that hides fear of rejection, or getting involved, or encroachment, or engulfment, or sexual inadequacy, or disloyalty to existing liaisons, or fear of intruding on the world of the other.

The reservations of newly-mets tend to be of two kinds. First, there is a serious reservation about one's own attractiveness, and not necessarily in the visual or bodily sense alone, although this is terribly important to most people; it is more a question of one's own worthiness to be included in the private world of another person. Second, there is a question about the other person's acceptability to oneself as a potential partner: "Is he my type?" "How far can I trust him?" "If I love him, will he exploit me?"

It goes without saying that people do not love everything and everybody. They *frame* in mentally what is lovable about another person and what is not. If the other person doesn't want to be loved in the way dictated by our imagery frame, he is "not my type." Human beings have an enormous capacity for pseudo-loving someone who is new and almost unknown; or to adore someone in fantasy at a far distance (like Jesus or a dead hero). But everybody is extremely limited in the capacity to love real and familiar persons, including one's own real self. The limits for giving and receiving love are determined by the love frames that are manufactured in the hearts of intimates.

The reason why "love at first sight" is always so overwhelmingly exciting is that it is an instant, emotional breakthrough, a hysterical brushing aside and an overdetermined denial of reservations about another person. Impulsive "love on sight" dramatically releases one person from the emotional stress of anxiety about being included or rejected by another. It's a delightful experience. But, as everybody knows, it doesn't last very long. With luck, it may signal the start of a genuine new relationship, but the real start and future course of any such intimacy will be determined by the way the couple copes with the first series of hurdles: the acceptance-rejection crisis.

"Falling" in love is always a form of hysteria. It is not a mutual, open exchange of mutual feelings. It is a unilateral interest in one's own feelings, fantasies, and needs for the other person. The other person then responds and calibrates his own interests with those of the "fallen" as best he can. The idea is to keep the fallen on the hook. But nobody accepts anybody unconditionally. Sartre was right when he said, "Hell is other people." And it should come as no surprise to anyone that few people fall in love gracefully. Most are "mad" or "sick" or at least insecure toward partners who have begun to mean a great deal to them. At this point, they are afraid to level and be realistic. The insecurity suffered by newly-loves makes them pose, play games, and manipulate each other in order to reinforce the still tenuous attraction. All new lovers become liars and actors. And even though they are excited, they are usually distraught, too.

As one attractive, unmarried female graduate student once put it in a seminar on intimacy:

STUDENT: Professor Bach, I hate myself most when I am in love.

DR. B: How come? Aren't you happy to love and be loved?

STUDENT: Yes! The way you put it, that would be fine: to love, feeling absolutely loving towards a guy, that would be great; also, feeling his loving me, receiving and accepting being loved. But that's not what I meant.

DR. B: That's what I heard. Correct me!

STUDENT: I meant I become very bitchy when I *fall* in love or when I have *fallen* in love. It's not a secure posture, is it?

DR. B: No, falling is definitely not secure.

STUDENT: When I really like a guy, I become aggressive, fighty, and feisty.

DR. B: Why?

STUDENT: I don't know why. I do know something happens to me. I become more critical, more aggressive . . . maybe to test the fellow? (*Pause.*) Or maybe I resent being "hooked." I resent him and myself for *falling* for him. Even the idea of falling for each other is absurd when you come to think about it, and I like him less when he "falls" for me! There's that word again, "falling." It makes me angry, on guard. I don't like to be vulnerable. We can do hurtful things to each other now. I can hurt him just by not returning his calls or any other silly thing we do can be interpreted as "rejection." It's a hateful state to be in and I don't like it. So we become ornery and pick fights with each other.

DR. B: Which is . . .?

STUDENT: His vulnerability, like mine, is our love for one another.

DR. B: Then why fight?

STUDENT: I guess it's because I want to play "rejection-insurance." I reject him first so that when he rejects me it will not be real. It's just his defense against my rejection of him.

This girl was reacting rationally toward the partial loss of self which is inherent in the falling-in-love process and can well be terrifying. It is somewhat like rebelling against a loss of freedom. This student was advised to be aggressive about preserving her identity, but that there was no ground for panic.

Suppose her boyfriend wanted to go to the beach. Her tendency might be to say "yes" because she is in love and "no" because she doesn't want him to have his own way. One way out of this trap is to ask the boyfriend, "Are you suggesting the beach just to please me?" Whatever the answer, the girl's follow-up question ought to be to herself: "Is this something I want to do? Is it one of my me-things or not?"

It is natural for intimate fighting to break out whenever Partner A behaves dissonant to (or outside of) the love frame of Partner B or when "A" fails to display "in-frame" behavior clearly enough. "B" will fight to keep "A" within the love frame, either by "kicking" him into it or "slapping" him when he is out of it. "A", loving to be loved by "B", may try to accommodate "B" for fear of rejection. Or he may fight "B" to broaden "B's" love frame because he recognizes that does not realistically reflect his real self. If "A" does not fight "B" for realistic framing, then "A" is guilty of collusion.

Collusion, provoked by self-doubt and fear of rejection, creates a "setup" for much more bitter fighting later on, usually around such themes as "You tricked me," "You're a phony," "You certainly aren't the person I used to love," "I'm terribly disappointed in you," or "How can anybody change so much?" Yet collusion is a common component of the early, romantic courtship phase when eager, reality-shy strangers grasp at all kinds of irrational untested fantasies about each other.

Quite possibly, this phase, when partners use stereotypes or excessive fantasies in lieu of realistic expectations, may even be essential to get strangers together and help overcome their strangeness. But as a prelude to establishing an enduring intimacy later on, it adds a real problem. By clinging to wishful

dreams, lovers subdue fears and ambivalence over new intima-
cies so they can make a deep commitment to the new partner.
But the sooner they can give up courtship dreams and accept
realities, the better off they'll be.

At any rate, courting partners should learn to check on their
real selves by starting to fight shortly after they become interested in each other.   The successful ones never stop.   The
later-to-be-unsuccessful intimates usually have quiet, courtly
courtships.   If they are particularly fearful of rejection, they
may pretend to be unconditionally pleased with everything the
partner does.   Their quiet courtesy breeds unchecked assumptions and unrealistic expectations of future bliss.   Courtly court-
ers may also use ingratiation, a style of "good-impression-mak-
ing" which we regard as illicit because it is a strategy of maxi-
mizing one's attractiveness by selective self-display and fakery.
The ulterior purpose of nonfighting courtship behavior, of
course, is to evade transparency and to avoid authentic encounter
for fear that the real self would not fit into the romantic early
love frame and that the faker would not be lovable.

Most people who use these and other dishonest tactics are by
no means sick or even unusually mean.   They are insecure,
eager, and perhaps desperate.   They know that the best defense
against the isolation of being a loner is to find a central place
in the heart of one intimate partner.   But they try to win that
place by phony tactics.   In the pursuit of centricity lovers harbor
irrational ambitions.   They try to become the whole world for
the partner because the more central one's place is, the more one
belongs, the more secure one feels in an indifferent world.

To be of central significance to a partner means to be close;
to share the peak moments of a lifetime as well as the trivial ups
and downs of daily existence; to be included and brought into
the private world of feelings, wants, and fears of the other; to
care and fuss about the other's growth, his triumphs and frustrations, his lot in life; to identify and empathize with his ways
of being and growing; to be fussed over and cared about by
him; to have a partner for sharing one's private concerns about
oneself, about life, growing, succeeding, failing; to give and take
pleasure and to facilitate in each other a sense of well-being;
to enjoy the safety of a private harbor in a sea of troubles.

People are hungry for evidence that they are of central significance to an intimate partner.   They don't just desire this

role. They need it. Without it, a person would be "a nobody" whose very sanity might eventually become threatened by an absence of self-confirmation. For all but the most hardened loners, game-players, and the psychiatrically sick, it is intolerable to confess, "I belong to no one."

But before a promising battle for central position in somebody's heart can even begin, one must first fight for acceptance, for inclusion in the other's world. Almost always, "B" has granted other people important places in his or her heart before "A" ever appeared on the scene. To make a place for himself in "B's" heart, "A" must at first put up with the others. "A" may try to move out the earlier arrivals or reduce them in importance to "B" so that "A" can become No. 1 in the center spot of his partner's heart. But this is not always easy and frequently the effort is unsuccessful, as the following case illustrates.

Lou Cramer, a perpetually worried-looking 43-year-old advertising account executive, divorced two years previously, had been going with his new girl, a divorcée named Sophie Burns, for only three weeks. Desperately upset, he came to fight training and said, "I've just spent the craziest weekend of my life." He reported:

"I want to get married again and succeed the next time around. I almost got pushed into it last weekend. Sophie likes to keep our relationship secret, especially from her roommate. I dated the roommate first but only for a while. Last Saturday at 9:30 A.M. Sophie phoned and said she was going to come right over and stay the weekend. Then her roommate called and said she'd found out about us. When Sophie arrived I told her about it and said, "Now we don't have to hide any more." She looked shocked and sick. She never gets angry, never raises her voice or uses profanity. I said: "You should feel good! Now we're rid of a clandestine situation. The true story is beautiful: We love each other! There's nothing to be ashamed of!" Finally, she mumbled, "If I can't trust you in a little thing like that, how can I trust you with my life? I really loved you but you spoiled it all!" Then she left. I was very disgusted. It was so depressing, the thought of having to go out and find somebody new. The silly dating game, I am so tired of playing that! Then I felt anger: What would I really get if she is that kind of person? Then she telephoned.

SOPHIE (*mellow*): Darling, I'm sorry. I got too upset. I guess it's not that important.

LOU (*perplexed*): How can we get along if you run away every time we have a disagreement. Why can't you stay and have it out?

SOPHIE: I didn't run away. I just wanted to be alone for a few hours.

LOU: How did I know it would only be a couple of hours? I thought we were through!

SOPHIE: I drove to the harbor and sat in my boat and thought and thought. Now I want you. Please come and get me.

(At 4:15 he picked her up.)

SOPHIE: I have to be back by six.

LOU (*flabbergasted*): I thought we were going to spend the weekend!

SOPHIE: I wasn't sure you wanted me. My brother-in-law called and invited me to dinner, so I accepted.

(Lou felt very annoyed and made her drive her own car. She followed to his place. He fixed a bourbon for her and a Scotch for himself. They started to pet. As always, she aroused him tremendously, but this time she refused intercourse.)

SOPHIE: No, darling, no. Once I have sex I'd want to stay. I can't go over to my sister's house for dinner if I make love to you. Let me go! But I tell you what I'll do. I'll be back just as fast as I can and I'll stay all night.

(At 10:00 P.M. she called. It was evident that she had had a lot to drink.)

SOPHIE (*happily*): We're still eating. There's going to be champagne with dessert. I'm so tired.

LOU (*angry*): You mean you're not coming, after all?

SOPHIE: Oh, no. I'll be over as soon as I can get away.

LOU (*furious*): You're not very dependable, are you?

SOPHIE (*surprised*): But darling, *I love you* and I'll be over. So long. (Lou said to himself: "To hell with her! She should have the guts to tell them that she had an appointment with me!")

At 11:30 P.M. when there was still no sign of Sophie, Lou went to bed. Sunday morning he called a girl in the same building and they played tennis. When he got back to his apartment at 3 P.M. Sophie called.)

SOPHIE (*anxious*): I've been trying to reach you all day!

LOU (*furious*): I simply can't understand what's going on between us. You tell me to spend the weekend with you and then you accept other engagements!

SOPHIE: I'm sorry! It'll never happen again. After this we'll be invited together *as a couple.*

LOU (*resigned*): OK. Come on over. There's a party next door and we're invited.

(At 3:30 P.M. she came over. They necked and she tried to go further, but he did not want to get excited again. He was proud of his self-control. They went next door to the party where she stuck close to Lou and whispered, "I want to be yours. I love you." As they left the party she said she had to go to the yacht club because her boat was being painted and a contract had to be signed.)

LOU: Fine. I'll drive out with you.

SOPHIE (*embarrassed*): I don't think you better. Dick, the fellow who co-owns my boat, will be there.

(Lou began to think Sophie was dating another fellow or maybe two or three. He walked her out to the car. They stood close.)

SOPHIE (*whispering*): I want to be yours. I want to give you babies. I want to cook for you, clean your house. I'll make you happy, very, very happy. I want you to take me now, marry me.

LOU: We've known each other only three weeks. It takes me longer to be sure.

(She seemed irked and drove off to see Dick. On Monday, Sophie called at 6:00 P.M.)

SOPHIE (*sweetly*): How come you didn't call me today?

LOU: Honestly, honey, you confuse me.

SOPHIE: What's so confusing? I want to be your wife.

LOU: But why do you always run off some place?

SOPHIE: I have normal obligations and must take care of them. What are you doing now?

LOU: Oh, nothing. I don't feel well.

(She came over, cooked him some soup, and massaged his back. He got excited. They started to make love. But when he tried to put on a condom, she turned away from him.)

SOPHIE: I'd only do it without that rubber. The rubber hurts.

(He refused. She cooled off, put on her clothes, and was ready to leave.)

SOPHIE (*sad*): You don't seem to really want me as I am.

LOU (*coldly*): I don't want you pregnant, no.

SOPHIE: What's the difference? We'll be married soon, any-how!

LOU: Let's not go over the same broken record: I'm not ready to get married.

SOPHIE: Because you don't know me well enough?

LOU (*icy*): No, honey, I know you well enough. And I won't marry you because I do know you well enough!

This series of "lost weekend" battles illustrates many of the difficulties experienced by potential intimates in the process of getting together and becoming significant to one another. Here is a couple strongly attracted to one another, starved for true intimacy. Each would like to get married to somebody. During their first three weeks of courtship they thought they had made such a good start that they not only became sexually involved but began to negotiate about marrying!

What went wrong? To begin with, they simply did not give each other sufficient opportunity to be in enough situations to-gether so they could collect adequate impressions and informa-tion about each other's lovableness. Wanting and desiring a partner is obviously not enough. In fact, it can become a blind-ing force. When an attraction is impulsive, new and strong, there is a tendency to narrow the relationship to an erotic love-bond, isolated from the realities of everyday existence. In the thrall of such overspecialized bonds not enough information can be obtained by either party to make a prediction of dur-ability and maintenance of the initial attraction. Too much is left to wishful fantasies and mere hope that the partners will stay lovable to each other.

Both partners of this "lost weekend" fight participated in a weekend marathon group meeting for premarital, marital, and postmarital (divorced) couples. The partners came independently to the 30-hour nonstop meeting. They participated honestly, confronted each other with their love-frames and left separately, never to see each other again. During the meeting it became abundantly clear to the group and to the couple that they "were not meant for each other." He was "not her type" and she was not his. The marathon group experience helped them to complete the process of weaning themselves away from each other after an abortive beginning.

The trouble was that their love-frames did not match nor mesh. The frames did not encompass their real selves. Also, the respective *we* images failed to match—which is an understatement because there was hardly any overlap between the two unilateral love-frames. Her love-frame could be summarized this way: "What turns me on in a man is complete confidence in himself combined with infinite tact and discretion." His love-frame went like this: "What arouses me in a woman is her complete loyalty and reliability. And, of course, she must look sexy."

She was sexy, all right, but she was far from reliable. She sprang surprises. She constantly shifted plans. This was her way of testing his ability to remain calm and sure of her in spite of the runaround she gave him!

Her idea of their we image centered on independent, autonomous interests and lots of freedom. His expectations of enduring intimacy centered on "sharing and doing everything together." Their *we* image overlapped in the areas of sex and money. But this was not enough to make the fight for the center of each other's heart rewarding. They both quit before they became hopelessly entangled.

This couple would have been better off never having said "hello" to each other in the first place, but quite a few loners are unable to take even the first tentative, probing step toward intimacy and to attempt matching their love-frames against those of anyone else. One good-looking, "successful" 25-year-old bachelor said, "I simply can't bring myself to dance with any girl I really like. I even have trouble talking to her unless she makes the first move toward me, and that hardly ever happens. When it did, once or twice, I never followed up. I was scared."

DR. BACH: Do you like being without a date?

HE: Of course not!

DR. B: Well, what are you doing about it?

HE: I have a pretty active fantasy life, but I never talk about it.

When this intelligent, heterosexual man later shared his inner world with a fight-training group, it developed that this otherwise productive young person preferred masturbation and imaginary intercourse (with the aid of pornography and sexy movies) to the risks of becoming involved with a real partner. He feared he would be rejected and that this would confirm his irrationally low evaluation of himself.

Once people do become emotionally involved and win their fights for acceptance, inclusion, and centricity, new questions are likely to arise: "Now that I am presumably in the center of his heart, how does he view me? What does he propose to do with me? And where do we go from here?"

Again, many partners evade these issues. They may be fight-phobic. But perhaps they just don't "know their own mind" yet. They may know that the relationship could take several turns, but they don't know which turn they prefer. Nor would they know how to embark for whatever goal they seek. For such undecided partners a good inner dialogue may set a constructive direction.

The following case of a 22-year-old girl who is having a love affair with her boyfriend, with no commitments made by either partner, shows that "talking to yourself" is far from "crazy."

SHE: My question revolves around the depth of our relationship, whether it is a fleeting affair or a serious friendship.

DR. BACH: The conventional part of you fights for marriage?

SHE: Yes, and sex has a lot to do with this. My conventional side tells me that if I press for marriage now I'll have better sex because I'll have a regular sex partner and it will be socially approved. I won't have to hide.

DR. B: Is anybody opposing your conventional side?

SHE: That would be the independent side of me. That side is saying: why hurry into marriage? Eventually yes, but

not now! Now you're interested in doing things independently, learning to live by yourself, having fun. Why
face the responsibility of marriage now? You can date
anyone you like, and yet not tie yourself down.

DR. B (*addresses the trainee's "independent" side*): Now, Miss
Independence, if I may interview this part of you: Would
you care to debate the points Miss Convention made?

SHE: Yes, I would say that sex doesn't have to occur just within
marriage to be good, beautiful, and meaningful.

DR. B: Does Miss Convention want to talk to Miss Independence
on the subject?

SHE: Well, Miss Convention says: "I think that sex is an expression of love between husband and wife and it's not a
park-bench affair between boyfriend and girlfriend. Besides, the marriage license isn't just a piece of paper, and
you know it. It is a social sanction. Miss Independence's
answer to this might be: "I don't need a social sanction.
I don't live at home where I had this kind of conventional
pressure. If he wants to come over he can stay, eat breakfast, we can make love, take a shower together, and who's
going to know or even give a god-damn?"

DR. B: In other words, as a single girl you don't present your
bedroom to the world. You only do that by the marriage
title of "Mr. and Mrs." Now, speaking to you as a whole:
Did you notice in yourself any different feeling, depending on whether you took the position of Miss Convention
or Miss Independence?

SHE: That's hard to say.

DR. B: Which one felt more confident? In which role did you
feel more like your own self?

SHE: I think there ought to be a compromise, with sexual relations now, and marriage in the background for later.

DR. B: So there are three parts of your inner debate: conformity, independence, and compromise. Does this mean
you will press your friend for a commitment to later marriage?

SHE (*emphatic*): No! The marriage plan exists only in my
fantasy. But I do want to find out what my relationship
to my boyfriend really is! I think uncertainty is the one
problem that even Miss Independence does not like. I

want to know: Where do I stand with him? What do I mean to him? Where are we going? Because if we're not going anywhere, why not have lots of men and have real freedom and independence?

DR. B: That's being "completely free"?

SHE: That's what real independence means to me. Now when other men come on strong I feel "I should be loyal to Bob." But Miss Independence says, "Why the hell should you? Has he committed himself?" If I am only a play girl, Miss Convention gets mad and calls me bad names!

DR. B: What names? Let her speak up.

SHE: She would say I'm a fool letting myself be used by the man for his own pleasure. If I were to run around with a lot of guys she would call me *a whore!* (*Pause.*)

DR. B: Do you now want to confront your friend Bob? (*Pause.*)

SHE (*thoughtful*): Not now. I think it's my own problem. I have to think where I am as a total person; where my relationships to men fit into my life.

DR. B: This inner debate will help you. It fills in where you're going and what the implications of the various alternatives are. I think it may be helpful if you listened to the tape recording of this inner debate so far. Listen for changes in your voice and check whether your confidence, hesitation, or fluency change, depending on which part of the inner debate you're taking.

(*They listen to the tape.*)

DR. B: Which side of your inner debate sounds more confident, and more adult? Which is weaker?

SHE: Miss Independence seems to have a stronger argument than Miss Convention, but there seem to be more than two sides. Miss Independence says the relation with men should be a meaningful, close relationship whether or not one is married. Now a third side comes along and says: "What difference does it make? I can just go out and see what other guys are like!" This is a side I hadn't realized was in me before. It is a whorish side that comes out and says, "If Miss Independence isn't going to be responsible and establish a meaningful relationship with one man, I come in and let you have fun with all!"

DR. B: You let a new voice in the inner dialogue speak up, a component you call the whore in you. Is there any real chance for her to take over?

SHE: No. I think this "whore voice" brings Miss Convention and Miss Independence together. Their combined forces are saying to me: "Well, you better find out what your relationship to your boyfriend is."

DR. B: Have you then decided to explore with your boyfriend and in your own mind where you two are going?

SHE (*relaxing for the first time*): Yes, and not only in my own mind! I want to confront him and find out what he thinks of me, and where he wants to go with me.

DR. B: All right, in other words, from this debate you have learned that next time you see your boyfriend you will have a program for exploratory action. What will your program be?

SHE: I haven't decided yet, but the general idea is to say: What is our relationship? I don't think it will be done exactly in this way; it'll be more indirect. I might tell him how I feel about him and more or less leave myself wide open to bring him out to say where he stands.

DR. B: But you will probe?

SHE: Well, it's about time because I've been putting off and putting off discussing my relationship with him by saying, well, I haven't known him that long, why rush things? I may scare him off by showing that I think seriously of him, love him, and that I feel very close to him. Now I say why should I put it off? I want to know where we stand!

DR. B: You want to know what direction you're going in, so you're now ready to risk scaring him off.

SHE: That's right, it's a risk. There is a certain hesitancy. I feel I want to do it, but can I put the issue to him?

DR. B: Perhaps you need a little more inner debate about this, but certainly the debate so far has already moved you a little closer to resolving this anxiety and toward active risking, rather than passive floating.

Everybody is afflicted with commitment jitters when it comes to milestone decisions about relationships with an Intimate Other. This uneasiness tends to reach uncomfortable peaks when society is summoned to witness the ultimate commitment at the time of the marriage ceremony. Everything that happened before took place largely or wholly in private conversation. It was all words. Even getting the license was not witnessed by anybody. But now comes the show! The guests will disperse after the wedding, but they'll be back. In a year or so, they will ask the couple, directly or indirectly, "How are you doing?"

Today every marriage is a horse race and every couple knows it. The spectators all but take bets: How good will this marriage be? How long will it last? What problems will this couple have? Will they make an addition to our social circle as a married couple (instead of just one unmarried friend, the way it was before they became a unit)? It is hardly surprising that such tensions breed exhausting prewedding fights.

Precommitment battles may start in relative calm over such issues as the guest list, whether to have the wedding at home or in church, whether the ceremony should be performed by a judge or a minister. But suppose the groom then "forgets" that they planned to keep the honeymon destination secret and tells his mother where they are headed. The bride could interpret this as his first serious breach of trust. From now on his every move will be watched and weighed with extra vigilance. Who will be his best man? That slob bachelor who kept trying to talk him out of the marriage? How will the groom behave at the rehearsal? Will he be late for church? Will Daddy get along with him if he loses his temper?

Meanwhile, as in every deep crisis, the bride will question her own image: Am I going to be too fat for my dress? Will my hair *ever* look right?

All this time, everyone is supposed to act overjoyed.

Comes the wedding and the reception. The couple is scheduled to leave, but the groom is having a few drinks and is enjoying himself:

FATHER-IN-LAW: Weren't you supposed to leave a couple of hours ago?

GROOM: That's our business.

Now the couple is in the car, ready to leave. Everybody has run out of rice. But the mother of the bride is still giving her little girl last-minute instructions. Finally, Mama tears herself away. The couple is alone . . . and upset.

HE: Won't you ever be able to tell your mother off?

SHE: Don't be cross, dear.

It would be pleasant to be able to avoid such stresses at happy times. It would also be an unrealistic expectation. And unrealistic expectations are, in all likelihood, one burden which the new Mr. and Mrs. are already toting along in abundant supply in their emotional dowry as they head from the dreams of courtship into the reality of married existence. The so-called honeymoon is, contrary to the "let's make nice" tradition, a good time for partners to start weaning each other gently but firmly away from this dowry of courtship dreams.

MEMOIRS OF AN EX-PROM QUEEN (EXCERPT) *

Alix Kates Shulman

My first job after the wedding money gave out was as a bookkeeping machine operator in a Wall Street bank at sixty dollars a week.   As Frank forbade me to be a waitress, and I dreaded being a salesgirl, there was little else for a twenty-one-year-old nontypist to do.   Without typing I was chronically "overqualified."   Without typing I couldn't even wangle interviews for the jobs listed in the *Help Wanted Female* section under *College Grad,* nor could I apply for the nontyping researcher, editor, or "trainee" jobs for which I supposed I was suited, listed under *Help Wanted Male.*

My bookkeeping machine (Burroughs F212) was formidable. I named her Trixie.   The work was taxing, but I liked the precision of it and, eager to master her, found a certain excitement in striking my balance at the end of each day.   Until our debits and credits balanced exactly, until every decimal error had been discovered and rooted out, Mr. Calley, the department supervisor, would not permit his girls to go home.   After my last deposit had been entered and the last check deducted, I would extract the subtotals, totals, and grand totals the machine had been storing up all day, push certain magic buttons, let the circuits run, and with suspended breath wait for Trixie to end her calculations and reveal in a small window on her face and printed on the record on her back two numbers which, if I had posted everything correctly all day long, would exactly, digit for digit, match.   Even my disappointment when the numbers differed was exhilarating.

At first I was slow in balancing, never passing a day without error.   Sometimes it was seven o'clock before I descended into the West Side IRT subway station with my book in hand, and almost eight before I surfaced again near Columbia.   But by attending to Trixie, setting myself records to beat and techniques to master, I gradually improved my performance until I was as good on my Burroughs as anyone.   And as though the suspense

* From MEMOIRS OF AN EX–PROM   Alix Kates Shulman.   Reprinted by
  QUEEN, by Alix Kates Shulman.   permission of Alfred A. Knopf, Inc.
  Copyright © 1969, 1971, 1972 by

were not intoxicating enough, the clattering of fifty cumbersome calculators all totaling at once in a single room provided me with a sense of solidarity against disaster I had never before felt in New York City.

It was broken only by a fifteen-minute morning coffee break, when I made eyes at New York out the window, and a precious solitary hour for lunch. At lunchtime I explored the caverns of Wall Street, thrilled that I, Ohio-born and twenty-one, was living among skyscrapers and traditions. I saw where the Stock Exchange had been scarred in the twenties by anarchist bombs; I ate hamburgers with college educations. I heard actors rehearsing in lofts, saw pushcart markets, tasted Indian curries and baklava, listened to choruses singing Bach in Trinity Church at noon. When the weather was fine, I took a sandwich to Battery Park, on the very tip of Manhattan Island. There, watching the ferries and tugs and cruise ships passing in the harbor, I fancied myself a boy joining one of the crews sailing off to Jamaica or Barbados or even the distant source of all mental and sensual goodies, Europe. When the weather was foul, I sat in the lounge and read my book, still hopeful of one day knowing everything. Only at night when I returned to Frank who, having polished off yet another tome toward his degree, was ready to help me out cooking our dinner in time for the news—only then did I know that neither would happen.

Not that Frank was to blame. Hardly. I had no doubt he felt almost as bad as I that I was no longer a student. Hadn't he married me half for my brains? No, I alone was to blame for being too tired to study at night and too distractable to read anything but fiction on the subway in the morning. And when I wanted to go to the movies in the evening or walk in Central Park on a weekend afternoon, Frank was too much the gentleman to allude to my lapsed ambitions. He intended no invidious comparisons as he said, "Look, I'd really rather stay home and work. I've got too much reading to do. But why don't you go on without me? You'll relax, and I'll be able to use the time." I felt guilty even asking him to interrupt his work, and didn't blame him for wishing me out of the way. My restlessness was not the easiest thing for a scholar to live with.

So I went off with a neighbor, or a friend from work who lived in the Village and introduced me to pot, or alone. And sometimes, in the huge Grant's Cafeteria on Broadway, or in the back section of the Thalia Theater, where I sat watching foreign films—sometimes I looked for Prince Charming, just in case he too happened to be out alone catching a breath of air or taking in a movie.

"Miss Raybel? Or is it Mrs. Raybel? "

"Mrs. Raybel."

"Mrs. Raybel, it has come to our attention that you are a college graduate," said the personnel manager, an elderly gentleman dressed by Brooks Brothers.

What could he want? Mr. Calley, the bookkeeping department supervisor, patting me kindly on the rear, had assured me, sending me down here, that I was not to be fired.

"In that case, we are going to offer you a promotion. We are prepared to transfer you to the Foreign Department at a starting salary of seventy-five dollars a week," he beamed.

"Doing what? " I asked.

"Translating."

I swallowed my surprise. French, my only foreign language, had always been my worst subject. "Translating what? " I asked.

"Letters, documents, letters of credit."

I knew I couldn't manage it, but the raise was substantial. "What languages? " I asked.

"You'll translate from all the languages into English, French, Spanish, German, Italian. Not Chinese," he smiled.

I nodded. What difference did it make whether I was unable to translate from one language or many? "My German may need a bit of brushing up," I offered.

"Oh, don't worry. You're a college graduate. You'll pick it up," he said. "We have some real foreigners up there to help you out. How's your typing? "

Real foreigners. Spanish sailors with bearded lips; Italians; German philosopher-refugees. "Pretty good," I lied, praying to be spared the humiliation of a typing test.

"Fine. You can start on Monday, then. Report to me first thing Monday morning, and I'll take you up to Foreign and introduce you around."

"Thank you."

"Good day."

We shook hands, and I returned to Bookkeeping to say goodbye to the women in the department and try one last time for perfect on Trixie.

At a party over the weekend I became acutely sensitive to the ubiquitous married *we:*

"*We* love Indian music."

"*We* were shocked to hear about Artie."

"*We* thought from the review *we* would love the new production of *Whim,* but *we* walked out at intermission, *we* found it so bad."

When Frank used it about me, I shouted before everyone, "Speak for yourself!"

It puzzled him, because the statement in which the offending word occurred was unobjectionable; in fact, true. But I felt misrepresented by it anyway. Trapped, suffocating in that abysmal *we.*

I lasted less than a month in the Foreign Department. A flirtation begun with the man at the next desk (a Wharton graduate on the Executive Training Squad whose assistant I was) ended abruptly when he was transferred to another branch. Once he was gone, I was ashamed of ever having taken up with him, even for a lunchtime diversion.

Nothing was working out. Frank had bought me a five-language commercial dictionary at the University Bookstore, and I studied German by listening to the *Threepenny Opera* sung in the original German. The singer, Lotte Lenya, the composer's extraordinary wife, became my new inspiration. I bought all her records. Most of her songs were about a prostitute, Jenny, who refused to be trampled on. *"Wenn einer tritt, dann bin ich es"*—"if somebody's to do the stepping, it'll be me." After work and the dinner dishes, I would sit listening to her songs, following the record jacket translation of the lyrics, memorizing Lenya's strange inflections. Sometimes I was moved to tears singing along with her, sometimes to fury. Even Frank peered suspiciously over his glasses when Lenya and I sang the one in which Jenny gets to decide who in the city shall be spared and who shall be killed (a fantasy twice removed, and doubly safe). *Kill them all,* says Jenny—*alle!* And when the heads roll, she says *Hoppla!*

But it was the wrong German for the bank, and even the dictionary was of little use. The job turned out to be a typing job after all, and they were bound to discover I couldn't type. I wondered if they would fire me before I quit, or if I would just stop going to work one day. The prospect of being fired was depressing, but there was unemployment to collect if I stuck it out. I didn't care; it was time to start exploring another section of the city anyway.

When Frank learned that he was to receive the coveted Haversham Ellis History Fellowship for the following year, he broke precedent and called me at the office.

"Hey, that's great, Frankilee!" I said, using his mother's diminutive.

"How about celebrating?" he said. "I'll meet you downtown after work."

It was an assistantship, far too prestigious for him to turn down. But it hardly paid enough to live on. Come September it would be his turn to work and mine to study according to our master plan, but that was obviously out of the question now.

I maintained a firm silence through both martinis, concentrating on the bartender's art. For me to be anything but supportive was perverse. I could certainly not be so selfish as to act out my "neurosis" and sabotage what was going to be an exceptional career. Self-destructive, too, since Frank's success would carry me up with him. If I could not be content with his success, the least I could do was wait, or state my terms. After all, I was still young. (Young!) My turn was coming. There were many dissertation widows at Columbia: none of them complained.

I tried to be gracious as we moved to a booth to map out our future. Publications and professorships, sabbaticals and grants to study abroad. The gates were open. Applying for the right grants with care would get us anywhere Frank chose to go.

"I hope you realize," I said at last, for the record, "I'm not moving out of New York City for any professorship, except maybe to Europe." I chastised myself for my failure of enthusiasm, but I no longer cared what Frank thought of me. Bitch? Okay. I could just see myself pouring tea at, say, New England University. Sasha Raybel, faculty wife.

"Don't worry," said Frank with his wry condemning smile, "no one would dream of asking *you* to make any sacrifices."

IT *

Donald E. Westlake

WHEN THE ALARM CLOCK woke Ralph Stewart that morning, there was a diaphragm in the bed. Karen's, of course. Looking at it, Ralph wondered if she knew it was no longer with her. No, probably not. Had the week at her mother's made her forgetful?

From the kitchen, Karen called, "Ralph! You getting up?"

"Sure, sure," Ralph said. He sat there, looking at it. She must think it was still with her. When she discovered it was gone, what a moment *that* would be.

"Ralph! Breakfast is ready and you're going to be late for work!"

"Sure, sure." Chuckling to himself, Ralph wrapped it in a Kleenex and tucked it away in the drawer of the night table on Karen's side. Then he padded off to brush his teeth.

. . .

After a week away, Karen was pleased to be back in her own kitchen again, though that wasn't what made her smile as she waited for Ralph to come in for breakfast. She was imagining the look on Ralph's face when he'd seen it lying there in the bed. At first she'd thought of peeking around the bedroom doorway to see what he'd do next, but he might have seen her and that would have spoiled the effect. Besides, it was even better this way, wondering what would be the first thing he'd say when he came through the kitchen door.

He came through the kitchen door. He said, "I'm starved."

Not a word from him during breakfast. He kissed her goodbye, said, "See you at six," grabbed his briefcase and ran.

Hadn't he seen it? She went into the bedroom and looked in the bed and it was gone. That was strange. He *had* found it, but he hadn't said a word about it. And he'd taken it away with him. Karen paled. Could it be? But there was no other explanation.

She'd been away for a week and Ralph must have thought it belonged to *somebody else.*

Who?

.   .   .

Ralph came into the apartment a little after six with a small smile already tugging at his lips.   What would she say?

She said, "Oh, there you are."   Coldly.

Chipper as a cricket, Ralph said, "Anything happen today, hon?"

"Nothing much," she said.   Coldly.

All evening, Ralph waited for her to say something, and she never did.   Also, there was a definite chill in the air, a definite chill.   Ralph began to feel irritated, both because his joke seemed to have fallen flat and because Karen was acting very distant, for some reason.   At ten o'clock, they had a sudden flare-up over whether to watch the spy show on channel two or the special about the Verrazano-Narrows Bridge on channel four.   Voices weren't raised, but anger quivered in their tones, and one or two cutting remarks were exchanged.   Ultimately, Ralph went down to the Kozy Korner and watched the spy show there.

When he got home, Karen was already in bed and asleep, or at least appearing to be asleep.   Ralph slid between the sheets and lay there a long while, staring at the ceiling.   She had never mentioned it.   Also, she was acting very cold and distant, for no good reason at all.   He'd been trying to avoid the thought, but as far as he could see, there was only one explanation.   She must think she'd lost it *somewhere else.*

Where?

.   .   .

After Ralph left for work the next morning, slamming the apartment door behind him, Karen sat at the kitchen table and cried for a quarter of an hour.   The argument over breakfast had been the most violent of their four years of marriage.   Ralph had said some things—

But one thing in particular, one unforgivable thing in particular.   To bring up Howie Youngblood again after all these years, to bring up an incident that had happened when she was very young and innocent, and it had been a college weekend, and she hadn't even *known* Ralph then, and she'd told him everything about it even before they were married, and to bring that up now, to throw it in her face like that, was unforgivable.

Of course, she knew why he was doing it. Trying to justify his own actions, that's all. She wondered if it could be that girl at Ralph's office, that Linda Sue Powers. Ralph very rarely mentioned her anymore, and when Karen had thrown the name out at breakfast that morning, Ralph had seemed to hesitate, as though maybe he felt guilty about something.

When Grace from down the hall came in for their usual mid-morning coffee, Karen said to her, "Grace, sometimes a person needs a trusted friend, someone she can talk to."

"Oh, Karen, you know me," Grace said, looking bright and alert. "Silent as the tomb."

So Karen told her everything. Except about putting it in the bed, of course; that was too personal and silly and hardly important anymore, anyway.

. . .

It was the first time Ralph had taken Linda Sue Powers to lunch. "I don't know why I should bother you with my troubles," he said, "We're hardly more than office acquaintances."

"Oh, I hope you think of me as more than *that,*" she said. She had very nice blue eyes. "I hope you think of me as your *friend,*" she said.

"I'd like to," Ralph said. And before he was done, he'd told her everything. Except about finding it in the bed, of course; that was unimportant by now and not the sort of thing to mention to a young lady.

. . .

The fight at the Culbertsons' party was just the climax to five weeks of border skirmishes and commando raids. The fight, which took place in front of 18 exceedingly interested spectators, lasted 20 minutes and culminated this way:

Karen: "And I suppose *you* haven't spent every night the past two weeks with that Powers woman?"

Ralph: *"Evening,* you filthy-minded bitch, *evening,* not night; we've been working at the *office.* And its left *you* plenty of time to howl, hasn't it?"

Karen: "Ralph, I want a divorce I want a divorce I want a *divorce!"*

Ralph: "Divorce? The way you carry on, I could practically get an annulment!"

.   .   .

The lawyer said, "We always require at least this one meeting between the principals, to see if any sort of reconciliation is possible. You two are both intelligent people; maybe this marriage can still be saved. What caused the estrangement, can you tell me that? What started it?"

Karen said, "I suppose it all started with Linda Sue Powers."

Ralph said, "I believe the name my wife is looking for is Howie Youngblood."

The lawyer had to shout and pound on his desk before they'd quiet down.

.   .   .

After the divorce, they met one last time at the apartment to divide up their possessions, neither trusting the other to go in first and alone. Ralph arrived with Linda Sue Powers. Karen brought along a pipe-smoking chap she didn't introduce.

They moved through the apartment together, their escorts waiting in uncomfortable silence in the living room, the principals talking in monosyllables as they said, "That's yours," or "I'll take that," or, "You can throw that out if you want." There were no arguments now, no squabbles, no rousing of passion. When they got to the night table, Karen opened the drawer. "So *that's* where you put it," she said, taking it out and unwrapping the Kleenex.

"A joke," he said. He sounded faintly bitter.

She nodded. "I know," she said. "I put it in the bed for a joke."

"You did?"

She frowned at the drawer. "And you—"

Then they looked at each other and they both understood; and for just a second, something very much like hope sprang up in their eyes. But then Karen shook her head and said, "No. There are things you said to me—"

Ralph said, "You accused me of some things—"

Karen said, "And there's that woman out there."

"Talking with that smokestack of yours."

They looked away from each other, their faces set. "Well," said Karen. She turned and threw it into the wastebasket.

Ralph said, "Aren't you going to take it with you?"

"I've got a new one," she said.

MARITAL LOVE AND HATE (EXCERPT) *

Israel Charny

So far, we have been reluctantly yielding to the fact of aggressiveness as a sadly inescapable quality of existence. However, the fact is that there are some aspects of aggressiveness that are really quite positive. We tend to forget these because so often aggressiveness ends up in destructive expressions that are so devastating that we naturally fear the very sources of such power without realizing that much aggressiveness can be constructive in its nature.

Thus, Coser, a sociologist, has pointed out how from a larger point of view of social organization aggression plays at least three positive functions: as a form of achievement as in the violence of revolutions against oppression; as a danger signal— a good example in our own time would be the demonstrations of American Negroes; and as a catalyst.[1]

In biological life, we have learned that aggression plays key *life-serving* roles in survival of the fittest (the basic Darwinian concept, of course); also for spacing out or apportioning territory to the species; also as a tonic for the stimulation and effecting of the whole symphony of drives; and even as a basis for the evolution of a bond of affiliativeness—and love.[2]

This last function of aggression is especially remarkable for our purposes. It is fantastic to see that only among those animals who show significant aggression within their species does there also evolve a love bonding; that without hating-killing there is no emerging counterpoint of loving. Shades of human lovers!

In psychological affairs, too, we have increasing evidence of the significance of aggressiveness as a life force; its absence marks weakness, lack of energy for projecting oneself, lack of stamina for creativity, lack of zest for recovery from emotional problems.

Aggressiveness is the hum of life, the spirit of being.

This has long been understood in popular, instinctive psychology: We are forever curiously gauging another man's real

* Reprinted with permission from
the author and *Family Process* 8
(March, 1969): 17–22.

strength by the vitality of his bearing and manner. In projec-
tive test studies of people, we look for indications of drive and
affect strength.

In treatment of various serious emotional disorders and mental illness, we find so often not only an excess of anger that is
burning up the person himself, but an excess that in many ways
is built on a basis of improper release or utilization of the natural
aggression one needs for successful living. Much of the treatment process is intended to teach people how to feel anger, and
share their anger with their family and associates without fearing that their anger will in fact destroy another.

In treatment of various sexual disorders, we frequently find
fears of one's aggression inhibiting the flow of sexual vigor; in
treatment an effort is made to help people be angry at the very
person they love and desire; also, on another level, to be physically penetrating and vigorous towards their sexual partner.

This last point is particularly significant for our consideration
of the marital relationship. For it reminds us that in the corner-
stone area of the basic sexual contract of marriage there is to be
a never-ending aggressiveness—a never-ending fusion of anger
with loving feeling. It is surprising that we have been so long
in coming to an extrapolation of this principle to the broader
range of the marital relationship; that the couple who can hate
each other *and* love each other may stay together, with some
real satisfaction no less, for all that they too must indeed endure many painful low points and troubling unsure experiences
of bitterness with each other.

Let us consider specifically some of the positive values of aggressiveness in the marital union:

1. Our spouse is a colleague, critic, teacher, and supervisor.

2. Our spouse is a reacting, stimulating, catalyzing force,
often irritating and provocative perhaps, but challenging us to
be more wise and creative.

3. From what we know of the structure of marriages, given
the particular characteristic of most marital unions as involving
people who differ quite dramatically on certain key psychological
characteristics, there is the possibility of each partner teaching
the other those qualities in which the one partner is quite strong
and in which the second partner is particularly weak.

A simple example is that the fair young maid who is socially
more comfortable and winning may be able to bolster the shakier,

more socially withdrawing man to dare experiment with becoming more winning socially. Since the oppositeness of people often also implies a degree of extremeness even on the part of the mate who seems blessed with the more positive side of a trait, conflict between spouses may also help reduce the too-good extreme. Thus, the sociable lady may also be a person who is too driven to socialize; and in conflict with a mate who tends to be more withdrawn but also possibly more given to inner depth, she may learn to quiet down, and search for more inner value in her interpersonal relationships.

4. An even more subtle but we believe important point about the oppositeness of marriage partners is that by and large we know that underneath whatever extreme is represented in the overt stance of a human being, there is so often an unconscious oppositeness in that person himself. In the conflicting interchange between mates, there is also a struggle around these unconscious opposites and hopefully, if the marriage struggle moves along constructively, there is also change developing on this level of the secret emotional understructure of each spouse.

For example, take the generally fair mate and the characteristically unfair mate in fights. The one generally seeks to pacify and to be reasonable. The other generally attacks and carries on as an unrelenting "hawk." Yet, often we find deep in the hawk considerable fairness and sensitivity; and in the fairer, more righteous fate, so often underneath there is a heck of a lot of unreasonable anger.

5. There is often value in a clash of forces insofar as it creates energy.

We now take for granted the miraculous physics of electrical potential as it involves plus and minus elements. So too may it be that the interplay of complementary qualities within us as individuals produces the energy of a search for a balanced expression of ourselves. And so too does the clash of various levels of difference and oppositeness between peoples such as a couple in marriage produce energy, vitality, zest, and power for life, for them and for their children stimulated by this environment.

Needless to say, if the wires are uninsulated, or if the amount of electricity transmitted is excessive for the wiring, or if you're standing in a puddle when you touch the hot wire, or if you do any of the other kinds of things that are wrong when you're dealing with electricity, you can burn yourself up! But if you learn to tap the energy, wire it, channel it appropriately to its goal points for activating other machinery, create on and off switches, circuit breakers, dimmers and whatnot, then there is the possibility of getting to a more creative state precisely because you do have power machinery working for you, and not just your own old hand tools!

The "How" of Marital Fighting and Loving

This is not the place for an extensive discussion of how couples might love and hate well. Interested readers are referred to a more popular presentation of this paper in which there is a fuller discussion of working "Principles for Survival in the Inferno".[3]

Some techniques and attitudes for marital fighting are these:

1.   It is natural and right to feel anger.

2.   There is much to be gained from learning how to fight with one's spouse openly, saying what we feel but not promiscuously, sharing our angers, but not overwhelming one another.

3.   It is very much wrong to hurt another person overtly, in *acts* against the other's person, but to *feel* like hurting another is a natural expression of anger.

4.   Feelings are not the same as actions; our feelings of anger in no way really punish or hurt the other party in a literal sense.

5.   Husbands and wives are far better off when they learn that in the course of marital fighting a good deal of unfairness, exaggeration, and extremes is natural.

6.   Our minds operate much like computers searching through all the accumulated data for just what we want to say; in a good, heated marital fight the machinery tries out many bits, including such part-truths or truths-of-the-moment as "I wish I had never married you." We should not believe that anything our rival spouse says is *fully* intended or the *whole* truth of his feelings, nor should we believe anything we think of is the full measure of what we feel and believe.

7.   For one's own sake, above all, and then too for the sake of one's children and for one's spouse, it is all to one's good to be committed increasingly to stay with one's marriage if at all possible—to work hard at reducing undue pain and at gaining the best this union can grow to create. Such commitment offers a sense of security and meaning to oneself and to one's family, especially when the going gets rough, as it always does.

8. Even when we hate, we love. Even the moments filled with our bitterest hate contain our love at one and the same time. How good to know this before one acts too strongly and realizes too late the damage done a person and a relationship one loves very much. An excellent emotional exercise in the heat of marital battle is to conjure up (silently! for Macys doesn't really tell Gimbels!) just how much one cares for one's now quite-hated-spouse; so as to experience one's hate and love as coexisting streams of feeling.

9. We would be wise to feel grateful for the stimulation of confrontations and challenges by our spouse.

10. Never fight in front of the children? On the contrary, fight fairly often in front of the children!, but fight wisely and well. The trick is not to put anger away so much as to show the children that when anger is experienced, it does not destroy either party, it is not acted out in overt violence, and that even certain regressive fighting behaviors that the parents allow themselves in the somewhat greater privacy of their away-from-the-children fighting are put aside out of respect for the child to whom they both are loyal.

There is much more to be said and much to be learned about effective marital fighting. As noted previously, at this writing we have been promised a major work is forthcoming from Bach, who has previously reported on his teaching couples how to fight as the key focus of his group therapy approach to marital disorders.[4] In general, we would suggest that the *how* of marital fighting and loving will yet be worked out through the efforts of many family researchers. The critical point of the hour, we have felt, is the need for a theory of marriage that acknowledges once and for all that marital fighting is inevitable, necessary, and desirable—not simply an unhappy byproduct of emotional immaturity or disturbance. The latter make for ineffective and immature fighting, or for a suppression of fighting with all their marriage-shattering consequences, but not for the fighting *per se* that is the legacy of all of us Adams and Eves.

A FINAL PERSPECTIVE: MARRIAGE AS A SMALL SCALE
BATTLEGROUND OF MAN'S CHOICES OF WAR OR PEACE

A final thought for twentieth century couples: In our marriages each of us is given a chance to participate in a worldwide and mankind-wide panorama of choices as to whether or not each man will allow his aggressiveness to mount into destructive, warring forms, or whether each of us will learn to feel angry and aggressive in *feelings* but not in violent destructive *action*.

In each marriage the choice is not between happiness and unhappiness, but between a respectful, cooperative state of nonviolent tension, where quite often we must experience anger though often we may also enjoy a more positive, empathizing, love; or a state of increasingly violent, demoralizing, depersonalizing destruction of one or another. And so it is in all of our universe that we must face as collective groups of people learning how to live with our differences, expecting there will be disagreements all the time and much anger, but learning how to create a lawful machinery for the expression and resolution of these differences, rather than succumbing to the age-old impulses to destroy and be destroyed.

OPEN MARRIAGE: A SYNERGIC MODEL *

NENA O'NEILL AND GEORGE O'NEILL

In the wake of increasing dissatisfaction with the prevailing pattern of traditional monogamous marriage, a number of alternative marriage styles have begun to emerge. These experimentations vary from those involving more than three persons in the basic pattern and include group marriage, communal life styles, and polygamous patterns (more often triadic, and more often polygynous rather than polyandrous) to modifications in the basic one-to-one monogamous configuration. This last group may be divided into those which are nonmarriage relationships (still monogamous but extra-legal) and those which represent innovations, changes, deletions, and additions to the standard expectations for those legally married. These modifications may include such various items as separate domiciles, extramarital sexual relations in group or partner-exchange contexts, or reversal of traditional role patterns; i. e., woman provides, man housekeeps. None of these patterns are particularly new in transcultural contexts since all have occurred elsewhere in other societies at one time or another. However, their proliferation and the motives which have impelled men and women in our society to increasingly seek innovations in our marriage style deserve closer scrutiny.

It is not enough to say that society is pluralistic and that these alternate patterns for marriage have appeared in response to the changes in our society and the development of different life styles. Even though one can foresee a future in which there is a range of marriage patterns to choose from, the questions still remain: Why have so many experimental forms appeared? And more important, what are the personal motivations for seeking these innovative styles? Compendiums of sociological explanations seemed somehow to pass over the personal dimensions involved. Yet these questions are exceedingly important for the future especially since that future will affect our styles of child-rearing and thus the perpetuation of those values we deem most humanistic and worthy of saving. Even excluding experimental family forms, Sussman has pointed out that even today some children may live in numerous variant forms of the traditional nuclear family dur-

* Reprinted from *The Family Co-ordinator*, October, 1972, pp. 403–409, by permission of the authors and the National Council on Family Relations.

ing their formative stages.[1]   Under these conditions some changes in our value system are to be expected.   The questions are which values and how many?

With the above questions in mind we began to explore contemporary marriage in 1967.*   The authors' interviews began first with those who were involved in experimental structures and in the greatest variations from the norm in traditional marriage.   It was felt that these innovators would have greater insight because they had already opted for change, and that they would perhaps be more articulate and perceptive about why they had chosen change.   The interviewers then moved on to the divorced, the non-marrieds,** the singles, the young, and to those who were either disillusioned or contented with traditional monogamous marriage.   As research was carried out in a primarily middle class setting, Cuber and Harroff's delineations of types of marriage relationships (i. e., conflict-habituated, devitalized, passive-congenial, the vital, and the total) gained increasing validity.[2]   During the research in the anthropological literature it was found that little

* In developing the concept of open marriage, the authors interviewed approximately 400 persons from 1967 to 1971. Informant respondents were 17 to 75 years of age, urban and suburban middle class in orientation and occupation, and approximately 75 percent were married or had been married. Thirty interviews, both formal and informal, with professional therapists and marriage counselors supplemented this data. The interviews included individual and couple in-depth sessions (frequently tape recorded), discussion in group settings, and short mini-interviews in a variety of social settings. While some topical and background questions were used (i. e., age, occupation, marital status, etc.: "What do you think the ingredients of a good marriage are?"), the interviews were primarily open-ended and exploratory in nature, focusing on eliciting information through face to face encounter, about values, feelings and attitudes toward marriage and changes they perceived as necessary for improvement.

** The term nonmarrieds applies to those relationships in which there is some commitment but which are not legalized. They can range in time from a few months to a life time. Premarital is an accurate term for only a portion of these relationships since some never intend to marry the nonmarriage partner, or the relationship is frequently considered only a temporary plateau before each has the sustaining personal resources to move on to another level, or another person. Formerly marrieds would probably comprise a separate category. The word cohabitation is also misleading as a coverall term for these relationships. Since cohabitation implies both a shared domicile and sex without legal marriage, it did not apply to some relationships encountered, e. g., a couple who did not share a domicile but did form a cohesive unit insofar as they shared all their spare time, vacations, and sex, and presented themselves as a couple in social situations. Therefore, the term nonmarriage relationship is suggested.

attention had been given to the interpersonal dimension of marriage or to the interrelation of the intrapsychic and ideological aspects of marriage.   However, it was felt that the anthropological perspective gave a holistic approach to the problems of contemporary marriage that was considered valuable.   While cultural ideologies and prescriptions for marriage behavior persisted, value orientation and actual behavior were changing, thus creating confusion for many.

THE PROBLEM

As exploratory insights to the problems evolved, the authors became increasingly convinced that the central problem in contemporary marriage was relationship.   The attempt to solve the problem by moving into group and communal situations did not seem to mitigate the problems we discovered in interpersonal relationships.   With the breakdown of many external supports for traditional marriage, the pressures on the interpersonal husband-and-wife relationship became intensified.   There was a need for that relationsip to provide more fulfillment and benefits both on a personal and interpersonal level.   Problems in marriage were manifested by the inability of the majority of individuals to find in the marital relationship both intimacy and opportunlty for developing their personal potential.   Understanding of the problem concluded in addition that:

1) Marital partners and those contemplating marriage expressed a need for intimacy and growth in a relationship where they could actualize their individual potential without destroying the relationship.

2) Most people did not have the skills in relating and in communication which would allow for growth in a noncritical atmosphere.   The typical dyadic marital role relationships had already been precut for them.   They were locked into a negative involuted feedback system.   This was their perception of their situation as well, although not with the same terminology.

3) Many of the innovations and experimental forms, although not all of them or all of the people involved in them, were a reflection and indication of this lack of skills in interpersonal relations.

4) Other important impediments to growth were the unrealistic expectations and myths stemming from the traditional mar-

riage format of the past, in particular, overriding emotional dependencies, and possessive jealousy.

This left us as the observers and researchers with the options of reporting the alternate styles with their attendant disillusionments and problems, or of choosing another path in utilizing the research. While one can catalogue all the sociological and technological forces that are contributing factors to the breakdown of marriage and the family, it offers little in the way of ameliorating the problems each individual faces when he comes to grips on an interpersonal basis with the old mores and patterns of institutions that have not changed, while his needs and the external socio-cultural conditions affecting his behavior *have* changed. Therefore, the authors chose to present a model for personal change and value reorientation that individuals could utilize on an interpersonal basis within their own marital situation.

The Action Model

The concept of open marriage, which is outlined elsewhere in detail,[3] is primarily based on the expression of desires for change and the perceived routes to change drawn from the interviews conducted over a period of four years and upon the actual changes already made in many relationships that were observed. The research conducted was utilized to create a model for change. In so doing the authors have stepped beyond the role of objective researcher reporting the data and findings into the realm of what can be termed action anthropology: that is, delineating a model for change by placing the problem areas in their cultural context. An attempt has been made to present the traditional marital configuration in its societal setting and to delineate the cultural imperatives and values implicit in these imperatives for examination by those involved in marriage relationships. The purpose, then, is to make it possible for individuals to become aware of the idealized precepts of the institution of marriage and the forces influencing their attitude toward, and their behavior in, marriage. Without an awareness of the present conditions, they cannot perceive the pathways to change. It is to be fully understood that some will choose to remain within traditional marriage where the perimeters and dimensions are defined for them by the norms. But for those who feel a need for change, awareness and insight are a necessary first step to determining or discovering what pathways are available.

Action anthropology is a variation on the theme of action research. In the past, action research has been associated with institutional or organizational change directed toward finding solutions to organizational or social problems.[4] The flow has been from the institutional level down to the individual in effecting change. More recently it has been recognized that individuals can initiate measures for change and reverse the flow to effect change on the institutional level. Weinberg has noted that this is a problem-solving, action-oriented society, and continues:

> On this action level, society and the person are both symbolic systems with varying capacities for solving problems. Both society and the person can respond to problems in terms of their knowledge and their capacity for decision making and executive knowledge. Both can communicate, plan, and implement programs to solve problems . . . . The individual deliberates about alternatives before selecting a problem-solving response.[5]

Today, the orientation toward methods of change must begin with the individual. The need for a measure of self-determination is paramount. Yet the individual is frequently overlooked as a primary force for change, the assumption being that his behavior is shaped by impinging social forces in the environment and that he has neither sufficient knowledge and perspective to perceive these forces, nor is adequately equipped to institute directive and self-motivated change. This attitude underestimates the individual. The sample encompassed a broad range of middle class informant-respondents. The majority expressed a desire for some feeling of self-determination and autonomy in their lives and marriage behavior. Many had already instituted it. Furthermore, most had a knowledge of what the problem areas were in marriage.

One quote is offered from an interview with a 23-year-old single woman, who was at that time in a nonmarriage relationship with a young man and seriously contemplating marriage:

> I don't want to say yes, yes we are going to be in love forever. It's like saying, yes, yes you know the ocean— and the next wave is going to look like this one, but I *can* say it is worth the risk *if* I feel I can do something about it. I want to be understanding, and start out with the attitude of, well it ain't going to be bliss but if I do

my homework I stand a very good chance, and knowing
what the chances are and stepping into it with your eyes
open, you got a chance of making your marriage work
. . . and there is a lot more homework to do today because people have to make decisions they never had to
make before in marriage, but those marriages will be better for it . . . it's not I'm doing this because I've
got to do it, it's doing this because I *chose* to do it, and
that's what it is, man is a thinking animal, therefore I
am. Once you get down to this kind of foundation and
you can build, you know, 'well begun is half done.'

THE OPEN MARRIAGE MODEL

Open marriage is presented as a model with a two-fold purpose:

1) To provide insights for individuals concerning the past patterns of traditional marriage, which has been termed closed marriage. Based on closed systems model, traditional marriage was
perceived as presenting few options for choice or change.

2) To provide guidelines, through an open systems model, for
developing an intimate marital relationship that would provide
for growth for both partners in the context of a one-to-one relationship. This does imply some degree of mutuality. It does
not imply that growth will always be bilateral, but rather that
there will be supportive assistance and tolerance during unilateral growth. Shostrom and Kavanaugh have delineated the
rhythmic relationship which best exemplifies this pattern.[6]
These guidelines have been designed in answer to the needs expressed by the majority of our informant-respondents for a relationship which could offer them more dimensions for growth
together than either could attain singly. The principle through
which this mutually augmenting growth occurs is synergy.
Many couples found that this synergistic self-actualizing mode
of relating became possible only through the revision and dele-
tion of some of the expectations of closed marriage.

Open marriage can then be defined as a relationship in which
the partners are committed to their own and to each other's
growth. Supportive caring and increasing security in individual
identities makes possible the sharing of self-growth with a meaningful other who encourages and anticipates his own and his
mate's growth. It is a relationship which is flexible enough to
allow for change, which is constantly being renegotiated in the

light of changing needs, consensus in decision making, in tolerance of individual growth, and in openness to new possibilities *for* growth. Obviously, following this model often involves a departure, sometimes radical, from rigid conformity to the established husband-wife roles and is not easy to effect.

In brief, the guidelines are: living for now, realistic expectations, privacy, role flexibility, open and honest communication, open companionship, equality, identity, and trust. The first step is for partners to reassess the marriage relationship they are in, or anticipate, in order to reevaluate expectations for themselves and for their partner. Couples in today's society are not educated for marriage or the requisites of a good human relationship, nor are they aware of the psychological and myriad other commitments that the typical marriage contract implies. The expectations of closed marriage—the major one being that the partner will be able to fulfill all of the other's needs (emotional, social, sexual, economic, intellectual, and otherwise)— present obstacles to growth and attitudes that foster conflict between partners. Awareness of these expectations and a realignment more in accord with a realistic appraisal of their capabilities are fundamental to instituting change and to solving their problems in relationship.

Living for now involves relating in the present rather than in terms of the past or in terms of the future goals which are frequently materialistic and concrete rather than emotional and intellectual in nature. The granting of time off, or privacy, can be used for examination of the self and for psychic regeneration. A way out of what many marital partners conceive as the role-bind involves working toward a greater role flexibility both in terms of switching roles temporarily or on a part-time basis, and as a therapeutic device for understanding the self and the position of the other partner. Open and honest communication is perhaps the most important element in an open relationship. The lack of communication skills creates a formidable barrier between husband and wife, yet these skills are the most important in sustaining a vital relationship, promoting understanding, and in increasing knowledge of self. Open companionship involves relating to others, including the opposite sex, outside the primary unit of husband and wife, as an auxiliary avenue for growth. Equality involves relating to the mate as a peer in terms of ways to achieve stature rather than through the status attached to husband and wife roles. Identity involves the development of the individual through interaction with mate and others and through actualizing his own potentials. Trust, growing through the utilization of these other guidelines and based on mutuality and respect, creates a climate for growth. Liking, respect, sexual intimacy, and love grow through the exercise of these elements.

Each progressive guideline becomes increasingly abstract. The system can be seen as an expanding spiral of evolving steps in complexity and depth in the marital relationship. The system operates through the principle of synergy, a concept drawn from medicine and chemistry, first utilized by Benedict in cultural, and later by Maslow in interpersonal contexts.[7, 8] In open marriage, the concept of *synergic build-up* is defined as a mutually augmenting growth system. Synergy means that two partners in marriage can accomplish more personal and interpersonal growth together than they could separately without the loss of their individual identities. Synergic build-up defines the positive augmenting feedback that can enhance mutual growth.

While only a limited few may be able to utilize all these guidelines in their totality and simultaneously, open marriage would best be considered a resource mosaic from which couples can draw according to their needs and their readiness for change in any one area.

The majority of the sample had already explored the possibilities for change in some of the areas covered by the guidelines. Many of these reflected only a change in attitude, while behavorial changes were acknowledged as difficult. The two areas of greatest difficulty were the conflicts arising from changing man-woman and husband-wife roles and the problems encountered in self-development.

The question of marital and extramarital sexual behavior, while ever-present, did not seem to be the central problem with which they were coping. While marital sex sometimes presented problems, many felt that the emphasis on sexual adjustment, in terms of manuals and the media, was exaggerated. Although many felt that they could not cope with sexual jealousy in terms of extramarital sex, they were on the verge of deciding that sex *per se* was not their central problem in the marriage. Numerous couples had already effected some degree of sexual latitude in their own relationships. Some had done so with tacit knowledge but without verbalized agreement. Others had done so in

various types of consensual arrangements, including group sex
and partner exchange. While some benefits were noted, it was
observed that by and large these experiences did not occur in a
context where the marital partners were developing their primary marriage relationship sufficiently for this activity to count
as a growth experience. Frequently it obscured relationship
problems, became an avenue of escape, and intensified conflicts.
For some, however, it did become a means of revealing other
problem areas in the marriage.

Underlying the marital couple's explorations into any area
of nonconformity, whether it was extramarital sex or the equally
important area of changes in typical role behavior (i. e., male-
female, man-woman, husband-wife), was the central problem of
relationship.* That is, how could the marital partners relate
in terms of their changing needs and those of society in a mutually beneficial fashion? Open marriage presents some of the
elements in interpersonal relationships that would allow for
change, for increasing responsibility for the self and for others,
and for increased understanding between husband and wife.

The open marriage model offers insights and learning guides
for developing more intimate and understanding marital relationships. An open relationship in marriage, as well as in any
interpersonal matrix, involves becoming a more open person.
Since the open-minded personality is one which can perceive
options and alternatives and make decisions about the paths to
change, efforts to help the marital couple in perception and skills

---

* Concerning these two areas of
change, the authors are least op-
timistic about the movement into
group marriage and communal living situations, which involve random or even structured sexual intimacy among many. No true group
marriage, as it is being explored in
our society, with equal sexual sharing among all partners has existed
according to the anthropological literature. Among all societies where
larger family structures exist, they
are maintained by elaborate kinship
ties and other supportive structures
interwoven with the institutional
framework of the society, thus goals
are integrated for the group or extended family. Certainly communal
or community situations where the
goals are banding together to share
economic, child care, or recreational
activities have many advantages
and hopefully will increase. But
when couples and individuals in
groups are pressed into situations
of total intimacy—including the
sexual dimension—for which they
have not been prepared either emotionally by training or by conditioning, the strain of the multistranded
relationships tends to fragment the
group. The goals of cooperation
and support are difficult to maintain under the pressure of emotional
conflicts which are intensified by
prescriptions for sexual intimacy.

should increase their ability to solve many problems in marriage.[9] However, it will not be easy for most couples. Emotional maturity, and the development of responsibility and confident identity cannot emerge overnight. But standing still, or merely exploring experimental structural forms without attention to the interpersonal factors only seems to be increasing the number of problems in marriage and decreasing the benefits to be gained from it. Open marriage is not intended to solve marital problems, but by using the open marriage model, the couple will at least be substituting problems which promote growth and learning for problems which are currently insoluable.

IMPLICATIONS

It is in the arena of interpersonal relations that marriage and the family will have to find new meaning and gain greater strength, no matter what the structural framework may be. Children cannot be taught the value of supportive love and caring, responsibility, problem-solving, or decision-making skills unless the parents have first developed these qualities in their own relationship. The inadequacy of organized institutions to instill these values and skills is only too apparent. Therefore, intimate, long-term relationships such as those of marriage and the family must provide them, and in order to do this they must be more rewarding and fulfilling for their members and there must be feedback and caring for each other's welfare.

Focusing on the methods for achieving a rewarding one-to-one relationship provides something that individuals can deal with and work with on a self-determining level. By encouraging personal responsibility, self-growth and bonding through the synergic relationship, the basic unit of husband and wife should become more rewarding and offer more avenues for fulfillment.

Building from within strengthens the individual, the couple, and then the family unit, and thus the entire social structure, since the fundamental unit of society is the family. Whatever form the family unit may be, its strength will still depend upon the rewards gained from interpersonal relationships. It is in this sense that the individual, and the married couple, can become not only a fulcrum for change but also a key factor leading to the strengthening of the social structure. Thus both family and society can be better equipped to cope with accelerating technological and cultural change. Hopefully, open families can evolve to an open society and eventually to an open world.

TERMINATION

INTRODUCTION

Eventually every human relationship ends. Although we all agree with this trusim, why, then, do we often view the termination of interaction as a disruption or a loss? Why isn't the ending considered as much an integral part of the process of relating as the beginning? Obviously, the termination of a relationship means a loss in our lives of something that is or was important in its consequences. We are often left with an emptiness and a set of questions. How did it happen? Couldn't I have controlled it? Why wasn't I more considerate when he/she was still here? And on the more threatening level, the termination of a relationship causes us to wonder if the loss is an indication that we are unloving and unlovable. Thus, either we consider termination as negative or we just avoid thinking about it.

It is not our contention that there is joy or pleasure in the end of a strong tie between two people. But two points are worth consideration. First, the termination of a relationship comes in a variety of forms and degrees. This is exemplified most painfully in the death of a loved one, or in divorce after years of marriage. Yet, death and divorce are only two forms of termination. Rejection, disengagement, mistreatment or inconsideration can be viewed as lesser forms of termination. In these losses, even the most disruptive, new meanings and self-understanding can be found. Growth may be facilitated by the termination of our closest relationships although, understandably, we try to avoid such situations.

Second, a human relationship is never really "finished". Our thoughts and actions are largely products of our experiences with others and the values we develop in interaction. From this perspective, any relationship we have affects us in some way in all subsequent interactions. If the earlier relationships have terminated, then our new ones, to some degree, have grown from those terminations as well as from the relationships that still exist.

Living involves deciding how we will relate to others. These decisions will be influenced by previously terminated relationships as well as by those which presently exist. Our decisions may involve taking the initiative, acting indifferently, even rejecting the relationship. Whatever we decide or whatever occurs with respect to one relationship affects us in others.

The readings in this section suggest the variety and possibilities of termination for new beginnings.

Two case studies of personal reactions to termination of trial marriages first presented by Crosby. Conclusions about the value of this life-style cannot be drawn from these studies only, as almost opposite conclusions were reached by each couple.

In the next reading, Jourard criticizes the static conception many feel is characteristic of marriage. He suggests that we continually redesign the marital relationship to facilitate growth and fulfillment in marriage by terminating boring and suffocating interaction patterns. Failure to do this does not inevitably result in divorce, but emotional divorce, the first of Bohannon's six steps, seems a logical extension.

The "amicable" divorce of Matthew and Anne Surrey may seem unbelievable if not inconceivable. Why should two people get a divorce if they can communicate so clearly on the conditions of their divorce? This is a factual account, although the names have been changed. Shideler explores the rationale of the Surreys as to why "divorce" in any other way would have been sacrilegious for them. Marriage meant living together in a way which did not require denial of their individuality. When their relationship changed so that this quality of life together was no longer possible, they chose divorce. Further, they chose to express their feelings about a divorce as solemnly as they had their decision to marry.

Loneliness is described in Waters' article as "caused by and dispelled by other persons." Another form of choice is involved in a refusal to seek beginnings to new relationships when we are confronted with an ending.

Finally, Mathews suggests we often do not work to achieve meaning from death. His determination to make the burial reflect the unique significance of his father's life was necessary to make the event meaningful. Perhaps more than other forms of termination, death may be the most difficult to accept because of the finality of the termination.

Termination of a relationship is not the end of meaning in life. It can open the door to new life, when seen from the perspective of the process of relating to others.

CASE STUDIES OF TRIAL MARRIAGE *

JOHN F. CROSBY

Case Study 3

We were to have been married in August, but the date was postponed indefinitely. I wasn't as sure as he of marriage, so since we both were to attend summer school, we rented a house together for two and a half months. Now, eight months later, I can look back through the journal I kept of those days and congratulate myself for having the courage to enter that trial marriage. Quickly, all the disillusionments of the early months of marriage set in—loss of romantic feelings, squabbling over everything, mutual feelings of being taken for granted, and sex becoming part of a daily routine. It was a highly emotional time for me, as I swung from great joy and tenderness to awful depression over what seemed such a failure—us. My predominating emotion was the sense of being "trapped," of "finality." One day in my journal I complained that I felt possessed, and longed for an "open-ended relationship. What I've got instead seems closed, and is pushing me down a narrowing funnel toward a wedding ring." Even on the "good" days when I thought maybe we could make it work, I called my feeling "resignation." I was trapped by love and a "duty" to return that love. Now I can see that my "trap" was partially self-made by my own emotional needs and insecurities.

Our house shook with conflict—over how to fry bologna, when to feed the dog, the dishes, sex—anything! Much of the conflict stemmed from the final uncovering of our *true* attitudes toward ourselves, each other, and life in general—but the fights were usually about the little surface annoyances. Communicating the real gripes was very difficult. Did I love him intellectually as well as emotionally? Why did I resent him so much—was he too dependent on me? At the time, I was too involved to sort out all the problems; I only felt the disappointments. We had friends, a newlywed couple, who were experiencing the same things. I'm so glad that mine was only a trial "marriage" be-

* From ILLUSION AND DISILLU-SION: THE SELF IN LOVE AND MARRIAGE by John F. Crosby. © 1973 by Wadsworth Publishing Company, Inc., Belmont, California 94002. Reprinted by permission of the publisher.

cause if I had been chained by a ring and a license, I don't know how I could have handled the intense disillusionment, the unavoidable conviction that we had made a mistake.

At the end, he left town as planned, and two months later I found strength to break our engagement. Now I see that not only were we not "right" for each other, but also that it was not the right season of my life for the responsibility of marriage—I still have much growing to do before I will be ready. As far as the ethical question of what we did, I do not see how we could have chosen a more "moral" action. We accepted our responsibility to ourselves, our possible children, and to society by trying to ascertain whether we could build a fruitful marriage *before* we made a final commitment. *If* we had married instead, and *if* it had lasted, I think we would both be very unhappy right now. Even my parents, who were understandably upset at first, now agree with me and share my happiness at having avoided a costly mistake.

My trial marriage was a time of dreaming, planning, fighting, and crying—a very painful time; but I know that I will never marry anyone until we have seriously tried our marriage on for size *first*.

Case Study 4

Bill is 23 years old. He has never been married but has been involved in a trial marriage which ended after four months.

"I don't understand it," Bill said to the therapist. "I thought everything would be great. Jean and I went together for about a year and we really hit it off. We did all kinds of things together. I could hardly stand to be away from her and I looked forward to every time we could see each other. Of course, we got close and we had a great time sexually. At first she was reserved but slowly she began to open up and relax. I swear, everything was wonderful. I didn't even think about anyone else—she was it. Even when I was away from her I couldn't imagine myself wanting sex with anyone else. I wanted to get married but . . . well, she wanted to try living together for a while. I kept fighting it by saying I didn't see what there was to gain—that we were like old married people anyway. She really surprised me—wanting a trial marriage kind of thing. Well, anyhow, I agreed and we got an apartment. For several weeks things were fine—but not for long. I don't get it yet—

all I know is when we started living together everything was spoiled. Boy, next time I won't try any of that trial stuff—it doomed us. We started fighting—really sort of picking at each other, blaming each other for little things, getting on each other's nerves. She claimed I was closed minded—that I was old-fashioned in the way I wanted to be the protector and the head of the house—you know, like I should let her make the decisions. I suppose I could have taken some of the changes but not the sex one. Boy—how could such a wonderful thing become so dull so fast? All of a sudden it was—like—well, like warmed-over coffee. Before it was exciting and full of challenge—and I really could hardly wait to give myself to her—and man, I mean "give" because it never was just a physical thing with us .   . But, it all went! Here we were living together and what should be the greatest thing became the worst."

REINVENTING MARRIAGE *

SIDNEY M. JOURARD

One man, one woman and no, or some, children, all living together in a household separate from others—this is the pattern, or better, the cliché, of marriage and family life that has evolved in the Western, industrialized world.

If this design evolved as an economic necessity, as the most efficient way for people to live in order to keep the economy going, and the social structure with its power elite unchanged, the design has been successful. In fact, throughout history people at the top have seldom lived the same pattern of marriage and family life as have the larger, working majority. The rich and aristocratic have invented ways to live that have scandalized the majority as much as they have evoked envy. The conventional marriage, while preserving the *status quo,* has failed to serve such important functions as facilitating personal growth and self-actualization in the married couple and their children. In fact, I see compulsive adherence to conventional definitions of husband-and-wife roles or son-and-daughter roles as a factor in disease.[1] Entrapment in forms of interaction that merely preserve a system imposes stress on those who are trapped, saps them of zest and morale, and contributes to illness.

As a psychotherapist, I have often been called upon to do "marriage counseling," and I have been struck by the incredible lack of artistry and creativity in marriage partners. Either person may be imaginative in making money or decorating a house, but when it comes to altering the design for their relationship, it is as if both imaginations had burnt out. For years, spouses go to sleep night after night, with their relationship patterned one way, a way that perhaps satisfies neither—too close, too distant, boring or suffocating—and on awakening the next morning, they reinvent their relationship *in the same way*. There is nothing sacred to the wife about the last way she decorated her house; as soon as it begins to pall, she shuffles things around until the new décor pleases her. But the way she and

* Sidney M. Jourard, 'Reinventing Marriage: The Perspective of a Psychologist' from THE FAMILY IN SEARCH OF A FUTURE, edited by Herbert A. Otto © 1970 by Meredith Corporation. Reprinted by permission of Prentice-Hall, Inc., Englewood Cliffs, N. J.

her husband interact will persist for years unchallenged and un-changed, long after it has ceased to engender delight, zest or growth.

I have similarly been impressed with the same lack of creativ-ity in inventing and reinventing oneself. A man can retire and, if one sees him asleep, his facial expression changes, the chronic neuromuscular patterns which define his "character" all dis-solve, and he is unconscious for a few hours.[2] On awakening, it is as if a button has been pushed; his facial musculature re-produces the mask that defines his physiognomy, he holds his body as he did yesterday, and he behaves toward everyone he encounters as he did yesterday. Yet, in principle, he has the possibility of recreating himself at every moment of his waking life. It is difficult but possible to reinvent one's identity, because man is human, the embodiment of freedom; his body and his situation are raw material out of which a way to *be* can be cre-ated, just as a sculptor creates forms out of clay or steel. The medium imposes limitations, but the sculptor has many degrees of freedom to create forms, limited only by the extent of his imagination, his courage, and his mastery of technique. The sculptor confronts a heap of clay, imagines a possible form that will be pleasing and meaningful to him, then sets about trans-muting this image into a structure that can be *perceived*.[3] He may create and then destroy dozens of approximations of his image, until finally he hits upon the form that "works." But that same sculptor, confronted by the "clay" of his being and the being of his wife, can neither imagine nor make new ways for him and her to interact that please, that fulfil needs and values other than the visible *form* of their relationship.

It is both possible and difficult to reinvent a relationship. The difficulty has to do with barriers to change that exist in persons and in the environment. If I begin to change my ways of being myself, I feel strange: I feel I am not myself. The dif-ferent ways of being may make me anxious or guilty. And so I may revert back to familiar, but stultifying, ways of being myself. If I persist in my efforts to reinvent myself, and begin to behave before others in new ways, they may become angered or affrighted. They don't recognize me. And they may pun-ish me in any way at their disposal for changing a part of *their* world—namely myself—without first "clearing it" with them. Much invaluable growth and change in persons has been invali-dated and destroyed by the untoward reactions of well-intentioned others. Perhaps it is because if I change a part of their world, the part that I embody, there is an invitation or demand presented to them to change *their* ways of being. They may not be ready or willing to change their ways. If I lack "ontological security," [4] I may withdraw my changed being from their gaze, wipe out the new version of myself and, in a moment of cowardice, reproduce the being I used to be. I then become an impersonation of a past identity.

When one is involved in a relationship like marriage, the difficulty in reinventing the relationship is compounded because there are two persons, two imaginations, and two sets of needs to be considered; two sets of change-possibilities are involved. But it is still possible for two people of good will to discuss images of possibility, reconcile differences that arise, and then set about trying to actualize themselves. It is possible to play games with a relationship, to experiment with new forms, until a viable way is evolved. What seems to thwart this kind of interpersonal creativity is failure in imagination on the part of either partner, dread of external criticism and sanctions, and dread of change in oneself.

One barrier to change in any institutional form is economic. People have to make a living, and they must find a way to interact with others which facilitates, or at least will not interfere with, the necessities of producing goods and maintaining the social, political and economic *status quo*. Societies that are under external threat and societies that have an insecure economic base are "one-dimensional" societies.[5] Their techniques for socializing the young and for social control of adults are powerful, and incontestable. Deviation from the norm is severely censured, by necessity, because the security of the whole society is endangered.

But in America, the most affluent nation that ever existed, objective reasons for enforcing conformity are diminishing. At last, we have the power and the wealth (despite protestations from conservative alarmists to the contrary) to ground *a fantastically pluralistic society*. Indeed, *not* to capitalize on our increased release from economic necessity, *not* to "play" creatively with such existential forms as marriage, family life, schooling, leisure pursuits, etc., is a kind of madness, a dread of, and escape from, freedom and the terror it engenders. Forms of family life that were relevant in rural frontier days, or in earlier urban life, that mediated compulsive productivity and produced a mighty industrial complex and immense wealth, are obsolete today. I think that our divorce rate and the refusal of many hippies, artists, and intellectuals to live the middle-class model for marriage and family life attests to this obsolescence. There exists, in fact, in this nation a great diversity of man-woman, parent-child relationships; only the middle-class design is legitimized. The other patterns, serial polygamy or communal living where the nuclear family is less strong, are viewed with alarm and scorn by the vast, conforming majority. These patterns exist as a kind of underground. But both the myriad ways for living married that are secretly being explored by consenting adults in this society, and the designs that have existed since time immemorial in foreign and "primitive" societies, represent a storehouse of tested possibilities available to those who would experiment with marriage. Polygyny, polyandry, homosexual marriages, permanent and temporary associations, anything that has been tried in any time and place represents a possible mode for existential exploration by men and women who dare to try some new design when the conventional pattern has died for them. *Not to legitimize such experimentation and exploration is to make life in our society unlivable for an increasing proportion of the population.*

If it is sane and appropriate for people to explore viable ways for men and women and children to live together so that life is maximally potentiated, then we must ask why it is not being done with more vigor, more openness, and more public interest. We must wonder why divorce laws are so strict, why alimony regulations are so punitive, and why people experience the end of one way of being married as so catastrophic that they may commit suicide or murder rather than invent new forms or patterns of life.

I suppose it is the task of sociologists to answer this question. But from both a clinical and existential point of view, something can be done.

I have encouraged couples who find themselves in a dead marriage but still find it meaningful to live together, to begin a series of experiments in their ways of relating. The image or metaphor that underlies this experimentation is the view of *serial polygamy to the same person.* I conjure up the image of two people who marry when they are young, who live a way of relating that gratifies needs and fulfills meaning up to the point of an impasse. One partner or the other finds continuation in that way intolerable. The marriage, in its legal form, is usually dissolved at this point. But it is also possible that the couple may struggle with the impasse, and evolve a new marriage with each other, one that includes change, yet preserves some of the old pattern that remains viable. This is their second marriage to each other.

The end of the first can be likened to a divorce, without benefit of the courts. The new marriage, whatever form it takes, will also reach its end. It may last as a viable form for five days or five years, but if both parties are growing people, it must reach its end. There is then a period of estrangement, a period of experimentation, and a remarriage in a new way—and so on for as long as continued association with that same spouse *remains meaningful for both partners.* Any one of these marriages may look peculiar to an outsider. For example, one marriage of perhaps seven months may take the form of separate domiciles, or weekend visits, or communication through the mails or by telephone. But the idea is that, for growing people, each marriage is, as it were, to a new partner anyway. So long as both partners are growing, they have had a polygamous relationship. The "new" spouse is simply the old spouse grown in some new dimensions.

This model of serial polygamy with the "same" spouse must be viewed as only one of the myriad possibilities for persons who desire marriages to try. The cultural storehouse can also be drawn upon for other models. We could even envision a new profession, that of "marriage-inventor," who would develop and catalogue new ways for men and women to cohabit and raise children, so that no one would be at a loss for new forms to try when the old forms have deadened and become deadly. It is curious to me that college courses and textbooks on marriage all turn out to be propaganda for the prevailing cliché of marriage for the middle class.

I could invent a course that might be called "Experimental Marriage," complete with laboratory. The laboratory would consist of households where every conceivable way for men, women, and children to live together would be studied and tested for its viability, its consequences for physical and mental health of the participants, its economic basis, etc. If the prevailing ways of marriage are outmoded, if men find it necessary to live with women or with somebody, on an intimate basis, and if children need parents, then experimentation is called for to make more forms of cohabitation available, on an acceptable basis, for everybody. The present design is clearly not for everyone.

There is an implication here for those counselors and therapists who engage in marriage- and divorce-counseling. Elsewhere I have discussed the politics of psychotherapy: [6] Is the therapist committed to the social *status quo,* or to a more pluralistic society? *If to the former, he then functions as an agent of socialization, a trainer of persons so they might better "adjust" to the* status quo. *If to the latter, he is more akin to a guru, or existential guide.* If he follows the latter model, then he will indeed function as a marriage counselor in ways different from his more conventional colleagues. He will encourage people who find themselves in marital impasses to explore new ways; he will be able to help his client invent a new way of being married to someone, rather than persuade him to perpetuate the conventional marriage form with his present partner in despair, or with a new partner in unfounded hope.

The inventive counselor of spouses or entire families, as I say, does not aim toward fitting human beings to a marital design that was invented by no one for no particular human beings. Rather, he is more akin to a consultant to artists whose creativity has dried up as they pursue tasks of vital concern to them. If Picasso, or Gilbert and Sullivan, ran out of ideas, or the courage to produce them in action, we might hope that they would have available to them a consultant who would help them turn their imaginations on again, and inspire them with the courage to produce what they imagined.

Since each man, woman, and child is a potentially creative artist in the invention of family roles, the marriage and family counselor should certainly be no less than a family-invention consultant. It happens that everyone is the artist-of-himself, whether he is reflectively aware of this or not. He is responsible for what he creates out of what he has already become. But the banality of self-creation that we see everywhere attests to alienation of each from his self-creative powers. The stereotype of family relationships in a society with an economic base that enables and requires creative diversity further attests to this alienation. A good therapist brings his patient back into contact with his powers. A good family counselor awakens his clients to the experience of their freedom or powers, and to their responsibility to reinvent their situation.

Concretely, this way of being a counselor requires that the counselor himself be more enlightened than his clients regarding barriers to inventing or changing patterns of life. It helps if he is himself continuously engaged in inventing and reinventing his own interpersonal life, so that he is, and exemplifies, a vital and growing person. His imagination and knowledge can then draw upon a repository of family life possibilities larger than that possessed by his clients. The criterion of a successful solution to marital and family-relationship problems is not the *appearance* of the relationship, but rather *the experience of freedom, confirmation, and growth* on the part of the participants. Thus, "seeking" spouses can be encouraged to try such things as: living apart from time to time; lending their children to foster parents for a while; trying to be radically honest with one another, etc. So long as the counselor is not himself existentially or professionally committed to one image of family life, he can encourage spouses to explore any and all possibilities, the criterion of their success being, not "saving the marriage" in its present form, but rather a richer, fuller experience of growing existence and honest relationship.

The group structure most effective for fighting an enemy is an army with its platoons and regiments. The group structure most effective for providing care and training to infants, as well as companionship, love, and sex for the adults, is the now-outmoded family structure. The family structure for the emerging age of affluence and leisure cannot be prescribed or described in advance—only invented.

THE SIX STATIONS OF DIVORCE *

PAUL BOHANNAN

Divorce is a complex social phenomenon as well as a complex personal experience. Because most of us are ignorant of what it requires of us, divorce is likely to be traumatic: emotional stimulation is so great that accustomed ways of acting are inadequate. The usual way for the healthy mind to deal with trauma is to block it out, then let it reappear slowly, so it is easier to manage. The blocking may appear as memory lapses or as general apathy.

On a social level we do something analogous, not allowing ourselves to think fully about divorce as a social problem. Our personal distrust of the emotions that surround it leads us to consider it only with traditional cultural defenses. Our ignorance masquerades as approval or disapproval, as enlightenment or moral conviction.

The complexity of divorce arises because at least six things are happening at once. They may come in a different order and with varying intensities, but there are at least these six different experiences of separation. They are the more painful and puzzling as personal experiences because society is not yet equipped to handle any of them well, and some of them we do not handle at all.

I have called these six overlapping experiences (1) the emotional divorce, which centers around the problem of the deteriorating marriage; (2) the legal divorce, based on grounds; (3) the economic divorce, which deals with money and property; (4) the coparental divorce, which deals with custody, single-parent homes, and visitation; (5) the community divorce, surrounding the changes of friends and community that every divorcee experiences; and (6) the psychic divorce, with the problem of regaining individual autonomy.

The first visible stage of a deteriorating marriage is likely to be what psychiatrists call emotional divorce. This occurs when the spouses withhold emotion from their relationship because they dislike the intensity or ambivalence of their feelings. They may continue to work together as a social team, but their attraction and trust for one another have disappeared. The self-regard of each is no longer reinforced by love for the other. The emotional divorce is experienced as an unsavory choice between giving in and hating oneself and domineering and hating oneself. The natural and healthy "growing apart" of a married couple is very different. As marriages mature, the partners grow in new directions, but also establish bonds of ever greater interdependence. With emotional divorce, people do not grow together as they grow apart—they become instead, mutually antagonistic and imprisoned, hating the vestiges of their dependence. Two people in emotional divorce grate on each other because each is disappointed.

In American society, we have turned over to the courts the responsibility for formalizing the dissolution of such a marriage. The legislature (which in early English law usurped the responsibility from the church, and then in the American colonies turned it over to the courts) makes the statutes and defines the categories into which every marital dispute must be thrust if legal divorce is possible. Divorce is not "legalized" in many societies but may be done by a church or even by contract. Even in our own society, there is only one thing that a divorce court can do that cannot be done more effectively some other way—establish the right to remarry. As long as your spouse lives, you cannot legally remarry until you are legally divorced. Because of the legal necessity of this one aspect, several other aspects of divorce are customarily taken care of by lawyers and judges. However, legal divorce itself does nothing but create remarriageability.

The economic divorce must occur because in Western countries husband and wife are an economic unit. Their unity is recognized by the law. They can—and in some states must—own property as a single "legal person." While technically the couple is not a corporation, they certainly have many of the characteristics of a legal corporation. At the time the household is broken up by divorce, an economic settlement must be made, separating the assets of the "corporation" into two sets of assets, each belonging to one person. This is the property settlement. Today it is vastly complicated by income tax law. A great deal of knowledge is required to take care of the tax positions of divorced persons—and if the lawyer does not have this knowledge, he must get assistance. Although the judges may ratify the property settlement, they usually do not create it unless the principals and lawyers cannot do so.

The coparental divorce is necessary if there are children. When the household breaks up, the children have to live somewhere. Taking care of the children requires complex arrangements for carrying out the obligations of parents.

All divorced persons suffer more or less because their community is altered. Friends necessarily take a different view of a person during and after divorce—he ceases to be a part of a couple. Their own inadequacies, therefore, will be projected in a new way. Their fantasies are likely to change as they focus on the changing situation. In many cases, the change in community attitude—and perhaps people too—is experienced by a divorcee as ostracism and disapproval. For many divorcing people, the divorce from community may make it seem that nothing in the world is stable.

Finally comes the psychic divorce. It is almost always last, and always the most difficult. Indeed, I have not found a word strong or precise enough to describe the difficulty or the process. Each partner to the ex-marriage, either before or after the legal divorce—usually after, and sometimes years after— must turn himself or herself again into an autonomous social individual. People who have been long married tend to have become socially part of a couple or a family; they lose the habit of seeing themselves as individuals. This is worse for people who married in order to avoid becoming autonomous individuals in the first place.

To become an individual again, at the center of a new community, requires developing new facets of character. Some people have forgotten how to do it—some never learned. The most potent argument against teen-age marriages is that they are likely to occur between people who are searching for independence but avoiding autonomy. The most potent argument against hurried remarriage is the same: avoidance of the responsibilities of automony.

Divorce is an institution that nobody enters without great trepidation. In the emotional divorce, people are likely to feel hurt and angry. In the legal divorce, people often feel bewildered—they have lost control, and events sweep them along. In the economic divorce, the reassignment of property and the division of money (there is *never* enough) may make them feel cheated.   In the parental divorce they worry about what is going to happen to the children; they feel guilty for what they have done.   With the community divorce, they may get angry with their friends and perhaps suffer despair because there seems to be no fidelity in friendship.   In the psychic divorce, in which they have to become autonomous again, they are probably afraid and are certainly lonely.   However, the resolution of any or all of these various six divorces may provide an elation of victory that comes from having accomplished something that had to be done and having done it well.   There may be ultimate satisfactions in it.

Divorce American style is a bewildering experience—so many things are happening at once.   We have never been taught what we are supposed to do, let alone what we are supposed to feel. I know a divorced man who took great comfort in the fact that one of his business associates asked him, when he learned of his divorce, "Do I feel sorry for you or do I congratulate you?" He thought for a moment and said—out of bravado as much as conviction—"Congratulate me."   It was, for him, the beginning of the road back.

THE EMOTIONAL DIVORCE AND THE PROBLEM

One of the reasons it feels so good to be engaged and newly married is the rewarding sensation that, out of the whole world, you have been selected.   One of the reasons that divorce feels so awful is that you have been de-selected.   It punishes almost as much as the engagement and the wedding are rewarding.

The chain of events and feelings that lead up to divorce are as long and as varied as the chain of events that lead up to being selected for marriage.   The difference is that the feelings are concentrated in the area of the weak points in the personality rather than the growing points of the personality.

Almost no two people who have been married, even for a short time, can help knowing where to hit each other if they want to wound.   On the other hand, any two people—no matter who they are—who are locked together in conflict have to be very perceptive to figure out what the strain is really all about.   Marital fights occur in every healthy marriage.   The fact of health is indicated when marital disputes lead to a clarification of issues and to successful extension of the rela-

tionship into new areas. Difficulties arise only when marital
conflict is sidetracked to false issues (and sometimes the dis-
covery of just what issue is at stake may be, in itself, an adequate conclusion to the conflict), or when the emotional pressures are shunted to other areas. When a couple are afraid to
fight over the real issue, they fight over something else—and
perhaps never discover what the real issue was.

Two of the areas of life that are most ready to accept such
displacement are the areas of sex and money. Both sex and
money are considered worthwhile fighting over in American
culture. If it is impossible to know or admit what a fight is
all about, then the embattled couple may cast about for areas
of displacement, and they come up with money and sex, because both can be used as weapons. Often these are not
the basis of the difficulties, which lie in unconscious or inad-
missible areas.

These facts lead a lot of people to think that emotional divorce occurs over money or over sexual incompatibility just
because that is where the overt strife is allowed to come out.
Often, however, these are only camouflage.

MONEY AND THE EMOTIONAL DIVORCE. One of the most tena-
cious ideas from our early training is "the value of a dollar."
When in the larger society the self is reflected in possessions,
and when money becomes one mode of enhancing the self—then
we have difficulty with anybody who either spends it too
lavishly or sits on it more tightly then we do.

Money is a subject about which talk is possible. Most middle-
class couples do talk about money; most of them, in fact, make
compromises more or less adequate to both. But in all cases,
money management and budgeting are endlessly discussed in
the American household. If communication becomes difficult,
one of the first places that it shows up is in absence of knowledge about the other person's expenditures.

I interviewed one divorced woman who blamed her ex-husband's spending practices and attitude toward money as a major factor in their divorce. She said that he bought her an expensive car and asked her to leave it sitting outside the house
when she was not driving it. *She* announced that *he* could not
afford it. He asked her to join a golf club. She refused, although she was a good golfer and liked to play—because *she*
told him *he* could not afford it. Whenever he wanted to use her

considerable beauty and accomplishments to reflect a little credit on himself for being able to have captured and kept such a wife, she announced that he could not afford it. After the divorce, it continued. Then one day, in anger, she telephoned him to say that she was tired of making sacrifices—this year she was going to take the children on a transcontinental vacation and that he would simply have to pay for the trip. He did not explode; he only thought for a minute and said that he guessed that would be all right, and that he would whittle down his plans for the children's vacation with him, so that it would come within the budget.

This woman told this story without realizing what she had revealed: that her husband was not going to push himself or them into bankruptcy; that he did indeed know how much things cost, and that he could either afford or otherwise manage what he wanted to give her. There was doubtless a difference of opinion about money—she, it appears, preferred to save and then spend; he preferred, perhaps, to spend and then pay. She, for reasons I cannot know from one extended interview, did not recognize his feelings. She *did* announce to him, every time that he wanted to spend money on her, that he was inadequate. I suspect it was her own fear that she would let him down. Without knowing it, she was attacking him where it hurt him and where her housewifely virtue could be kept intact, while she did not have to expose herself or take a chance.

I am not saying that there are not spendthrift husbands or wives. I am saying that if differences that lie beyond money cannot be discussed, then money is a likely battleground for the emotional divorce.

SEX AND THE EMOTIONAL DIVORCE. Among the hundreds of divorcees I have talked to, there is a wide range of sexual attitudes. There were marriages in which sexual symptoms were the first difficulties to be recognized by the couple. There were a few in which the sexual association seemed the only strong bond. I know of several instances in which the couple met for a ceremonial bout of sexual intercourse as the last legitimate act before their divorce. I have a newspaper clipping that tells of a man who, after such a "last legal assignation," murdered his wife before she became his ex-wife. And I know one divorce that was denied because, as the judge put it, he could not condone "litigation by day and copulation by night."

Usually, when communication between the spouses becomes strained, sexual rapport is the first thing to go. There are many aspects to this problem: sexual intercourse is the most intimate of social relationships, and reservations or ambivalences in the emotions are likely to show up there (with unconscious conflicts added to conscious ones). The conflicts may take the extreme form of frigidity in women, impotence in men. They may take the form of adultery, which may be an attempt to communicate something, an unconscious effort to improve the marriage itself. It may be an attempt to humiliate the spouse into leaving. Adultery cannot sensibly be judged without knowing what it means to a specific person and to his spouse in a specific situation. Adultery is a legal ground for divorce in every jurisdiction in the United States, and indeed in most of the record-keeping world.

Because sexuality is closely associated with integration of the personality, it is not surprising that disturbance in the relationship of the spouses may be exposed in sexual symptoms. Except in some cases in which the marriage breaks up within a few weeks or months, however, sexual difficulties are a mode of expression as often as they provide the basic difficulty.

GROWING APART. Married people, like any other people, must continue to grow as individuals if they are not to stagnate. Only by extending themselves to new experiences and overcoming new conflicts can they participate fully in new social relationships and learn new culture. That means that no one, at the time of marriage, can know what the spouse is going to become. Moreover, it means that he cannot know what he himself may become.

Some of this growth of individuals must necessarily take place outside of the marriage. If the two people are willing and able to perceive and tolerate the changes in one another, and overcome them by a growing relationship directly with the other person, then the mutual rewards are very great, and conflicts can be resolved.

Inability to tolerate change in the partner (or to see him as he is) always lies, I think, at the root of emotional divorce. All marriages become constantly more attenuated from the end of the honeymoon period probably until the retirement of the husband from the world of affairs. That is to say, the proportion of the total concern of one individual that can be given to the other individual in the marriage decreases, even though the precise quantity (supposing there were a way to measure it) might become greater. But the ties may become tougher, even as they become thinner.

When this growing apart and concomitant increase in the toughness of the bonds does *not* happen, then people feel the marriage bonds as fetters and become disappointed or angry with each other. They feel cramped by the marriage and cheated by their partner. A break may be the only salvation for some couples.

In America today, our emotional lives are made diffuse by the very nature of the culture with which we are surrounded. Family life, business or professional demands, community pressures— today all are in competition with one another for our time and energies. When that happens, the social stage is set for emotional divorce of individual couples, because the marriage relationship becomes just another competing institution. Sometimes emotional divorce seems scarcely more than another symptom of the diffuseness.

EMOTIONAL DIVORCE AND GRIEF. Emotional divorce results in the loss of a loved object just as fully—but by quite a different route of experience—as does the death of a spouse. Divorce is difficult because it involves a purposeful and active rejection by another person, who, merely by living, is a daily symbol of the rejection. It is also made difficult because the community helps even less in divorce than it does in bereavement.

The natural reaction to the loss of a loved object or person (and sometimes a hated one as well) is grief. The distribution of emotional energy is changed significantly; new frustration must be borne until new arrangements can be worked out. Human beings mourn every loss of meaningful relationship. The degree depends on the amount of emotional involvement. Mourning may be traumatic—and it may, like any other trauma have to be blocked and only slowly allowed into awareness. Mourning may take several months or years.

Divorce is even more threatening than death to some people, because they have thought about it more, perhaps wished for it more consciously. But most importantly—there is no recognized way to mourn a divorce. The grief has to be worked out alone and without benefit of traditional rites, because few people recognize it for what it is.

When grief gets entangled with all the other emotions that are
evoked in a divorce, the emotional working through becomes
complicated—in a divorce one is very much on his own.

THE LEGAL DIVORCE AND THE PROBLEM OF GROUNDS

Judicial divorce, as it is practiced in the United States today,
is a legal post-mortem on the demise of an intimate relationship.
It originated in Massachusetts in the early 1700s as a means for
dealing with the problems that emotional divorce caused in
families, at the same time that all going households could continue to be based on holy matrimony. Legal divorce has been
discovered and used many times in the history of the world, but
this particular institution had no precursors in European history. The historical period in which it developed is important. In those days it was considered necessary that the state
could profess its interest in the marriage and the family only in
the guise of punishing one of the spouses for misconduct.
Thus, the divorce itself was proclaimed to be the punishment of
the guilty party. Whether divorce as a punishment was ever a
commonsensical idea is a moot point—certainly it is not so today.
Yet, our law still reflects this idea.

Thus, if the state is to grant divorces to "innocent" spouses
as punishment to offending spouses, it must legalize certain
aspects of the family—must, in fact, establish minimal standards of performance in family roles. Marriages break down in
all societies; we have come, by state intervention, to solve some
of these breakdowns with the legal institution of divorce. Until
very recently, no country granted its citizens the clear right to
divorce, as they have the clear right to marry. The right is always conditional on acts of misbehavior of the spouse, as misbehavior has been legally defined and called "grounds." Whatever the spouse does must be thrust into the categories that the
law recognizes before it can be grounds for divorce.

This way of handling divorce has some strange and unintend-
ed effects. It has made lawyers into experts in several aspects
of divorce; there are no recognized experts in other aspects of
divorce. Therefore, lawyers are called upon to assume responsibility for more and more aspects of the institution—and in
many they have no training in others there is no possible legal
base from which they can operate. The difficulty in legal divorce in America seems to lie in two related situations: the uncertainty of the population and even of the legal profession about

what the lawyers are supposed to do, and the absence of institutions paralleling the legal institutions to handle the non-legal problems.

DIVORCE LAWYERS AND WHAT THEY DO. If you want a physician, you look in the yellow pages and find them noted, most of them with their specialties spelled out. With lawyers it is not so—there is only a list. It is an unfortunate by-product of the ethical commitment of the American Bar Association not to advertise that attorneys cannot list their special competences. It is my opinion that, at least as far as family lawyers are concerned (the only exception now allowed is patent law), this ruling should be changed.

The legal profession is committed to the proposition that any lawyer—or at least any firm of lawyers—should be able to handle any sort of problem. Legally, divorce is indeed a simple matter; that is part of the trouble. Any competent lawyer can indeed write the papers and make the necessary motions. The difficulty comes in the counseling aspect of divorce practice.

Every divorcing person must find his lawyer—and it may be difficult. It may be done through friends, business associates, clergymen, but it is surprisingly often done in the yellow pages. Perhaps there is no other situation in our country today in which a person in emotional distress is so faced with buying a pig in a poke. Clients who are inexperienced may not realize that they can fire a lawyer faster than they can hire him. They worry along with a lawyer they neither like personally nor trust professionally.

Because lawyers are for the most part untrained in family psychology and sociology, and because there is no practice—not even the criminal law—in which they are dealing with people in such states of emotional upset, divorce becomes a "messy" or "dirty" kind of practice—these are their words. In the hierarchy of lawyers by specialties (and there is a rigid and fairly overt hierarchy), the divorce lawyer and criminal lawyer rank approximately at the bottom—allowing, of course, for such considerations as ethics, financial success, social rank, and the like. My own opinion is that the more emotional the problems a lawyer handles, the further down the lawyers' pecking order he ranks. Corporation lawyers are at the top; corporations have no emotions. Divorcees and criminals have little else.

Lawyers also dislike divorce practice because it is not lucra-
tive. Many divorcees think lawyers take advantage and over-
charge them. In most divorce cases, the legal fees—both of
them—are paid by the husband, and are set by the judge at the
time of the divorce hearing. Many lawyers think that the fees
that the court sets are ridiculously low—another reason that they
do not like to take divorce cases. Many lawyers make additional
charges for the many other services they perform for divorcees.
Divorce lawyers tend to work on an hourly rate, though probably all of them adjust the rate to the income of their
client.

Most divorcees, on the other hand, do not appreciate how much
work their lawyers actually put in. Because the court hearing seldom takes more than a few minutes, and because the
papers are often not a thick bundle, the assumption is that comparatively little effort went into it. The divorce lawyers I know
earn their fees; the good ones always contribute a lot of personal advice, care, and solace without charge.

Many divorce cases do not end when the decree is final. Money must be collected; ex-husbands may use non-payment of
alimony as the only sanction they have over ex-wives; financial
positions and obligations change. For these and many other
reasons, the divorcee may come back to the lawyer sooner
or later. One divorced woman summed it up, "Every divorcee
needs a good firm of lawyers."

But the greatest difficulty arises from the fact we started with:
divorce lawyers are forced, in the nature of the law, to put
the "real situation," as they learn it from their clients, into language that the law will accept. If a divorce action is to
go to court, it must first be couched in language that the courts
are legally permitted to accept. Both marriage counselors and
lawyers have assured me that reconciliation is always more difficult after grounds have been discussed and legal papers written
than when it is still in the language of "reasons" and personal
emotion. Legal language and choice of grounds are the first
positive steps toward a new type of relationship with the person
one of my informants called "my ex-to-be." Discussion of
grounds often amounts, from the point of view of the divorcing
person, to listing all the faults that the spouse ever committed,
then picking one. Since everyone has faults, this is not difficult
to do. (There is an old joke that goes the rounds of divorce
lawyers about the conscientious young man who came to his

lawyer and said he wanted a divorce, but was not sure he had grounds. The cynical lawyer raised his eyes and asked, "Are you married?")

We all know that grounds and reasons may be quite different. The divorcing person usually feels that he should not "tattle" and selects the "mildest" ground. Yet, every person who institutes a suit for divorce must wonder whether to use "adultery" if in fact it occurred, or to settle for the more noncommittal "mental cruelty." Does one use drunkenness when divorcing an alcoholic? Or desertion? Or does one settle for "incompatibility?"

WHAT THE COURT DOES. The judges in a divorce court are hard-working men who must become accustomed to a veritable chaos of emotional confusion. Some of them do the job well, with great knowledge and commitment. Others feel that they have themselves been sentenced, that no human being should be asked to stand very much of it, and hope to be in some other court soon.

The usual divorce in court takes only a few minutes—sometimes as little as two or three and seldom more than fifteen or twenty. Many divorcees are disturbed to discover this fact, having thought all their grievances would be heard and, perhaps, they would "get some justice." Many report, "It's a weak-kneed system. I don't feel that it really did the job." Others are constantly aware that they perjured themselves—about grounds, about residence, perhaps about facts. Some divorcees feel virtuous for using "mental cruelty" as a ground and tell all their friends "the real reason"—thereby alienating friends. Others take a pragmatic attitude about the legal proceedings: "What do I care? I got what I wanted, didn't I?"

The court action seems short and ineffective at the time—not traumatic. Most divorcees, in retrospect, cannot remember the details of it; in part, I think, because there is little to be remembered. Divorce dockets are crowded in all American cities. Judges do not have time to give each case the thought and time the divorcing parties think it deserves—realizing that one's monumental troubles are not worth the court's time can often act as a restorative, but sometimes as a depressant. Many judges agree that they would like to have more time to make specific investigations and suggestions in each case—to convince themselves that attempts have been made to discover whether these two people should in fact be divorced—whether divorce is a reasonable solution to their problems. Though judges do take time with some cases, most would like to be able to take more.

One of the reasons that the divorce institution is so hard on people is that the legal processes do not provide an orderly and socially approved discharge of emotions that are elicited during the emotional divorce and during the early parts of preparation for the legal processes. Divorces are "cranked out" but divorcees are not "cooled out."

THE ECONOMIC DIVORCE AND THE PROBLEM OF PROPERTY

The family household is the unit of economic consumption in the United States. As such, middle-class households must have a certain amount of domestic-capital equipment besides personal property such as cars and television sets. In most households, these items "belong to the family," even though they may be legally owned in the name of one of the spouses.

Behind the idea of fair settlement of property at the time of divorce is the assumption that a man cannot earn money to support his family if he does not have the moral assistance and domestic services of his wife. The wife, if she works, does so in order to "enhance" the family income (no matter how much she makes or what the "psychic income" to her might be). Therefore, every salary dollar, every patent, every investment, is joint property.

In most states, the property settlement is not recorded in the public records of divorce, so precise information is lacking. However, in most settlements, the wife receives from one-third to one-half of the property. As one sits in a divorce court, however, one realizes that in many divorces the amount of property is so small as to need no settlement or even to cause any dispute. Judges regard settlement as the province of lawyers, and generally agree that the lawyers have not done their jobs if the matter comes to court.

Many wives voluntarily give up their rights to property at the time they become ex-wives. Some are quite irrational about it— "I won't take *anything* from *him*!" Sometimes they think (perhaps quite justly) that they have no moral right to it. Others, of course, attempt to use the property settlement as a means of retaliation. The comment from one of my informants was, "Boy, did I make that bastard pay." It seems to me that irrational motives such as revenge or self-abnegation are more often in evidence than the facts of relative need, in spite of all that judges and lawyers can do.

The property of the household is never, in the nature of household living, separable into two easily discernible parcels. Even in states that lack common-property laws, the *use* of property is certainly common within the household and subject to the rules of the household, of course, but (except for clothes or jewelry or tools) usually not the exclusive property of any specific member of the household. Whose, for example, is the family car? Whose is the hi-fi? Whose is the second-best bed? And whose is the dog?

ALIMONY. The word "alimony" is derived from the Latin word for sustenance, and ultimately from the verb which means "to nourish" or "to give food to." The prevailing idea behind alimony in America is that the husband, as head of the family, has an obligation to support his wife and children, no matter how wealthy the wife and children may be independently.

At the time of divorce, the alimony rights of the wife are considered to be an extension of the husband's duty to support, undertaken at the time of marriage. Therefore, alimony means the money paid during and after the divorce by the ex-husband to the ex-wife (rarely the other way around).

There is, however, another basis on which some courts in some American jurisdictions have looked on alimony—it can be seen as punishment of the husband for his mistreatment of the wife. Where this idea is found, the wife cannot be entitled to alimony if she is the "guilty party" to the divorce. In most states, the amount of alimony is more or less directly dependent on whatever moral or immoral conduct of the wife may come to the attention of the court. A woman known to be guilty of anything the court considers to be moral misconduct is likely to be awarded less than an "innocent" wife. The law varies widely on these matters; practice varies even more.

The most important thing about the award and payment of alimony is that it is done on the basis of a court order. Therefore, if it is not paid, the offending husband is in contempt of court. The institution of divorce is provided, as we have seen before, with only one formal sanction to insure the compliance of its various parties. And that is the court.

The amount of alimony is set by the court, on the basis of the wife's need and the husband's ability to pay. Both her education and training and his may be taken into account; the state of health may be relevant. Sometimes the length of the marriage is a consideration—a short period entitling the wife to less alimony. The age of the children, the moral behavior of each spouse, the income tax position—all these things and undoubtedly many more will affect the court's decision about alimony.

Either ex-spouse may petition the court to have alimony arrangements changed, upon any change in either the ex-wife's need or the ex-husband's ability to pay. It cannot, however, be changed on the basis of the postmarital behavior of either party. Some courts listen with sympathy to an ex-husband's request to reduce alimony at the time of his remarriage; almost all alimony is arranged so that it stops entirely at the time of the ex-wife's remarriage.

CHILD SUPPORT. Courts and citizens are both much clearer about child support than they are about alimony. The principle is obvious to all: as long as he is able to do so, the responsibility for supporting children lies with their father. Whether a man is morally and legally obliged to support his children depends only on one factor: his ability to do so. In assessing child support payments, the court looks simply at his ability to pay, including his health, and to the needs of the child. The amount may be set by the court; it is always ratified by the court.

The principles behind the idea of child support are simple. However, the functioning of the child support aspects of the divorce institution are anything but simple. The difficulty arises, again and as usual, because of the lack of sanctions aside from the court, and from the further fact that court action is expensive and usually slow. The father who does not pay the stipulated child support is in contempt of court, and can be brought back into court on that basis. In order to avoid clogging the courts, some states have found various ways in which the payments can be made to the state and forwarded to the mother or other guardian of the children. This, too, is expensive. There seems to be no really adequate means, as yet, of dealing with men who do not make support payments.

Some mothers try to stop the visitation of fathers who do not make support payments—and some courts uphold them. Although most divorced parents realize that "fighting through the children" is harmful to the children, not all succeed in avoiding it.

THE COPARENTAL DIVORCE AND THE PROBLEM OF CUSTODY

The most enduring pain of divorce is likely to come from the coparental divorce. This odd word is useful because it indicates that the child's parents are divorced from each other—not from the child. Children do not always understand this: they may ask, "Can Father divorce *me?*" This is not a silly or naïve question; from the standpoint of the child what was a failure in marriage to the parents is the shattering of his kinship circle.

The children have to go somewhere. And even when both parents share joint legal custody of the child, one parent or the other gets "physical custody"—the right to have the child living with him.

The word "custody" is a double-edged sword. It means "responsibility for the care of" somebody. It also means "imprisonment." The child is in the custody of his parents—the criminal is in the custody of the law. When we deal with the custody of children in divorces, we must see to it that they are "in the care of" somebody, and that the care is adequate—we must also see that the custody is not punitive or restricting.

Legal custody of children entitles the custodial parent to make decisions about their life-styles and the things they can do which are developmentally important to them—educational and recreational and cultural choices. In the common law, the father had absolute property rights over the child—the mother had none, unless she inherited them at the death of the father. About the time judicial divorce was established in America, custody preferences shifted until the two parents were about equal. With the vast increase in the divorce rate in the early third of the twentieth century, the shift continued, giving the mother preference in both legal and physical custody. We rationalize this practice by such ideas as mother love, masculine nature, or the exigencies of making a living.

Custody of the children, once granted to the mother, will be taken away from her by the courts *only* if she can be shown to be seriously delinquent in her behavior *as a mother.* Her behavior *as a wife* may be at stake in granting the divorce or in fixing the amount of the alimony—but not in granting custody. A woman cannot be denied her rights as a mother on the basis of having performed badly as a wife, or even on the basis of her behavior as a divorcee if the children were not threatened physically or morally. Similarly, a man cannot be penalized as a father for his shortcomings as a husband.

The overriding consideration in all cases is that the court takes what action it considers to be "in the best interests of the child." The rights of children as human beings override, in our morality and hence in our law, all rights of the parents as parents, and certainly their rights as spouses. We have absolutely inverted the old common law.

It is generally considered that a child's best interests lie with his own parents—but if they do not, what is called "third-party custody" can be imposed by the court. Courts do not like to separate children from at least one parent—but sometimes there is no alternative "in the best interests of the child."

A man is always, either by statute law or by common law, obliged to take financial responsibility for his minor children. If there are overriding circumstances that make it impossible for him to work, then that responsibility devolves on their mother. Sometimes a mother refuses her ex-husband the right to support his children as a means to deny him the right to see them—some men accept this, but few would be forced by a court to accept it if they chose to question its legality.

The rights of the parent who has neither legal nor physical custody of the child are generally limited to his right of visiting the child at reasonable times. This right stems from parenthood and is not dependent on decrees issued by a court. The court may, of course, condition the rights of visitation, again in the best interests of the child.

CHILDREN AND ONE-PARENT HOUSEHOLDS. Children grow up. The association between parent and child and the association between the parents change with each new attainment of the child. The child grows, parents respond—and their response has subtle overtones in their own relationship. In divorce, their responses must necessarily be of a different nature from what it is in marriage. In divorce, with communication reduced, the goals of the spouses are less likely to be congruent—the child is observed at different times and from different vantage points by the separated parents, each with his own set of concerns and worries.

Coparental divorce created lasting pain for many divorcees I interviewed—particularly if the ex-spouses differed greatly on what they wanted their children to become, morally, spiritually, professionally, even physically. This very difference of opinion about the goals of living may have lain behind the divorce. It continues through the children.

The good ex-husband/father feels, "My son is being brought up by his mother so that he is not my son." A divorced man almost always feels that his boy is being made into a different kind of man from what he himself is. Often, of course, he is right. The good ex-wife/mother may be tempted to refuse her ex-husband his visitation rights because, from her point of view, "He is bad for the children." This statement may mean no more than that the children are emotionally higher strung before and after a visit, and therefore upset her calm. But the mother may think the father wants something else for the children than she does, thus putting a strain on her own efforts to instill her own ideals and regulations.

It is difficult for a man to watch his children develop traits similar, if not identical, to those he found objectionable in their mother and which were among those qualities that led to the emotional divorce. The child becomes the living embodiment of the differences in basic values. A man may feel that "she" is bad for the children even when he has the objectivity to see also that the children will not necessarily develop unwholesome personalities, but only different personalities from those they might have developed through being with him.

The problem for the mother of the children is different—she has to deal with the single-parent household, making by herself decisions, which she almost surely feels should be shared. She does not want somebody to tell her what to do, as much as somebody to tell her she is right and make "sensible suggestions." Like most mothers, she wants support, not direction.

There is a traditional and popular belief that divorce is "bad for children." Actually, we do not know very much about it.

Although social scientists no longer put it this way, there is still in the general population a tendency to ask whether divorce "causes" juvenile delinquency. Obviously, if the child's way of dealing with the tensions in the emotional divorce of his parents is to act out criminally, he has turned to delinquency. But other children react to similar situations with supercompliance and perhaps ultimate ulcers. The tensions in divorce certainly tell on children, but the answers the children find are not inherent in the institution of divorce.

The more fruitful question is more difficult: "How can we arm children to deal with themselves in the face of the inadequacies and tensions in their families, which may lead their parents to the divorce court?" At least that question avoids the scapegoating of parents or blaming it all on "society"—and it also provides us a place to start working, creating new institutions.

TELLING CHILDREN ABOUT DIVORCE. It is a truism today that parents should be honest with their children, but parents apparently do not always extend this precept to being honest with their children about divorce. One of the most consistent and discouraging things found in interviewing American divorced persons came in response to my question, "What have you told your child about the nature of divorce in general and your own in particular?" The question was almost always followed by a silence, then a sigh, and then some version of, "I haven't told them much. I haven't had to. They know. You can't kid kids."

It is true, generally, that children are not easily deceived. But it is not true that they know instinctively why something is happening. Children today are comparatively sophisticated about divorce—until they are involved in it.

Children who live in and with the institution of divorce have a lot to learn that other children may never have to learn. The most important ideas to be communicated to them deal with the nature of the new life they will lead. It may be reasonable, in some cases, not to acquaint them with the facts of the emotional and legal divorces. But the new situation—custody, visitation, the new division of labor in the household—can be explained quite clearly so that the child can do his adjusting to a fairly predictable situation.

Of equal importance, they must be taught purposefully and overtly some of the culture of the family that does not occur in the ex-family. That is to say, children in divorce must pick up by instruction what they would have learned by habituation or osmosis in an unbroken healthy home.

The children must learn how to deal with the "broken orbit" of models for the roles they will play in life. A boy cannot become fully a man—or a girl a woman—if they model themselves only on the cues they pick up from one sex alone. A woman cannot teach a boy to be a man, or a girl a woman, without the help of men. And a man cannot teach either a boy to be a man or a girl to be a woman without the help of women.

All of us interact with members of both sexes. Our cues about the behavior of men come from the responses of women, as well as from the responses of men. Children—like the rest of us—must have significant members of both sexes around them.

Obviously, children of even the most successful homes do not model themselves solely on their parents, in spite of the importance parents have as models. There are television models (boys walk like athletes or crime busters); there are teachers, friends, storekeepers, bus drivers, and all the rest. But the child who lives in a one-parent home has to adjust to a different mixture of sex-role models. The big danger may be not so much that a boy has no father model in his home, but that his mother stops his walking like Willie Mays or a television cowboy because she doesn't like it. And worst of all, she may, without knowing it, try to extinguish in him the very behavior patterns he has learned from his father: especially, if she does not want to be reminded of his father.

Children who live in one-parent homes must learn what a husband/father is and what he does in the home—and they have to learn it in a different context from children of replete homes. They must learn what a wife/mother is in such a home. Children are taught to be husbands and wives while they are still children. In the one-parent home the children have to be taught actively and realistically the companionship, sexual, coparenting, and domestic aspects of marriage.

It is important to realize that these things can be taught. Yet, it is in this very process of teaching the child that the parent may reveal a great deal of bitterness and hostility toward the ex-spouse. The good parent has to teach the child without denigrating or idealizing the other parent.

A noted psychoanalyst has told me that in her opinion there are only two things children learn in two-parent homes that cannot be taught in one-parent homes; one is the undertone of healthy sexuality that is present in a healthy home. Nothing appears on the surface save love—but the sexual tone of married love permeates everything. Even in the most loving one-parent home this is something that can, perhaps, be explained to children, but something that they will have trouble feeling unless they experience it elsewhere. The other thing that is difficult to teach, she says, is the ambivalence of the child toward both parents. When the relationship of father-child is none of the business of the child's mother, or the relationship of mother-child outside the ken and responsibility of the child's father, then the illusion can be maintained by the child that father is wholly right and mother wholly wrong, or father wholly unjustified and mother completely innocent. It is seldom true.

In short, the ex-family must do many of the things that the family ordinarily does, but it does them with even more difficulty than the family. It is in the coparental aspects of the divorce that the problems are so long-lasting—and so difficult. And the reason, as we have seen, is that a child's mother and father are, through the child, kinsmen to one another, but the scope of activities in their relationship has been vastly curtailed.

THE COMMUNITY DIVORCE AND THE PROBLEM OF LONELINESS

Changes in civil status or "stages of life" almost invariably mark changes in friends and in significant communities. We go to school, and go away to college. We join special-interest groups. When we are married, we change communities—sometimes almost completely except for a few relatives and two or three faithful friends from childhood or from college.

When we divorce, we also change communities. Divorce means "forsaking all others" just as much as marriage does, and in about the same degree.

Many divorcees complain bitterly about their "ex-friends." "Friends?" one woman replied to my question during an interview, "They drop you like a hot potato. The exceptions are those real ones you made before marriage, those who are unmarried, and your husband's men friends who want to make a pass at you."

Like newly marrieds, new divorcees have to find new communities. They tend to find them among the divorced. Morton Hunt's book, *The World of the Formerly Married*, provides a good concise report on these new communities. Divorcees find —if they will let themselves—that there is a group ready to welcome them as soon as they announce their separations. There are people to explain the lore that will help them in being a divorcee, people to support them emotionally, people to give them information, people to date and perhaps love as soon as they are able to love.

There are, of course, some people who avoid other divorcees. Such people tend to disappear into the population at large, and hence are more difficult to find when we study their adjustments.

But the community divorce is an almost universal experience of divorcees in America. And although there are many individuals who are puzzled and hurt until they find their way into it, it is probably the aspect of divorce that Americans handle best.

THE PSYCHIC DIVORCE AND THE PROBLEM OF AUTONOMY

Psychic divorce means the separation of self from the personality and the influence of the ex-spouse—to wash that man right out of your hair. To distance yourself from the loved portion that ultimately became disappointing, from the hated portion, from the baleful presence that led to depression and loss of self-esteem.

The most difficult of the six divorces is the psychic divorce, but it is also the one that can be personally most constructive. The psychic divorce involves becoming a whole, complete, and autonomous individual again—learning to live without somebody to lean on—but also without somebody to support. There is nobody on whom to blame one's difficulties (except oneself), nobody to shortstop one's growth, nobody to grow with.

Each must regain—if he ever had it—the dependence on self and faith in one's own capacity to cope with the environment, with people, with thoughts and emotions.

WHY DID I MARRY? To learn anything from divorce, one must ask himself why he married. Marriage, it seems to me, should be an act of desperation—a last resort. It should not be used as a means of solving one's problems. Ultimately, of course, most people in our society can bring their lives to a high point of satisfaction and usefulness only through marriage. The more reason, indeed, we should not enter it unless it supplies the means for coping with our healthy needs and our desires to give and grow.

All too often, marriage is used as a shield against becoming whole or autonomous individuals. People too often marry to their weaknesses. We all carry the family of our youth within ourselves—our muscles, our emotions, our unconscious minds. And we all project it again into the families we form as adults. The path of every marriage is strewn with yesterday's unresolved conflicts, of both spouses. Every divorce is beset by yesterday's unresolved conflicts, compounded by today's.

So the question becomes: How do I resolve the conflicts that ruined my marriage? And what were the complementary conflicts in the spouse I married?

Probably all of us marry, at least in part, to defend old solutions to old conflicts. The difficulty comes when two people so interlock their old conflicts and solutions that they cannot become aware of them, and hence cannot solve them. Ironically, being a divorced person has built-in advantages in terms of working out these conflicts, making them conscious, and overcoming them.

WHY WAS I DIVORCED? Presumably the fundamental cause of divorce is that people find themselves in situations in which they cannot become autonomous individuals and are unwilling to settle for a *folie à deux*. Divorcees are people who have not achieved a good marriage—they are also people who would not settle for a bad one.

A "successful" divorce begins with the realization by two people that they do not have any constructive future together. That decision itself is a recognition of the emotional divorce. It proceeds through the legal channels of undoing the wedding, through the economic division of property and arrangement for alimony and support. The successful divorce involves determining ways in which children can be informed, educated in their new roles, loved and provided for. It involves finding a new community. Finally, it involves finding your own autonomy as a person and as a personality.

AUTONOMY. The greatest difficulty comes for those people who cannot tell autonomy from independence. Nobody is independent in the sense that he does not depend on people. Life is with people. But if you wither and die without specific people doing specific things for you, then you have lost your autonomy. You enter into social relationships—and we are all more or less dependent in social relationships—in order to enhance your own freedom and growth, as well as to find somebody to provide for your needs and to provide good company in the process. Although, in a good marriage, you would never choose to do so, you *could* withdraw. You could grieve, and go on.

These are six of the stations of divorce. "The undivorced," as they are sometimes called in the circles of divorcees, almost never understand the great achievement that mastering them may represent.

AN AMICABLE DIVORCE *

Mary McDermott Shideler

Matthew and Anne Surrey
announce
an amicable divorce

Their friends and relatives
are invited not to take sides
and to keep in touch
with both of them

For the time being still
both at home at
1492 Columbus Circle
Middle City, Midwest

An amicable divorce sounds like a contradiction in terms. Usually we assume that either the couple was driven to that step by bitter conflict leading to permanent alienation if not violence, or else they had entered marriage so flippantly that its dissolution leaves them utterly indifferent to each other. Either way, the word "amicable" is not appropriate to describe the process or its aftermath.

Many people, indeed, especially in our churches, are likely to feel that if the couple remains amicable their marriage ought not to be dissolved. Marriage is too serious an affair, they believe, to be terminated unless it becomes intolerable, and when it has reached that stage, the break will necessarily be drastic. Other attitudes toward marriage and divorce are being developed, but are seldom enough understood that it is worth examining how the one particular couple whom I have named Matthew and Anne Surrey approached their divorce and met certain of its problems, especially in the light of their Christian commitment and of their desire that the dissolution of their marriage, like its institution, should be solemnized with a religious ceremony.

I

In the dozen years of their marriage, Matt and Anne had separated twice—at least once for more than a year—in order to obtain for themselves and give each other the kind of breathing space that they needed in their search for a way to solve their problems without violence. Each thoroughly liked and respected the other. They continued to share many interests. But now, their relationship had become destructive of their individual selves and therefore of their union. The details do not matter. Here was simply the not uncommon situation where in order to grow or even endure, each needed something that the other could not give without destroying his or her very identity as a person, and each was compelled to express in his or her own life something essential which undercut the other's well-being. They could laugh and weep together, but they could not build. The time had come for them to go their own ways, not bound and not keeping the other in bondage. "Nothing short of necessity," Anne told me, "could have pried us apart."

Those reasons did not satisfy the judge who presided over the final hearing. Apparently Anne's testimony that Matt had never physically abused her, that their previous separations had ended with reconciliations, perhaps the fact that they had no children, conveyed to him an impression that they were treating the institution of marriage frivolously. And he was clearly shocked at Matt's presence in the courtroom, since the divorce was not being contested, the more because he sat with Anne and her witness before the court was in session, the three of them conversing decorously but in as friendly a manner as if they were waiting for the curtain to rise at a theatre. The judge plainly interpreted the case as one of "easy come, easy go," and his moral sensitivities were outraged. In conclusion, he said in so many words that he was exceedingly reluctant to grant this divorce, and did so only because the new laws in that state required him to.

For the legal making or breaking of a marriage, nothing more than such bare formalities are prescribed. The other rituals associated with marriage—the parties before the wedding, the ceremony in the presence of families and friends, the official announcements—are unnecessary, but they are notably enriching. They are means for initiating the couple and their associates into the new conditions of their lives. Far from being

merely decorative, these rites of passage are psychologically and
sociologically of great importance. Unfortunately, no such rites
have yet been established for divorce, which is also the beginning of a new life. So the Surreys, recognizing their value and
wanting them, improvised their own.

Because the Surreys are not only intelligent and perceptive,
but also imaginative, their rites accurately reflected their attitudes and convictions. Central for them was the affirmation
that their divorce was not the cutting of a fabric but its unravel-
ling. Their marriage was not a rag to be consigned to a trash
can, but a network whose threads were to be disentangled and
sorted out into those which could be used again, and those which
should be discarded. Moreover, they wanted to make their affirmation in both secular and religious terms. Between the time
they filed for divorce and the time when Anne left town several
days after it had been granted, two private and three public
forms of expression emerged, not including their appearance in
court.

II

First, together Matt and Anne told their closest friends of
their intention. Together they received the brunt of the initial
surprise and regret, answered any questions, and gave any explanations asked for. Whatever the procedure accomplished for
them, it saved their friends from the considerable embarrass-
ments which can follow when one party to the divorce confides in
someone who has been close to both parties.

Second, the Surreys continued to inhabit the same house, to
run their household as before, and to go places as a couple in
their usual way. Partly this was because they were not financially able to maintain separate households. But also, throughout they remained friends—possibly better friends than while
they were married; and the continuation of their domestic arrangements was a way of demonstrating publicly that extremely
important fact. Let those who consider the Surreys' behavior
another evidence of frivolity take note that almost invariably, a
request, a criticism, a gesture, will have a different impact if not
a different meaning when it is made in the context of marriage,
and when it is made in the context of friendship or of a professional relationship (as with a priest or doctor or lawyer). Some
people can be freer with each other and hurt each other less when
they are not married than when they are, especially in the nuclear

family where all one's emotional eggs are being carried by a single other person.

If marriage be interpreted narrowly as the licensing of sexual relations, instead of broadly as the commitment to become a family, the Surreys' living together after they filed for divorce will appear scandalous. To the Surreys' themselves, it was not only natural but right thus to affirm the mutual love and respect that endured even when they had discovered that the two of them could no longer constitute a family. To quote another woman, replying to her lawyer's expression of surprise that she should be so friendly with the man she was divorcing, "But I'm not married to all my friends! "

One view of marriage which is popular today says that friendship is (or should be) its basis. Another, falsely called "romanticism," says that love of a particular kind is enough for a successful marriage. Neither of these, however, takes adequate account of the blazing truth that above all else, marriage in our society is a *working* relationship, a matter of building together a common structure by working toward a common goal: maintaining a household, bringing up children, serving the community, or whatever. In the absence of a working relationship, neither mutual love (romantic or other), nor friendship, nor common interests will make a marriage more than tolerable. The essential is dedication to the same task. Husband and wife can have different vocations and occupations, and still be a family as long as their work is compatible and each is willing—and able —to serve the other in his or her vocation. But the exalted emotions are the icing on the cake, not the substance of the dinner.

III

The third of the Surreys' rites of passage was a party—today, the most pervasive and flexible of social rituals. Because the date of the hearing was postponed at the last minute, the observance preceded the event, but its character was in no way changed because of that dislocation.

Like all the Surreys' parties it was informal. Twenty or thirty people turned up in the course of the evening, many bringing contributions of beer, to sit on the floor of the tiny living room, or gather where they could in the rest of the house. Many commented on how much they liked both Matt and Anne, and how sorry they were about the divorce. None in my sight or hearing criticized either by so much as a lifted eyebrow, or implied fault or blame, or seemed to think it out of place for them to announce the beginning of their lives apart with the same kind of fanfare that proclaims the beginning of a life together.

The high point of that party was the cutting of a wedding cake, complete with figures of a bride and groom on top. The company gathered about the table. Anne took the knife and Matt laid his hand on hers. They looked up to make sure that the friend who had brought his camera was ready to record the event. They brought the knife down accurately between the dolls, so that one fell over on each side. The noisy chatter started again, not quite drowning Anne's announcement that it was a spice cake, the flavor chosen for its symbolic meaning.

If the divorce had bitter overtones, the party would have been unbearable for everyone. As it was, there was pain, but only the clean pain that characterizes even the happiest weddings. The wound of separation is deep in marriage as well as in divorce, but it need not fester. And while its presence may give the festivities the tinge of a deeper color, it should not be allowed to dominate the pattern of rejoicing. Appropriately, emotions are mixed in an amicable divorce as well as in a happy wedding. But the priorities are kept clear, and private grief is expressed privately not because one is hypocritical, but from a sensitivity to the fitness of things. It is too profound, too intimate, to be publicized.

IV

That same intensity led the Surreys to make the religious ceremony a private one. Necessarily it was conducted in a home rather than a church or chapel: what denomination today would "sanctify" a divorce? Nor has any denomination that they knew of provided such a liturgy as this, which they asked me to write for them, and which they and my husband amended slightly before it was performed on the evening of the day when their divorce decree was signed.

When Matthew and Anne arrived at our house with the two other friends they had invited, they were too keyed up from the hearing to do anything but tell their tale, with its funny moments as well as tense and sober ones. Bit by bit, the sharing of the narrative diminished their tension. When all of us were inwardly quiet, Anne put on the phonograph Egon

Petrie's recording of his own transcription of "Sheep May Safely Graze." As it ended, the Service for the Dissolution of a Marriage began.

OFFICIANT: Let us stand in a circle. (We did so, with Matt on his left, and Anne on his right.)

ALL: Oh Lord, how excellent is thy Name in all the earth.

OFFICIANT: Dearly beloved, we have gathered here to solemnize the end of one time in Matthew's and Anne's lives, and the beginning of another. We are so made that we cannot live in isolation from our fellow men, but neither can we live too closely joined with them. We are social beings, but also individual selves, and it is the rhythm of union and separation that enables us to live in the communion which sustains our selves, and in the solitude which nourishes our community. As it is written: (Here he read Ecclesiastes 3:1–8, 11–14)

Thirteen years ago, the time was right for Matthew and Anne to be joined in holy matrimony. Then they needed for their growth in grace and truth the visible bond of marriage. Now the time has come when that bond is hampering both their growth as individual persons, and their common life. They have resolved, therefore, to sever the ties of their marriage, though not of their mutual love and honor, and have asked us, their friends, to witness that affirmation of their new lives, and to uphold them in their new undertakings.

Matthew Surrey, do you now relinquish your status as husband of Anne, freeing her from all claims upon and responsibilities to you except those that you willingly give to all other children of God?

MATTHEW: I do.

OFFICIANT: Do you forgive her any sins she has committed against you, and do you accept her forgiveness, thus freeing her from the burdens of guilt and sterile remorse?

MATTHEW: I do.

OFFICIANT: Do you release her with your love and blessing, in gratitude for the part she has played in your life, in knowledge that her part in you will never be forgotten or despised, and in faith that in separation as in union, you both are held in the grace and unity of God?

MATTHEW: I do.

(The same questions were asked of Anne, and she replied in the same way.)

OFFICIANT: Matthew, what sign do you give Anne as a token of your forgiveness and your release of her?

MATTHEW: Her wedding ring reconsecrated to her freedom. (He placed it on the third finger of her right hand)

OFFICIANT: Anne, what sign do you give Matthew as a token of your forgiveness and your release of him?

ANNE: His wedding ring reconsecrated to his freedom. (She placed it on the third finger of his right hand)

OFFICIANT: Let us pray. Almighty and loving God, who has ordered that seasons shall change and that human lives shall proceed by change, we ask thy blessing upon thy children who now, in their commitment to thee, have severed their commitment to each other. Send them forth in the bond of peace. When they meet, sustain them in their liberty. Keep them both reminded that thy love flows upon and through them both. Sanctify them in their lives, deaths, and resurrections, by the power of thy Holy Spirit, and for the sake of thy Son, Jesus Christ, our Lord.

ALL: Amen.

OFFICIANT: The peace of God which passes all understanding keep your hearts and minds in the knowledge and love of God, and the blessing of God Almighty, the Father, the Son, and the Holy Spirit, be among you and remain with you always. Go in peace.

ALL: In the name of the Lord. Amen.

Spontaneously each person put his arms around those closest to him, and for several minutes there were tears and laughter, hugging and kissing, in a glorious affirmation. Awaiting them were home-made bread of that morning's baking, and wine that flashed red.

Two days later, the mail brought the last of their symbolic expressions, the notification printed in Gothic type: "Matthew and Anne Surrey announce an amicable divorce. . . ."

LONELINESS *

Donis M. Waters

Have you ever been lonely? No, this isn't the start of a popular song. It's an honest question. *Have* you ever been lonely? Have you ever felt that some elusive something was missing in your life, something you couldn't quite name but whose absence left you with an acute sense of emptiness and longing? Have you ever been in a crowd and suddenly felt as if you were watching them from a great distance? Of course you have, for loneliness is the one form of human misery that plagues us constantly from birth to death. It is also the one human misery over which we have the least control because it is both caused by and dispelled by other persons.

Opinions differ as to a precise definition of loneliness. As a sociologist I could say that loneliness is a lack of satisfactory interpersonal relations. A psychologist might say that loneliness is an intense state of depression characterized by self-pity and emotional isolation. However, these definitions sound far too academic and impersonal to describe the spirit-crushing, overwhelming grip of loneliness. I prefer the definition my seven-year-old offered. He said, "Loneliness? That's like when you're standing outside in the cold and you look through the window and see everyone nice and warm and eatin' cake and popcorn and stuff, and you want to go in and have some too but you can't 'cause the door's locked, and you yell and you cry but everyone's having such a good time they don't hear you so you just stand there and watch. That's loneliness!" What more can I add? That's loneliness. Being left out when you want to be in—being cold when you want to be warm—standing on the fringe and watching life go by—having nothing to look forward to, no one to care and no one to care for—that's loneliness.

Man is born with a gregarious instinct, a basic drive that draws him toward the human community, not only for physical contact, but for *emotional communication*. In this one term, emotional communication, can be found the whole of man's psychic needs: love, acceptance, security, sympathy, friendship, achievement and finally the need most often overlooked, the need to be needed. The necessity to fulfil these psychic needs is a constant, compelling

* Taken from LIFE TOPICS SERIES,
published by Alba House Communications, Canfield, Ohio 44406.

force which dictates our mental attitudes as relentlessly as bodily needs dictate our physical actions. When these psychic needs are denied us, when we lose our emotional communication, we fall prey to a misery we alone can not relieve—loneliness.

Temporary loneliness, although it may be unpleasant, will not bring any lasting damage, but intense, chronic loneliness has driven men to the extremes of human tolerance, to the desperation which leads to alcoholism, drug addiction, insanity, violence and even death. With a little forethought, a little effort, a little determination, our loneliness need never reach these proportions.

There is a way to overcome loneliness, and for lack of a more sophisticated term I call it the mutual benefit formula. If our loneliness is caused by the indifference and neglect of other people then it must be relieved by other people. Yet we can very seldom rise above our pride and sense of self-sufficiency long enough to *admit* we need other people. This, then, must be the first step toward relieving our loneliness—admitting we need the companionship, the attention, the thoughts of other people. From there we can proceed to the second step—letting others *know* we need them.

Perhaps this is the bitterest step, for it means swallowing a good dose of that false pride and admitting to ourselves that we are not as self-sustaining as we think we are. But how do we go about letting others know our need? Do we just walk up to them bold-faced and say, "I'm lonely and I need you"? Not necessarily, although to our family and close friends there is certainly no harm in using this direct approach. But why not try a more subtle, indirect approach—instead of asking for friendship and attention, why not offer them?

Look at the problem this way: If loneliness is caused and relieved by other people, then there must be someone whose loneliness we have caused or can relieve, someone who is facing the same situation we are—need versus pride. Doesn't it stand to reason that if we were to seek out that person and relieve his loneliness, he in turn would respond with the warmth, friendship and solicitation that answers our own need?

Examples of this mutual benefit formula can be seen everywhere—the neighborhood spinster with the open cookie jar, the widow in volunteer gray, the aging grandfather with stories and sage advice, the dedicated relief worker, the doctor, the priest, the missionary—people who are so busy offering themselves to others they have no time in their lives and no room in their hearts for loneliness.

THE TIME MY FATHER DIED *

JOSEPH W. MATHEWS

Sometime past noon, November ninth the last, our telephone rang. It was for me, person-to-person. My oldest sister, Margaret, was calling. "Joe, Papa just died!"

We children never called him Papa while we were growing up. He was mostly "Dad." But in the last decade or so, out of a strange mellowing affection, we started, all seven of us, referring to our father as Papa.

My Papa dead!—just seven days before he was ninety-two.

Within the hour I began my journey to my father. I find it difficult to express how deeply I wanted to be with him in his death. Furthermore he had long since commissioned my brother and me to conduct the celebration. My brother unfortunately was out of the country and I had quiet anxiety about executing it alone.

The late afternoon flight was conducive to contemplation. I thought of the many well-meant condolences already received.

"Isn't it fine that your father lived to be ninety-two?"

"It must be easier for you since he lived such a long life."

Certainly I was grateful for such comments. But I found myself perturbed too. Didn't they realize that to die is to die, whether you are seventeen, forty-nine, or one hundred and ten? Didn't they know that our death is our death? And that each of us has only one death to die? This was my father's death! It was no less significant because he was most of a hundred. It was his death. The only one he would ever have.

The family had already gathered when I arrived in the little New England town. We immediately sat in council. The first task was to clarify our self-understanding. The second was to embody that understanding in the celebration of Papa's death. Consensus was already present: the One who gives us our life is the same that takes it from us. From this stance we felt certain broad implications should guide the formation of the ceremony.

> Death is a very lively part of a man's life and no life
> is finished without the experience of death.

* Joseph W. Mathews.

Death is a crucial point in the human adventure which somehow transposes to every other aspect of life.

Death is to be received in humble gratitude and must ever be honored with honest dignity.

Together we concluded that the death of our father must be celebrated as a real part of his history, before the final Author that gave him both his life and his death, with integrity and solemn appreciation.

The very articulation of these lines of guidance worked backward laying bare our own inward flight from death. They also made more obvious the efforts of our culture to disguise death. I mean the great concealment by means of plush caskets, white satin linings, soft cushions, head pillows, Sunday clothes, cosmetics, perfume, flowers, and guaranteed vaults. Empty of symbolic meaning, they serve but to deceive—to simulate life. They seem to say, Nothing has actually happened, Nothing is really changed. What vanity to denude death! All our pretenses about it only strengthen its power to destroy our lives. Death stripped of meaning and dignity becomes a demon. Not to embrace death as part of our given life is finally not to embrace our life. That is, we do not really live. This is the power of unacknowledged death. I ponder over the strange smile on faces of the dead.

To symbolize the dignity of our father's death, the family thought to clothe him in a pine box and to rest him in the raw earth.

I remember the men of the war I buried. There was great dignity in the shelter—half shrouded, in the soiled clothing, in the dirty face, in the shallow grave. I say dignity was there. Death was recognized as death. Death was dramatized as the death of the men who had died their own death.

A sister and brother-in-law were sent to make arrangements. They asked about the coffin. A pine box was out of the question. None was to be had. The undertaker, as they called him, explained that caskets ranged from one hundred to several thousands of dollars.

Interpreting the spirit of the common mind, our emissaries asked for the $100 coffin.

"What $100 coffin? replied an astonished undertaker.

"Why the one you mentioned."

"Oh no, caskets begin at $275."

"Did you not mention a $100 coffin?"

"Yes. Yes. But you wouldn't want that. It is for paupers. We bury only the paupers in the $100 coffins."

This thought racked the psychic foundations of my sister and her husband. They retreated for further consultation. None of the rest of us, it turned out, were emotionally prepared for the pauper twist. Actually, the tyranny of the economic order over us was exposed. Our deepest emotions of guilt, love, sorrow, regret were all mixed up with this strange tyranny. In short, we could not move forward with our decision until we first agreed to set up a small memorial for Papa that would be used for charity in the little community.

By this time, assuming that no one would want to put his father away as a pauper, the undertaker had placed Papa in the $275 casket. Having recovered some equilibrium we protested. He was understandably upset by our stand and insisted that we come to his showroom. We all went together, including Mama, who has been weathering the storms of life now for more than fourscore years. Caskets of all kinds filled the place. We asked about the pauper's coffin.

"We keep that outside in the storehouse." Anticipating our next request he hurried on. "No, I can't bring that into my show-room."

In the back I saw a wooden rough box which reminded me of the pine coffin. We talked, the undertaker and I. He was really a very sensitive man. Certainly he had a living to make. When I offered to pay him more for the other expenses of the funeral, he refused. But he mellowed a bit. He remembered when he lived in upper New York state as a little boy. His grandfather had been an undertaker too. Grandfather had used rough pine boxes out in the country to bury people in. In his recollecting he found a kind of meaning in our decision for the pauper's coffin. He even brought it into the showroom where Mama and the rest of the family could see it.

Immediately it was opened, another mild shock came. The pauper's coffin was exactly like any other coffin—pillow, white satin, and all. Except the white satin wasn't really white satin. It was the kind of shiny material you might buy at the ten-cent store. Everything was simply cheap imitation. We had hoped for something honest. Despite the disappointment, we took the pauper's box. And Papa was transferred to his own coffin.

I did not want to see my father until I could have some time with him alone. Several hours before the funeral I went to where he waited. I can scarcely describe what I saw and felt.

My father, I say, was ninety-two. In his latter years he had wonderfully chiseled wrinkles. I had helped to put them there. His cheeks were deeply sunken; his lips pale. He was an old man. There is a kind of glory in the face of an old man. Not so with the stranger laying there. They had my Papa looking like he was fifty-two. Cotton stuffed in his cheeks had erased the best wrinkles. Make-up powder and rouge plastered his face way up into his hair and around his neck and ears. His lips were painted. He . . . he looked ready to step before the footlights of the matinee performance.

I fiercely wanted to pluck out the cotton but was afraid. At least the make-up could come off. I called for alcohol and linens. A very reluctant mortician brought them to me. And I began the restoration. As the powder, the rouge, the lipstick disappeared, the stranger grew older. He never recovered the look of his ninety-two years but in the end the man in the coffin became my Papa.

Something else happened to me there with my father in his death. Throughout childhood, I had been instructed in the medieval world view. This by many people who were greatly concerned for me. My father, my mother, my Sunday school teacher, yes, my teachers at the school and most of my neighbors. They taught me the ancient Greek picture of how when you die there's something down inside of you that escapes death, how the real me doesn't die at all. Much later I came to see that both the biblical view and the modern image were something quite different. But I wondered if the meeting with my father in his death would create nostalgia for the world view of my youth. I wondered if I would be tempted to revert to that earlier conditioning in order to handle the problems of my own existence. It wasn't this way.

What did happen to me I am deeply grateful for. I don't know how much I'm able to communicate. It happened when I reached down to straighten my father's tie. There was my father. Not the remains, not the body of my father, but my father. It was my father in death! Ever since I can remember, Papa never succeeded in getting his tie quite straight. We children took some kind of pleasure in fixing it before he went out. Though he always pretended to be irritated at this, we knew that he enjoyed

our attention. It was all sort of a secret sign of mutual acknowl-
edgment. Now in death I did it once again. This simple little act
became a new catalyst of meaning. That was my Papa whose
tie I straightened in the coffin. It was my father there experiencing his death. It was my Papa involved in the Mystery of his
death as he had been involved in the Mystery in his life. I say
there he was related to the same Final Mystery in death as in life.
Somehow the dichotomy between living and dying was overcome.

Where is thy victory, O death?

Death is indeed a powerfully individual happening. My Papa
experienced his death all alone. About this I am quite clear. I
remember during the war I wanted to help men die. I was never
finally able to do this. Sometimes I placed a lighted cigarette in
a soldier's mouth as we talked. Sometimes I quoted for him the
Twenty-third Psalm. Sometimes I wiped the sweat and blood
from his face. Sometimes I held his hand. Sometimes I did
nothing. It was a rude shock to discover that I could not in the
final sense help a man to die. Each had to do his own dying,
alone.

But then I say, death is something more than an individual experience. It is also a social happening. Papa's death was an
event in our family. All of us knew that a happening had happened to us as a family and not just to Papa. Furthermore, the
dying of an individual is also an internal occurrence in the larger
communities of life. Indeed it happens to all history and creation
itself. This is true whether that individual be great or small.
The inner being of a little New England town is somehow changed
by the absence of the daily trek of an eccentric old gentleman to
the postoffice who stopped to deliver long monologues on not very
interesting subjects to all who could not avoid him. Perhaps we
don't know how to feel these happenings as communities. Maybe
we don't know how to celebrate them. But they happen.

Finally, death is a happening to that strange historical cadre
the Church. This body, however vaguely, is more self-conscious-
ly aware of this. It is clearly there in ancient rites by which it
celebrates the event of death.

We wanted to celebrate Papa's death as his own event but we
wanted also to celebrate it as a social happening. Most of all,
we wanted to celebrate Christianly. But this is not so simple.
The office of the funeral suffers a great malaise in our day. Perhaps even more than other rites. There are many causes. The

undertaker, in the showroom episode, spoke to this with deep concern. His rather scathing words disturb me still.

"Funerals today have become no more than disposal services!"

"What of those conducted by the Church?" I ventured.

"Church indeed! I mean the Church." he said.

His professional posture was here set aside. Pointing out that most funerals today are held outside any real sense of Christian community, he spoke of the tragedy of keeping children away from death. He spoke of adults who sophisticatedly boast of never having engaged in the death rite. He spoke of the over-all decrease in funeral attendance. He especially rued the empti-ness of the rites because they were no longer understood. And he caricatured the clergy as the hired disposal units with their artificial airs, unrealistic words, and hurried services.

"What we all seem to want nowadays," he said, "is to get rid of the body as quickly and efficiently as is respectably allowable, with as little trouble to as few folk as possible."

These solemn words were creatively sobering. The funeral em-bodied the full office of worship. We who gathered acted out of all three parts. We first confessed our own self-illusions and re-ceived once again the word of cosmic promise of fresh beginnings. Then we read to ourselves from our classic scriptures recounting men's courage to be before God and boldly expressed together our thanksgiving for the given actualities of our lives. Thirdly, we presented ourselves to the Unchanging Mystery beyond all that is and corporately dedicated our lives once more to the task of af-firming the world and creating civilization.

The point is, we did not gather to console ourselves. We did not gather to psychologically bolster one another. We did not gather to excuse anybody's existence or to pretend about the world we live in. We celebrated the death of my father by recol-lecting and acknowledging who we are and what we must there-fore become. That is, we assembled as the Church on this occa-sion in our history, to remember that we are the Church.

In the midst of the service of death the "words over the dead" are pronounced. I had sensed for a long time that one day I might pronounce them over Papa. Now that the time had come I found myself melancholy beyond due. It was not simply that it was my father. Yet just because it was my father, I was per-haps acutely sensitive. I mean about the funeral meditation, as it is revealingly termed.   Memories of poetic rationalizations of our human pretenses about death gnawed at my spirit.   Some that I recalled actually seemed designed to blanket the awareness that comes in the face of death, that death is a part of life and that all must die.   I remembered others as attempts to explain away the sharp sense of ontological guilt and moral emptiness that we all experience before the dead.   The very gifts of grace were here denied, whether by ignorance or intent, and the human spirit thereby smothered into nothing.   I remember still other of these meditations even more grotesque in their disfigurement of life —undisguised sentimentalities offering shallow assurances and fanciful comforts.   How could we shepherds of the souls of men do such things to human beings?   Perhaps after all, I was not unduly depressed.

Coincidental with these broodings, my imagination was vividly assaulted by another image.   It was a homely scene from a television western.   A small crowd of townsfolk were assembled on Boot Hill to pay last respects to one who had lived and died outside the law.   A very ordinary citizen was asked to say "a-few-words-over-the-dead."   He spoke with the plainness of wisdom born out of intimate living with life as it actually is.   Protesting that he was not a religious man, he reminded the gathered of the mystery present in that situation beyond the understanding of any one or all of them together.   Then he turned and spoke words to the dead one.   He spoke words to the family.   He spoke words to the townsfolk themselves.   In each case his words confronted the intended hearer with the real events and guilt of the past and in each case he offered an image of significance for the future. There was comfort in his words.   But it was the honest, painful comfort of coming to terms with who we are in the midst of the world as it is.   It impressed me as deeply religious, as deeply Christian.   For my father, I took this pattern as my own.

At the appointed place I, too, reminded the assembled body of the Incomprehensible One who is the ground of all living and dying.   I, too, announced a word to the assembled townsfolk, and to my family, and to my father.

I looked out at the members of the funeral party who represented the village where my father had spent his last years.   They were sitting face to face before one another, each caught in the gaze of his neighbor.   In that moment, if I had never known it before, I knew that a community's life is somehow held before it whenever it takes, with even vague seriousness, the death of one of its members. I saw in its face its failures and fears, its acts of injustice, callousness, and irresponsibility. I saw its guilt. I saw its despair. They would call it sorrow for a passing one. But it was their sorrow. Indeed it was, in a strange way, sorrow for themselves.

In the name of the Church, I spoke, first, of all this which they already knew yet so desperately needed to know aloud. And then I pronounced all their past, remembered and forgotten, fully and finally received before the Unconditioned Being who is Lord both of life and death.

I looked out at my family. There was my mother surrounded by her children and her children's children. What was going on in the deeps of this woman who had mixed her destiny with that of the dead man for the major share of a century? What of sister Margaret who knew so well the severity of her father? What of the son who had never won approval? Or the son-in-law never quite received. What of the one who knew hidden things? What of the rebellious one? What of the specially favored? What of Alice? What of Arthur? What of Elizabeth? I knew, as I looked, perhaps all over again, that the sorrow at death is not only that of the loss of the cherished and the familiar. It is the sorrow of unacknowledged guilt, postponed intentions, buried animosities, unmended ruptures. The sorrow of the funeral is the pain of our own creatureliness, of self-disclosure, and of self-acknowledgment. It is the pain of turning from the past to the future. It is the pain of having to decide all over again about our lives.

In the name of the Church, I spoke of these things written so clearly upon our family countenance. And then in fear and joy pronounced all our relations with Papa and one another as cosmically approved by the One who gives us our lives and takes them from us once again.

I looked at my father. And I knew things in a way I had not known them before. It wasn't that I knew anything new. But my knowing was now transposed so that everything was different. I knew his very tragic boyhood. I knew the scars it engraved on his soul. I knew his lifelong agonizing struggle to rise beyond them. I knew his unknown greatness. I knew his qualities next to genius that never found deliverance. I knew his secret sense of failure. I knew things he never knew I knew. I knew the dark nights of his soul. I knew, well, what I knew was his life. His spirit's journey. That was it. It was his life I knew in that moment. It was frozen now. It was all in now. It was complete. It was finished. It was offered up for what it was. This was the difference made by death.

In the name of the Church, I spoke his life out loud. Not excusing, not glorifying, just of his life as I saw it then. And then I pronounced it good and great and utterly significant before the One who had given it to history just as it was. Not as it might have been, not as it could have been abstractly considered, not as I might have wanted it to be or others felt it should have been, not even as Papa might have wanted it altered. I sealed it as acceptable to God, then, just as it was finished.

The celebration ended in the burial grounds.

The funeral party bore Papa to his grave. There was no drama in the processional. It was just empty utility. The death march, once explosive in symbolic force, had lost its power. I allowed myself to be swept along in silent frustration. I was sad for Papa. I had pity for those of us who bore him. I grew angry with myself.

The sun had already fallen behind the ridge when we came to the burial ground. It was on a remote New England hillside (they call it a mountain there). I remember clearly the sharp, cold air and how the very chill made me feel keenly alive. I remember also how the dark shadows dancing on the hills reminded me of life. But I remember most of all the clean smell of God's good earth freshly turned.

I say I smelled the fresh earth. There was none to be seen. What I did see is difficult to believe. I mean the green stuff. Someone had come before us and covered that good, wonderful raw dirt, every clod of it, with green stuff. Everything, every scar of the grave, was concealed under simulated grass: Just as if nothing had been disturbed here: Just as if nothing were going on here: Just as if nothing at all were happening. What an offense against nature, against history, against Papa, against us, against God.

I wanted to scream. I wanted to cry out to the whole world, "Something *is* going on here, something great, something significantly human. Look! Everybody, look! Here is my father's death. It is going on here!"

The banks of flowers upon the green facade only added to the deception. Was it all contrived to pretend at this last moment that my father was not really dead after all? Was it not insisting that death is not important, not a lively part of our lives, not thoroughly human, not bestowed by the Final One? Suddenly the great lie took on cosmic proportion. And suddenly I was physically sick!

This time I didn't want to scream. I experienced an acute urge to vomit.

A sister sensitively perceived all this and understood. She pushed to my side and gave me courage. Together we laid aside the banks of flowers. Together we rolled back the carpet of deceit. God's good, wonderful clean earth lay once again unashamedly naked. I drank it into my being. The nausea passed.

Mind you, I'm not blaming anybody. Not anybody really, save myself. I just hadn't anticipated everything. I have no excuse but I was taken by surprise, you understand. And I so passionately wanted to celebrate Papa's death with honesty and integrity and dignity—for his sake, for our sake, for God's sake.

We lowered Papa then in his pauper's box deep into the raw ground. Then began the final rites. There were three.

I lifted up the Bible. It was a sign. We were commemorating Papa's journey in the historical community of the faithful. However distantly, however feebly, however brokenly, he had walked with the knights of faith, Abraham, Amos, Paul, Augustine, Thomas, Luther, Wesley, Jesus. By fate and by choice these were his first companions of the road. I recalled aloud from their constitution which I held in my hands. The heroic formula from Job is what I meant to recite: Naked I came from my mother's womb, and naked shall I return; the Lord gave, and the Lord has taken away; blessed be the name of the Lord. What came from my lips were the words of Paul. "If I live, I live unto the Lord; if I die, I die unto the Lord; so whether I live or whether I die, I am the Lord's."

I lifted up a very old, musty, leatherbound volume of poetry. This too was a sign. We were ritualizing Papa's own unique and unrepeatable engagement in the human adventure. Papa was an individual, a solitary individual before God. It was most fitting that a last rite should honor this individuality. Such was the role of the volume of hymn-poems. From it Papa had read and quoted and sung in monotone for as long as any of us including

Mama could recall.   The words I joined to the sign were from this
collection.   The author was a friend of Papa's.

> God moves in a mysterious way, his wonders to perform;
> He plants his footsteps on the sea and rides upon the
>   storm;
> Blind unbelief is sure to err, and scan His works in vain;
> God is His own interpreter and He shall make it plain.

The third sign celebrated the fact that Papa was a participant
in the total wonder of creation and that his life and death were
good because creation is good.   What I mean is that Papa was
God's friend.   My last act was to place him gladly and greatfully
on behalf of all good men everywhere in the hands of the One in
whose hands he already was, that Mysterious Power who rules
the unknown realm of death to do with him as He well pleaseth.
I ask to know no more.   This I symbolized.   Three times I
stooped low, three times I plunged my hands deep into the loose
earth beside the open pit, and three times I threw that good earth
upon my Papa within his grave.   And all the while I sang forth
the majestic threefold formula,

In the name of the Father and of the Son and of the Holy Ghost.

And some of those present there for the sake of all history and
all creation said Amen.

EPILOGUE

Self is never static. No relationship is ever the same today as it was yesterday nor will it be the same tomorrow. Repeatedly we face the impact of gender, love, sex, conflict and termination upon our self and upon all relationships. For instance, from tentative professions of "I love you" in third grade notes, through secret yearnings for the teacher, to dating and commitment, we ask with Browning "How do I love you?" and respond "Let me count the ways". The readings on love posed the question for a relationship of infatuation or "puppy love", the newness of "I love you", early marriage, changing expressions of love through the experiences of family life, to one statement of ideal love in marriage.

There have been no "answers" presented in these readings. Indeed, there may be no one answer to any of the realities of our lives. There may be only varied ways in which these realities may be encountered, dealt with, and the next day faced, with the awareness that similar situations will arise again throughout our lives.

There is meaning in these experiences that has the potential for growth of our self. The process by which we acquire and develop a self is done only in relation to other selves. It is ever-changing, ever-challenging. As we work through these encounters we hope to approach our full potential as human beings. When we face these realities constructively and creatively, there is hope for meaningful relationships of significance.

ENDNOTES FOR
FEMALE-MALE RELATIONSHIP

Jack O. Balswick and Charles W. Peek

1. M. Mead, *Sex and Temperament in Three Primitive Societies* (New York: William Morrow, 1935).

2. W. H. Manville, "The Locker Room Boys," *Cosmopolitan*, 1969, 166, pp. 110–115.

3. *Ibid.*, p. 111.

4. A. Averback, "The Cowboy Syndrome," Summary of research contained in a personal letter from the author, 1970.

5. R. O. Blood and D. M. Wolfe, *Husbands and Wives: The Dynamics of Married Living* (Glencoe, Illinois: The Free Press, 1960), p. 172.

6. J. O. Balswick, "The Effect of Spouse Companionship Support on Employment Success," *Journal of Marriage and the Family*, 1970, 32, pp. 212–215.

7. N. Hurvitz, "Marital Strain in the Blue Collar Family," in A. Shostak and W. Gomberg (eds.), *Blue-Collar World* (Englewood Cliffs, New Jersey: Prentice-Hall, 1964).

8. M. Komarovsky, *Blue-Collar Marriage* (New York: Random House, 1962).

9. L. Rainwater, *Family Design: Marital Sexuality, Family Size, and Contraception* (Chicago: Aldine, 1965).

10. M. Komarovsky, *Blue-Collar Marriage, op. cit.*, p. 156.

11. J. O. Balswick, "The Effect of Spouse Companionship Support on Employment Success," *op cit.*

Suzanne K. Steinmetz

1. R. M. Somerville, *Introduction to Family Life and Sex Education* (Englewood Cliffs, New Jersey: Prentice-Hall, 1972), p. 78.

2. J. Aldous, "Occupational Characteristics and Males' Role Performance in the Family," *Journal of Marriage and the Family*, 1969, 31, pp. 707–712.

3. *Ibid.*, p. 708.

4. A. Shomberg, "The Concept of the Breadwinner," as quoted in A. Michel (ed.), *Family Issues of Employed Women in Europe* (Leiden, The Netherlands: E. J. Brill, 1971), p. 12.

5. R. O. Blood and D. M. Wolfe, *Husbands and Wives* (Glencoe, Illinois: The Free Press, 1960).

6. B. Settles, "New Roles—New Life Styles for Men." Paper presented at the University of Delaware, November, 1972.

7. S. Steinmetz, "The Sexual Context of Social Mobility: Discrimination in Social Research." Paper presented at the Annual Meeting of the National Council on Family Relations, October, 1972.

8. G. Victor and P. Wilding, *Motherless Families* (London: Routledge and Kegan Paul, 1972).

9. W. B. Watson and A. T. Barth, "Questionable Assumptions in the Theory of Social Stratification," *Pacific Sociological Review*, 1964, 7, pp. 10–16.

10. W. Blackstone, *Commentaries on the Laws of England* (London, 1862).

11. United States Department of Health, Education and Welfare, *Women and Social Security: Law and Policy in Five Countries* (Washington, D. C.: Government Printing Office, 1973), p. 77.

12. *Ibid.*, p. 75.

13. *Ibid.*, p. 78.

14. *Ibid.*, p. 93.

15. *Ibid.*

16. *Ibid.*

17. "Wifely Breadwinners," *Parade*, September 2, 1973, p. 5. p. 73.

18. *Time*, May 14, 1973.

19. A. S. Rossi, "Naming Children in Middle Class Families," *American Sociological Review*, 1965, 30, pp. 499–513.

20. W. J. Goode, *World Revolution and Family Patterns* (New York: The Free Press, 1963).

21. *Ibid.*, p. 355.

22. B. Moore, *Social Origins of Dictatorship and Democracy* (Boston: Beacon Press, 1966), p. 165.

23. E. P. Stevens, "Machismo and Marianismo," *Society*, 1973, 10, pp. 57–63.

24. A. R. Hochschild, "A Review of Sex Role Research," in J. Huber (ed.), *Changing Women in a Changing Society* (Chicago: University of Chicago Press, 1973), p. 1012.

25. See, for example: I. Nye and L. Hoffman, *The Employed Mother in America* (Chicago: Rand McNally, 1963).

26. An interesting discussion of this point can be found in: R. Brandwein, "The Single Parent Family Revisited." Paper presented at the Annual Meeting of the Society for the Study of Social Problems, August, 1973.

27. G. Victor and P. Wilding, *Motherless Families, op. cit.*

28. *Ibid.*

29. From a personal communication with Barbara Settles.

30. W. R. Gove, "Sex, Marital Status and Suicide," *Journal of Health and Social Behavior*, 1972, 13, pp. 204–213.

31. *Ibid.*, p. 208.

32. S. S. Bellin and R. H. Hardt, "Marital Status and Mental Disorders Among the Aged," *American Sociological Review*, 1958, 23, pp. 155–162.

33. L. M. Adler, "The Relationship of Marital Status to Incidence of and Recovery From Mental Illness," *Social Forces*, 1953, 32, pp. 185–194.

34. G. Gurin, *Americans View Their Mental Health* (New York: Basic Books, 1960).

35. N. M. Bradburn, *In Pursuit of Happiness* (Chicago: National Opinion Research Center, 1963).

36. G. Knupfer, W. Clark and R. Room, "The Mental Health of the Unmarried," *The American Journal of Psychiatry*, 1966, 122, pp. 841–851.

37. L. Srole, *Mental Health in the Metropolis: The Midtown Manhattan Study* (New York: McGraw-Hill, 1962).

38. *Ibid.*

39. N. M. Bradburn and D. Caplovitz, *Reports on Happiness* (Chicago: Aldine, 1965).

40. Personal communication with Evan Stark.

41. M. Mead, *Sex and Temperament in Three Primitive Societies* (New York: William Morrow, 1935).

42. M. Weisinger, "Men—Don't Be Ashamed to Cry," *Parade*, September 16, 1973, pp. 24–27.

43. J. O. Balswick and C. Peek, "The Inexpressive Male: A Tragedy of American Society," *Family Coordinator*, 1971, 20, pp. 363–368.

44. R. M. Somerville, *Introduction to Family Life and Sex Education*, *op cit.*

Betty Rollin

1. B. Friedan, *The Feminine Mystique* (New York: Norton, 1963).

2. P. Wylie, *Generation of Vipers* (New York: Farrar and Rinehart, 1942).

3. P. Roth, *Portnoy's Complaint* (New York: Random House, 1969).

4. M. Hunt, *Her Infinite Variety: The American Woman as Lover, Mate and Rival* (New York: Holt and Rinehart, 1962).

ENDNOTES FOR LOVE

Alan M. Dahms

1. E. Berne, *Games People Play: The Psychology of Human Relationships* (New York: Grove, 1964).

2. E. Albee, *Who's Afraid of Virginia Wolfe?* (New York: Atheneum, 1966).

3. S. Beckett, *Waiting for Godot* (New York: Grove, 1954).

4. A. Camus, *The Stranger* (New York: Knopf, 1958).

5. J. Farber, *The Student as Nigger* (North Hollywood, California: Contact, 1969).

6. L. F. Baum, *The Wizard of Oz* (New York: Grosset and Dunlap, 1900).

7. D. Morris, *Intimate Behaviour* (London: Cape, 1971).

8. J. D. Salinger, *The Catcher in the Rye* (Boston: Little, Brown, 1951).

9. G. Greer, *The Female Eunich* (London: MacGibbon and Kee, 1970).

10. G. Allen and C. Martin, *Intimacy, Sensitivity, Sex and the Art of Love* (Chicago: Cowles, 1971).

11. United States Commission on Obscenity and Pornography, *The Report* (Washington, D. C.: Government Printing Office, 1970).

12. United States Commission on Marihuana and Drug Abuse, *Marihuana: A Signal of Misunderstanding* (Washington, D. C.: Government Printing Office, 1972).

13. J. Garrity, *Sensuous Woman: The First How-To Book For The Female Who Yearns to be All Woman* (New York: L. Stuart, 1970).

14. "M", *Sensuous Man: The First How-To Book For the Man Who Wants to be a Great Lover* (New-York: L. Stuart, 1971).

15. R. Chartham, *The Sensuous Couple* (New York: Ballantine, 1971).

16. "P", *The Sensuous Child* (New York: L. Stuart, 1971).

17. D. Morris, *Intimate Behaviour, op cit.*

18. *Ibid.*

19. A. Camus, *The Stranger, op cit.*

20. J. Heller, *Catch 22* (New York: Simon and Shuster, 1961).

ENDNOTES FOR
SEX

John A. Blazer

1. L. J. Friedman, *Virgin Wives—A Study of Unconsummated Marriages* (Springfield, Illinois: Charles C. Thomas, 1962).

2. *Ibid.*

3. *Ibid.*

4. *Ibid.*

Clark E. Vincent

1. R. A. Nisbet, *The Sociological Tradition* (New York: Basic Books, 1966) pp. 3–106.

2. C. E. Vincent, "Interfaith Marriage: Problem or Symptom?" in J. E. Zahn (ed.), *Religion and the Face of America* (Berkely: University of California Press, 1969), pp. 67–85; and C. E. Vincent, "Sources of Sexual Communication Difficulties in Marriage," in C. E. Vincent (ed.), *Human Sexuality in Medical Education and Practice* (Springfield, Illinois: Charles C. Thomas, 1968), pp. 440–459.

3. J. H. Gagnon, "Sexuality and Sexual Learning in the Child", *Psychiatry,* 1965, 28, pp. 212–228.

4. R. Brecher and E. Brecher (eds.), *An Analysis of Human Sexual Response* (New York: New American Library, 1966); and W. H. Masters and V. E. Johnson, *Human Sexual Response* (Boston: Little, Brown & Co., 1966).

5. *Ibid.*

ENDNOTES FOR
CONFLICT

John F. Crosby

1. R. May, *Love and Will* (New York: W. W. Norton, 1969), p. 148. Reprinted by permission.

2. From G. R. Bach and P. Wyden, *The Intimate Enemy* (New York: William Morrow, 1969), Chapter 1. Reprinted by permission.

3. From V. Frankl, *Man's Search For Meaning* (New York: Washington Square Press, 1959), p. 160.

Israel W. Charny

1. L. A. Coser, "Some Social Functions of Violence," in M. E. Wolfgang (ed.), *Patterns of Violence: The Annals of the American Academy of Political and Social Science*, 1966, 364, pp. 8–18.

2. *Ibid.* and K. Lorenz, *On Aggression* (New York: Harcourt, Brace & World, 1966).

3. I. W. Charnez, "Love and Hate, Honor and Dishonor, Obey and Disobey." In co-operative, nonviolent tension: the need for a revised marriage contract and a revised offer of help by the marriage counselor. Presented to the Family Workshop, Family Service of Chester County, Pennsylvania, September, 1967.

4. G. Bach, Symposium, "Hate and Aggression." *Voices: The Art and Science of Psychotherapy*, 1965, 1.

Nena O'Neill and George O'Neill

1. M. B. Sussman, "Family Systems in the 1970's: Analysis, Politics and Programs," *The Annals of the American Academy of Political and Social Science*, 1971, 396, pp. 40–56.

2. J. F. Cuber and P. B. Harroff, *Sex and the Significant Americans* (Baltimore: Penguin Books, 1965).

3. N. O'Neill and G. O'Neill, *Open Marriage: A New Life Style for Couples* (New York: M. Evans, 1972).

4. L. Festinger and D. Katz, *Research Methods in the Behavioral Sciences* (New York: Holt, Rinehart and Winston, 1953).

5. S. K. Weinberg, *Social Problems in Modern Urban Society* (Englewood Cliffs, New Jersey: Prentice-Hall, 1970), p. 4.

6. E. Shostrom and J. Kayanaugh, *Between Man and Woman* (Los Angeles: Nash, 1971).

7. A. H. Maslow and J. J. Honigmann (eds.), "Synergy: Some Notes of Ruth Benedict," *American Anthropologist*, 1970, 72, pp. 320–333.

8. A. H. Maslow, "Human Potentialities and the Healthy Society," in H. A. Otto (ed.), *Human Potentialities* (St. Louis: W. H. Green, 1968).

9. M. Rokeach, *The Open and Closed Mind* (New York: Basic Books, 1960).

ENDNOTES FOR
TERMINATION

Sidney M. Jourard

1. See my book, *The Transparent Self* (Princeton, New Jersey: Van Nostrand, 1964) especially Chapters 6, 9, 15, for the sick-making potentialities of various family and occupational roles.

2. Wilhelm Reich has discussed "Character" in terms of neuromuscular patterning; significantly enough, he speaks of both character—*and* muscular armor. See W. Reich, *Character Analysis* (New York: Orgone Institute Press, 1948).

3. My existentialist bias is showing here, as rightly it should. See S. M. Jourard, *Disclosing Man to Himself* (Princeton, New Jersey: Van Nostrand, 1968) especially chapter 14 for a discussion of creativity that applies as much to the creation of self and of relationships as it does to such productions as a painting, a symphony, a dance or a sculpture.

4. See R. D. Laing, *The Divided Self* (London: Tavistock, 1960).

5. See H. Marcuse, *One-Dimensional Man* (London: Routledge and Kegan Paul, 1964).

6. S. M. Jourard, *Disclosing Man to Himself, op. cit.*

*

AUTHOR INDEX

References are to Pages

SUBJECT INDEX

END OF VOLUME